The Politics of Community Policing

Law, Meaning, and Violence

The scope of Law, Meaning, and Violence is defined by the wide-ranging scholarly debates signaled by each of the words in the title. Those debates have taken place among and between lawyers, anthropologists, political theorists, sociologists, and historians, as well as literary and cultural critics. This series is intended to recognize the importance of such ongoingconversations about law, meaning, and violence as well as to encourage and further them.

Narrative, Violence, and the Law: The Essays of Robert Cover, edited by Martha Minow, Michael Ryan, and Austin Sarat

Narrative, Authority, and Law, by Robin West

The Possibility of Popular Justice: A Case Study of Community Mediation in the United States, edited by Sally Engle Merry and Neal Milner

Legal Modernism, by David Luban

Surveillance, Privacy, and the Law: Employee Drug Testing and the Politics of Social Control, by John Gilliom

Lives of Lawyers: Journeys in the Organizations of Practice, by Michael J. Kelly

Unleashing Rights: Law, Meaning, and the Animal Rights Movement, by Helena Silverstein

Law Stories, edited by Gary Bellow and Martha Minow

The Powers That Punish: Prison and Politics in the Era of the "Big House," 1920–1955, by Charles Bright

Law and the Postmodern Mind: Essays on Psychoanalysis and Jurisprudence, edited by Peter Goodrich and David Gray Carlson

Russia's Legal Fictions, by Harriet Murav

Strangers to the Law: Gay People on Trial, by Lisa Keen and Suzanne B. Goldberg

Butterfly, the Bride: Essays on Law, Narrative, and the Family, by Carol Weisbrod

The Politics of Community Policing: Rearranging the Power to Punish, by William Lyons

Laws of the Postcolonial, edited by Eve Darian-Smith and Peter Fitzpatrick

The Politics of Community Policing

Rearranging the Power to Punish

William Lyons

Ann Arbor

THE UNIVERSITY OF MICHIGAN PRESS

Published in the United States of America by
The University of Michigan Press
Manufactured in the United States of America
♾ Printed on acid-free paper

2002 2001 2000 1999 4 3 2 1

A CIP catalog record for this book is available from the British Library.

Library of Congress Cataloging-in-Publication Data

Lyons, William, 1960–
The politics of community policing : rearranging the power to punish / William Lyons.
p. cm. — (Law, meaning, and violence)
Includes bibliographical references and index.
ISBN 0-472-10953-7 (alk. paper)
1. Community policing—Washington (State)—Seattle. 2. Law enforcement—Washington (State)—Seattle. 3. Seattle (Wash.)—Social conditions. 4. Seattle (Wash.)—Politics and government. I. Title. II. Series.
HV7936.C83 L86 1999
363.2'3'0973—dc21 98-40135
CIP

It is right to be against violence. And it is easy to be against violence. But those who tell us that the answer to civil strife is simply more police and bigger jails, who blame a few agitators or a handful of criminals—such men betray the future of the American nation. Violence is wrong, but it is also a reminder. It is a reminder that millions of American citizens have been shut out from the blessing of American freedom. It is a reminder of our common failure to ensure opportunity for the black man, and the American Indian, for the Mexican-American and the Puerto Rican—for all of the oppressed in our midst. It is a reminder that the American promise is still unfulfilled. . . . We must reject absolutely the leadership of fear, the cries of those who find repression more congenial than justice, and anger more popular than compassion.

—Senator Robert Kennedy, "Crisis in Our Cities," in *The Critic* (1967)

Fear is the foundation of most governments; but it is so sordid and brutal a passion and renders men in whose breasts it predominates so stupid and miserable that Americans will not be likely to approve of any political institution which is founded on it.

—John Adams, "Thoughts on Government" (1776)

Contents

List of Figures ix

List of Tables xi

Acknowledgments xiii

Chapter 1. Competing Stories about Community and Policing 1

Chapter 2. Community (Policing) 15

Chapter 3. (Community) Policing 35

Chapter 4. Communities and Crime on the South Side of Skid Road 57

Chapter 5. The Emergence of the South Seattle Crime Prevention Council 77

Chapter 6. Policing Reform in Southeast Seattle 105

Chapter 7. Reciprocity in Police-Community Partnerships 135

Chapter 8. Getting Back to Mayberry 163

Appendix 187

Notes 197

Bibliography 227

Index 239

Figures

1. Seattle city map with SSCPC area shaded 6

2. Rainier Valley neighborhoods, 1990 61

3. Rating of privately owned facilities, 1991 73

4. Rating of public services, 1991 73

5. Rating of publicly owned facilities, 1991 73

6. SSCPC 15-point plan 97

7. Police precinct map of Seattle, 1990 99

8. Geographical distribution of Part I offenses, 1988 100

9. Location of initial targets and property owned by core SSCPC members, 1989–95 148

Tables

1. Valley Income by Topographic Community, 1989 — 62

2. Racial Composition of Southeast Seattle, 1960–90 — 64

3. Community Survey Priorities, 1991 — 72

4. Disposition of Complaints for Selected Cities, 1988 — 122

5. Seattle Police Department Complaints, Contact Log Entries, and Investigations, 1978–88 — 122

6. Number of Hot Line Calls through May of Each Year, 1989–93 — 138

7. Budgetary Allocations from Proposition 1 — 144

8. Initial Targets Established by the Partnership — 147

9. Breakdown of 332 NARs Collected in Fourth Quarter, 1988 — 150

10. Changes in Number of Complaints of Police Misconduct, 1987 to 1988 — 156

11. Change in Total Part I Offenses, 1988 — 161

Acknowledgments

This study of community policing is motivated by my concern for American democracy. As the decline of community life and the concentration of power in state and corporate bureaucracies intersect with increasingly inescapable violence on urban streets and in our homes, it is not surprising that our concerns about community, democracy, and public safety have joined forces in a reform like community policing. While the analysis presented here is critical of community policing in a city identified by the National Institute of Justice as a model, my hope is that a better understanding of the stories we tell about community and policing will provide us with a resource we can use to nurture its democratizing elements and resist its disciplinary mechanisms over the long run. This, however, remains an empirical question.

Whatever the reader finds here, I offer humbly and with thanks to many friends who have assisted and supported me through this long process. Stuart Scheingold, Michael McCann, and Christine DiStefano, each in their own characteristic ways, provided me with essential support and critical feedback in the process of creating a first draft of this manuscript. Michael Taylor, David Olson, Wesley Skogan, Austin Sarat, and Michael Musheno each read all or parts of earlier drafts and provided me with valuable, critical comments. Julie Drew, Helena Silverstein, Bob VanDyk, Jeff Jacobson, Steve Snow, Karen Stuhldreher, Rich Sherman, Dan Grundmann, Howard Faye, Matt Diamond, Mark Gardner, Lisa Miller, Trish Oberweis, Ina Chang, Elaine Chang, Colleen Kelly, Tim Hall, and many others contributed in very real ways to my personal and intellectual growth, as manifest in this work. I also wish to thank Chuck Myers, the reviewers at the University of Michigan Press, my research assistant Michael Lawrence, and my colleagues here at the University of Akron. My most heartfelt thanks to each of you.

Between the time I completed the research and finalized the manuscript I had the opportunity to work for the Seattle Police Department as manager of the Research and Grants Division. Chief Stamper's administration is not a part of this study, but all the officers and staff I had the pleasure of working with taught me much about policing, politics, and power. While I am thankful to all who shared their insights with me, special thanks are due to Nancy McPherson. I have never before worked with anyone of such courage, energy, and integrity. I am also grateful to have forged friendships with Pam McCammon, James Koutsky, Emmet Kelsie, Glenda Belcher, Ray Nakanishi, Dan Fleissner, Norm Stamper, and many others. These relationships and our shared experiences continue to enrich my personal life and professional work.

Finally, I wish to thank my family. You understood my need to complete this project my way and never gave up on nurturing those relationships that make life worth celebrating. (And, no, this does not mean you have to read the whole book!) We each share both a burden and a privilege in constructing a life, and through those stages of this project when only the burdens felt manifest your love remained a steadfast and profoundly appreciated privilege. You constantly reminded me that it is what we become through our work, not what we produce alone, that measures our achievements. No one taught me more about politics and integrity than my dad. No one taught me more about being organized, planning, and caretaking than my mom. My parents showed me in their lives the value of hard work, family, and integrity. They taught me to love, laugh, and celebrate life. And I hope, as they have, that I can place kindness and respect at the center of all my relationships. For all these reasons I humbly wish to dedicate this book to my parents.

Chapter 1

Competing Stories about Community and Policing

The beating of Rodney King by several officers from the Los Angeles Police Department drew national attention to the urban crime control problem. In an election year response, President George Bush offered the Justice Department's Weed and Seed Program. The mayor of Seattle saw this as an opportunity to be more responsive to community concerns. Seattle applied for and received a Weed and Seed grant to target gang activity in the Central District, a primarily lower income, black neighborhood. The grant provided more than $1 million in the first year, with the potential for much more in subsequent years, for law enforcement agencies to lead an effort to weed out undesirable elements in the target community and seed for community revitalization to keep them out.[1]

On June 6, 1992, in a small storefront chapel in Seattle's Central District, the Coalition to Stop Weed and Seed met to share information. Speakers told the 50-plus attendees that Weed and Seed would turn *their* communities into concentration camps, subject only *their* children to stricter federal sentencing requirements, suspend *their* civil rights, seize *their* property, and cut off *their* welfare benefits. The basic message was "Weed and Seed does not meet *our* needs."

Citing an American Civil Liberties Union (ACLU) report, speakers argued that Weed and Seed would lead to a more powerful, but less accountable, federal policing presence in their communities. "Operation Weed and Seed substitutes federal law enforcement and sentencing for local law. And federal drug sentencing laws are draconian. Under federal law, an offender can be imprisoned for up to three times as long as a similar offender sentenced under Washington state law. Under 'Weed and Seed' Seattle's white neighborhoods would be governed by state law and our black neighborhoods would suffer under harsher federal law."[2]

The coalition of groups opposed to Weed and Seed had been concerned about crime control long before Weed and Seed appeared on the political agenda, and the tactics they discussed reflected their desire to do more than just criticize. They discussed various measures to mobilize the community: forming new community councils; informing property owners about potential seizures; and organizing demonstrations, phone trees, a clergy coalition, and a legal defense fund. They discussed two electoral strategies: one ballot initiative to abolish the at-large election of city council members and return to a city council elected by district, and another to recall Norm Rice, Seattle's first African American mayor. They also heard from a committee planning alternative arrangements for the provision of public safety, including the creation of a community-based civilian review board.[3]

The Weed and Seed controversy highlights the difficulties inherent in government attempts to be responsive to community needs. Agreement on the importance of public safety did not mean agreement on the best way to achieve it. An editorial columnist for the *Seattle Times* argued that, while state law enforcement agencies viewed Weed and Seed as a responsive solution to the problems of drug use and gang activity in high-crime neighborhoods, many residents of the target neighborhoods saw such programs as part of the problem.[4] Mayor Rice tried to calm community fears about accountability by pointing out that Weed and Seed would expand Seattle's popular community policing program, but this did not calm the fears expressed by the coalition. The communities most victimized by crime in Seattle remained concerned not only about crime but also about the way crime control was provided.

Since 1993, the New York City Police Department (NYPD) has been a poster child for community policing. Like the Weed and Seed controversy in Seattle, the New York case highlights the competing messages, the fears of crime and official misconduct, constitutive of community policing. The brutal beating of Abner Louima by officers of the NYPD sent a powerful message, a message one officer involved explained as constitutive of a new style of policing, a political message that we are now living in "Giuliani time." According to Andrew Karman,

> Some officers have gotten the message that they were unleashed, that their handcuffs were taken off. In the Louima case, when the

> officer said, "It is Giuliani time," he was saying the rules of the game have changed. He was saying he felt that, "Mr. Louima, you don't have any protectors anymore."[5]

Despite the fact that this case exploded in the media more than a year after a highly critical Amnesty International report was dismissed by Mayor Giuliani, he still maintained that there was no connection between police brutality and New York's much-publicized policy of "zero tolerance" for minor crimes—a policy some believe accounts for a substantial portion of the decline in crime and most were certain would make Giuliani virtually unbeatable in the upcoming elections. The *Washington Post* reported, just prior to the Louima beating, that crimes reported in the city had dropped from more than 700,000 in 1990 to less than 400,000 in 1996 and murders had dropped from 2,005 in 1992 to 985 in 1993. At the same time, misdemeanor arrests increased from just over 120,000 in 1990 to almost 200,000 in 1996 and complaints of police misconduct rose from more than 3,000 in 1990 to just under 6,000 in 1995.[6] While Mayor Giuliani's public approval ratings were over 80 percent at the beginning of 1997, levels of police brutality, according to the 1996 Amnesty report, had "reached an extremely worrying level."[7]

Mayor Giuliani's rush to take credit for the dramatic drop in crime was not matched by a rush to accept responsibility for Abner Louima's tragedy. The fear-inducing message announced to Abner Louima and other similarly power-poor members of New York communities screamed what is generally whispered: the disciplinary harmonies that accompany the democratic melodies in stories about community policing. "This is Giuliani time" conveys a simple, painfully clear message: you are not part of the community we are partnering with when we tell our stories about community policing. This officer's succinct message also recognizes that there are competing stories associated with former New York Mayor Dinkins, perhaps contrasting stories told at community meeting time and press conference time with stories screaming through toilet bowl plungers at ass-kicking time. With the recent publication of Kelling and Coles's celebration of the NYPD as the vanguard of community policing, it is difficult not to also hear a message about "rearranging the power to punish," further privileging the "illegalities" of powerful public and private leaders and punishing the "illegalities" characteristic of the least advantaged in the stories and practices constitutive of community policing in New York.[8]

Mayor Giuliani is, no doubt, correct to point out that there is no *necessary* connection between more aggressive policing of minor disorders and police brutality. But the mayor built powerful electoral alliances by zealously (fanning and) responding to the fears of middle-class voters with stories about the virtues of anticipatory policing practices. And he failed to anticipate with an equivalent zeal the entirely foreseeable consequences of his "zero tolerance" stories on police practice, media coverage, and the city's least advantaged residents. This sent a political message about who was invited to join the community being constructed in stories about community policing.[9] Failing to anticipate the foreseeable consequences with an equally zealous, anticipatory "zero tolerance" of unaccountable police power links aggressive crime control policies to the beating of Abner Louima and reveals an important reason to deconstruct prevailing stories about *community* and *policing* in community policing. While "Getting Back to Mayberry" may be an unambiguously positive image for some, it is also an image of a community that has never had a safe place for people like Abner Louima or Rodney King.

Through my analysis of community policing in Seattle, I have come to see the politics of community policing as constituted—in large part—by discursive struggles to define *community* and *policing*. This study, therefore, is an analysis of the politics of community policing as the construction of competing stories, in environments characterized by power imbalances, requiring attention to the political utility of prevailing stories, including how particular stories impact agency, resources, and legitimation. Stories about community policing turn out to be both disciplinary and democratizing, but not in an undifferentiated way. Community policing colonized community life, increasing the capacity of the Seattle Police Department to shield itself from critical public scrutiny. It also manifested the potential for more democratic forms of social control in police attention to individual rights and impartial law enforcement, a brief episode of reciprocity in the police-community partnership, community police teams, and the resilience of stories about community revitalization in the struggle to define community policing. The meaning of community policing, then, has remained contingent on struggles to control political, economic, and social resources for the power to say what policing is and who communities are.

The City. Seattle is located on a long north-south peninsula with

Puget Sound on its west and Lake Washington on its east. Incorporated as a city in 1869, Seattle is governed under a mayor-council form of government. A city of more than half a million residents, Seattle occupies 143 square miles of land, including 5,000 acres of parks. The Seattle Police Department (SPD), with some ups and downs, has been a reliable player in Seattle politics since it was first organized in 1886. In 1994, the final year of this study, the Seattle Police Department employed 1,266 sworn officers and 633 civilians. The ratio of police officers to population was 1 to 420, compared to a national average of 1 to 454. The number of police officers per 1,000 population was 2.38, compared to 2.20 nationally. And the ratio of sworn to civilian employees was 2 to 1, compared to 3.46 to 1 nationally.[10]

The Neighborhoods. Southeast Seattle is a set of neighborhoods running from Skid Road to the southern edge of the city and was the target area for the South Seattle Crime Prevention Council (SSCPC) (see fig. 1). This study focuses on the activities of the SSCPC from its creation in 1988 to 1994, when Police Chief Patrick Fitzsimons retired. Southeast Seattle is a largely residential area with the highest concentration of people of color in the city (see appendix). After World War II, decisions by public and private leaders in the city contributed to economic decline and rising crime in the southeast. Beginning in the 1970s, loose coalitions of community activists fought the city in an attempt to preserve their communities, including efforts to improve public safety. The pressure they applied to a reluctant police administration led to the formation of the SSCPC, an association that the National Institute of Justice called a "model partnership between citizens and police."[11]

Because the pressure to experiment with new forms of policing came from within the community and overcame strong opposition from Chief Fitzsimons, the emergence of community policing in Seattle offers a unique opportunity to examine the "hidden transcripts" constitutive of community policing.[12] Unlike nearly all other cities, where community policing initiatives began with the chief or the mayor, in this case they began in the neighborhoods and provide a picture of what more decentered stories about community and policing look like and how they integrate the competing stories of various communities around a shared interest in enhancing their capacity to subject unaccountable power in their neighborhoods to critical public scrutiny. This case is also illustrative of voluntary cooperation at the community level that succeeded in pressuring a notoriously stubborn city bureaucracy

Fig. 1. Seattle city map with SSCPC area shaded. (From National Institute of Justice 1992.)

to form a partnership, succeeded in linking crime prevention efforts to other ongoing struggles to revitalize the southeast, succeeded in ensuring that the new chief was seriously committed to community policing, and succeeded in cooperating with other citizen groups and the police to impact crime rates in their neighborhoods.

The Approach. I focus on competing stories for several reasons. First, this analytical strategy serves as a way of hearing many different voices in the text without granting immediate credibility to any one of them.[13] Second, I use stories as interchangeable with narratives, both meaning temporally ordered tales about history with a plot, a moral or vision with political utility in the present, and closure.[14] Stories are the small arms of neighborhood struggle, the heavy artillery deployed in city newspapers, and the building blocks of discourses.[15] My focus on stories is an attempt to explicate the political messages and power-knowledge nexus at the heart of an emerging discourse on social control: community policing. Third, I prefer to use the term *stories* (rather than *narratives, messages,* or *discourses*) because its common language meaning is consistent with my more analytical usage, thereby increasing the accessibility of this text to a broader audience without compromising the clarity of my argument. Finally, those police officers and community activists I studied did in fact tell stories about community and policing; and their stories mattered to them both as tales with a moral relevant to current political conflicts and as resources to draw upon in their ongoing struggles over the power to say what policing is and who the community will be. One Seattle police officer, recognizing the importance of discursive struggle, noted that "if we don't tell our story, the community will make up their own stories."[16]

Further, my analysis distinguishes between prevailing and competing stories about community and policing. The critical distinction here is empirical. Competing stories were more decentered, focusing on what can be done, by any of a variety of state and nonstate actors, to reduce crime and violence in a way that is consistent with resilient communities. Prevailing stories were state centered, focusing on policing as an activity of law enforcement professionals and the community as a resource to be more effectively tapped by these state agents. There was no single prevailing story about policing or community. Stories about policing, for instance, ranged from nostalgic visions to managerial strategies. But there are identifiable themes common to prevailing stories, which highlight the boundaries of an emerging discourse on social control. First, prevailing stories construct history and the present to support state-centered stories about professional policing. Second, prevailing stories draw discursive resources from references to empowering communities with specified capacities while narrowing the possibility of more empowered communities by ignoring the relational basis of these capacities, that is, social capital and reciprocity (discussed below). And, third, prevailing stories integrate more decentered stories about community and policing only to the extent that these normalize deference to state agency and strengthen state capacities to surveil public and private space.

I begin my analysis with a central assumption in stories about community policing. A core assumption in the logic of community policing is that innovative police practices can mobilize now latent informal mechanisms of social control embedded within communities.[17] These mechanisms, like social capital, inhere within the reciprocal relational networks that constitute communities. Advocates expect police-community partnerships to empower citizens by reducing fear—thereby making policing more efficient and effective to the degree that it revitalizes communities with specified capacities—that is, it invests in the social capital of those communities most victimized by crime and violence.

Social capital provides a way of thinking about the relational basis of communities capable of mobilizing informal social controls and how to invest in these capacities. Social capital, like financial capital, is a resource that can be mobilized as a form of collective power. Unlike financial capital, however, social capital cannot be separated from the collective activities (relational networks) that created it; it inheres within reciprocal relationships and can be mobilized by members of these networks as a resource. SSCPC success in pressuring the Seattle Police Department to form a partnership and change the way policing works in the southeast can be attributed, in part, to their long-term investment in social capital. Their initial success in reducing crime can also be attributed to the relatively reciprocal relationships they established with other communities in the southeast, police officers, and police leaders in the South Precinct just prior to and including the first year of their partnership. And the eventual atrophy of the SSCPC can be traced to their failure to preserve this horizontal and vertical reciprocity and ensure that the way crime was controlled continued to contribute to the social capital required to enable communities with the capacity to subject unaccountable forms of power in their neighborhoods to critical public scrutiny. For these reasons, I focus on social capital and reciprocity as the key contextualizing factors for understanding when the more democratic face of community policing is more likely to prevail over its disciplinary face.

A Dialectic of Democratic and Disciplinary Mechanisms of Social Control. Stories about stronger communities and more democratic policing turn out to be inseparably linked to a widening of the web and thinning of the mesh of disciplinary mechanisms of social control.[18] When stories about community policing recognize, as most do, that the police cannot do it alone, that police-community partnerships can contribute to a community's capacity to mobilize informal social controls, and that partnerships will be able to tailor police practices to the particular problem solving efforts appropriate for different times and places, this candor manifests a democratic impulse.[19] This is the part of the story that focuses on dramatic drops in crime rates, attributing a portion of this success to the political will to invest in social capital by experimenting with more reciprocal forms of police-community partnerships and recognizing that the way we fight crime also impacts the distribution of agency, resources, and the power to punish.

These more conventional measures of crime-control success, and the democratic triumph manifest in reducing the disorders and violence that plague our least advantaged communities "cannot be deconstructed away," according to Stanley Cohen. "If anything, these criteria need extension by seeing freedom from fear as a universal human right."[20] In more decentered stories about community policing, this extension emerges as a right to be free from the fear of unaccountable power that undermines the resilience of communities, including fear of gangsters and unaccountable state agents. While these and other more democratic aspects of community policing are real, they are not the entire story.

As police departments and other powerful public and private agents work to place their stories about community and policing in the forefront of public debate, the disciplinary potential within these stories becomes more salient. As Cohen notes about accountability, so is the case with the democratic impulses in community policing more generally. "Democratic notions such as accountability are easily transferred by the old bureaucracies into self-protecting ideologies."[21] In Seattle from 1988 to 1994, this linking of democratic and disciplinary stories supported police colonization of the model partnership, transforming an active and reciprocal partner into a docile and dependent client, displacing more democratic forms of moderation into normalization, and replacing more critical forms of public scrutiny with citizen surveillance plugged directly into state information systems. I see this as a dialectic of discipline and democracy because the same capacities supported either form of power, depending on the degree to which these were embedded within more or less reciprocal relational contexts. The more democratic forces (subjecting unaccountable forms of power to critical public scrutiny or moderating competing demands) and the more disciplinary powers (to surveil or normalize) both require a degree of transparency and a linked capacity to gather information and construct more or less persuasive stories. When this transparency directs power and information in panoptic fashion, only in the direction of the state, it encourages docility and dependence; when it directs power and information more reciprocally, to support multiple forms of agency, the same capacities can enable strong and active resistance to prevailing stories and strengthen more decentered stories about community and policing in the discursive struggle to define community policing.

The dialectical relationship between democratic and disciplinary mechanisms of social control is what Foucault and Cohen highlight when they note that within each disciplinary discourse there are also resources for resistance to it.[22] While prevailing stories about community policing privilege state agency, they also highlight the contingency and indeterminacy of effective social control efforts. While problem solving partnerships inject a still more "preservationist" slant to police-community relations, they also mobilize a potentially "insurgent" language that can be applied to a variety of substantive problems beyond its utility as a procedural device to enhance the power and privilege the agency of police departments.[23] It can be powerfully mobilized by citizens and officers to contest department stories about problems and solutions, crime and crime control. When state agents present disorder as the most policy-relevant root cause of crime, this can justify harsh, proactive, and disciplinary attacks on disorderly individuals formerly known as homeless persons. However, as the Kelling and Coles's book ironically demonstrates, this requires the state to engage in a discursive struggle over the naming of these individuals and the chronic social problems and political cowardice their plight represents.[24]

Here we can see the interweaving of democratic and disciplinary impulses. While Kelling and Coles seek to highlight the importance of fighting disorder through a much thinner mesh of discursive power more widely cast, they also highlight the inherently relational nature of social control. In the Seattle case, for instance, the focus on disorder did not remain limited to supporting aggressive order maintenance by professional law enforcement agencies; it also contributed to seeing disorder as a visible consequence of a cascade of activities that only became visible within precommunity policing stories in the form of street crime. While prevailing stories construct disorder as an activity of the poor, the discursive focus on disorder also expanded the scope of the conflict to include physical disorder (pressuring property owners to maintain their properties), social disorder (pressuring both the supply and demand side of the drug and vice markets), and political disorder (pressuring city and police officials to address a broad array of community concerns in an integrated fashion).[25]

At the same time, aggressive order maintenance supported displacing culpability and reparations from the powerful original sinners responsible for the decline of Southeast Seattle onto the victims of neighborhood blight. A democratic impulse to more aggressively address the problems that victimize the least advantaged strengthened the capacity of state agents to, as Kelling and Coles recommend, redefine chronic social and political problems as police problems. The policing of disorder mobilized disciplinary mechanisms of social control—quickly removing "disorderly" individuals from public view in a spectacle reminiscent of public floggings. The publicity of this spectacle, however, also makes "the uninterrupted play of calculated gazes" available to citizens seeking to hold now more visible and exposed state agents accountable for their exercise of power, a task made moderately more feasible by the state's justification of these practices as consistent with our democratic traditions.[26] In this sense, the gaze is not so much uninterrupted as fragmented; the spectacle is not replaced with a single web of surveillance, but efforts to construct a spectacle out of the routine work practices of police officers also subjects police leaders (including mayors, like Rice and Giuliani) to critical public scrutiny. They are expected to justify their failure to balance their official zeal by responding with equivalent force and foresight to the fears of all city residents.

Seeing the presence of the sovereign is an important nondisciplinary characteristic of community policing, since, as Foucault notes, "[t]he scarcely sustainable visibility of the monarch is turned into the unavoidable visibility of the subjects. And it is this inversion of visibility in the functioning of the disciplines that was to assure the exercise of power even in its lowest manifestations."[27] In this case, the state remains visible, both the seeker of information and a subject in communication. "Visibility is [indeed] a trap."[28] It is a paradox facing state agents seeking to tap into the resources constitutive of communities. In community policing, the legitimation of state power becomes more anonymous, but the exercise of this power by the state becomes more visible.

Foucault had great expectations for the police capacity to fill in the microphysics of power constitutive of a disciplinary society. But the expected role may not be attainable because the legitimation efforts examined here depend in part on a police capacity to enable *both* democratic and disciplinary forms of social control. If the police are to be "an apparatus that must be coextensive with the entire social body and not only to the extreme limits that it embraces, but by the minuteness of the details it is concerned with," it seems unlikely that it can do this without also inviting the additional constraints inherent in efforts to mobilize informal social controls within an indeterminate and contingent network of social relationships.[29] The police, according to Foucault, "had to be given the instrument of permanent, exhaustive, omnipresent surveillance, capable of making all visible, as long as it could remain itself invisible."[30] The degree to which this is a persuasive vision of our collective future remains an empirical question, but in this study of community policing the police remain visible, and their capacity to surveil remains impermanent, partial, and continuously mixed with the linked capacities of citizens to see the police and (sometimes) subject the police department to critical public scrutiny.

The Power to Say What Policing Is and Who Communities Are. The meaning of law and order in Southeast Seattle is being worked out in the interactions between and among police and citizens. The historical context in which these meaning struggles take place is prefigured by anger, violence, distrust, racism, and accountability concerns. Each of these represents a discursive and relational constraint on police control over the rearranging of the power to punish. If the "exercise of power consists of guiding the possibility of conduct," as Foucault argues, then the disruptive subjects opposed to Weed and Seed or enraged by the beating of Abner Louima are voicing concerns from their lifeworlds in the form of demands to participate in the power to guard against the possibility of police misconduct.[31] Their voices tell stories about subjecting the unaccountable power of gangsters *and* agents of the state in their neighborhoods to critical public scrutiny.

The data and analysis presented here are based on a case study of one police-community partnership: the South Seattle Crime Prevention Council. This data was compiled from three primary sources: in-depth interviews with community activists, police officers, elected officials, and police administrators; observations of SSCPC meetings (and analysis of their meeting minutes), Seattle City Council meetings, and other related meetings for the period 1988–94; and extensive research into materials published by the Seattle Police Department, neighborhood and city newspapers, and archival materials on the history of Southeast Seattle.

My approach starts with a focus on the core assumptions among police reformers about the role of community in community policing because embedded within these assumptions are key resources for competing stories about community and policing. If community policing is effective and efficient because it involves policing in a way that enables communities with specific and identifiable capacities, then my first level of inquiry asks how effective the Seattle Police Department has been in developing new policing strategies that can be expected to enable communities to reclaim these capacities (informal mechanisms of social control). If the practice of community policing has not enabled communities with these capacities—and I argue that it has not—then my second level of inquiry investigates the system of urban social control that is emerging under the label "community policing."

In Southeast Seattle, competing stories about policing and community were interwoven within the relationships that created and were created by a formal police-community partnership: the South Seattle Crime Prevention Council. In this relational context, police power was both constrained and manifest as a "capacity to secure outcomes where the realization of these outcomes depends upon the agency of others."[32] Throughout the period of this study, the prevailing stories about policing remained state centered, expanding the department's mandate to fight the fear of crime as well as crime itself. More decentered stories were a part of these prevailing stories only to the extent that they reinforced this state agency.

The police chief in this period (1988–94) showed little interest in policing in a way that would bring officers closer to the people they served or in stories about policing that might have enabled communities to use the police department as a resource to build their own capacities to mobilize informal social controls. The discursive power of community revitalization withered within prevailing stories as it was interwoven into the larger, ongoing political struggles in the city and within the police bureaucracy. This meant that even in a National Institute of Justice model of community policing (Seattle) there was nearly no change in police organization, patrol orientation, community-based crime prevention, or accountability six years after the first police-community partnership was established.[33]

Chapter 2

Community (Policing)

Community has furnished a discursive framework within which social policies have been conceived, designed, implemented, and legitimated. Nowhere has this been more prominently so than within the realm of criminal justice. . . . Ideas of community have been invoked explicitly or evoked implicitly as explanations for and as means of curing social disorder.

—Lacey and Zedner (1995: 301)

I. Introduction

There are two reasons to take a closer look at the stories about community in community policing. First, community revitalization is central to the logic of stories about community policing. Advocates assume that a more proactive policing of disorder, including fear reduction and problem solving partnerships, will revitalize communities and enable citizens to contribute their informal forms of social control to the provision of public safety. Community-level informal social controls are central to what advocates claim will be innovative, efficient, and effective about community policing. Police-community partnerships to address neighborhood problems are expected to empower citizens in communities to overcome their fears and contribute to the coproduction of social order.[1]

A second reason to make explicit the stories about community implicit in stories about community policing is the dominance of state-centered stories about policing. Prevailing stories about policing and community obscure the power relations manifest in these stories and the practices they justify. This includes power imbalances between community groups and police departments, as well as across and within communities. "Appeals to 'community' thus appear to represent," according to Crawford, "the site at which shifts in the legitimate responsibilities of individuals, organizations, and the state are currently being played out and contested [and] the absence of any theory of power relations between communities is deafening by its silence."[2] While Crawford is critiquing a communitarian approach to community, this failure to account for power imbalances characterizes prevailing stories about community policing. With power relations made less visible, the intersection of stories about police and community form a "discursive alliance" around a concept of community whose political utility to the state can be found in its cultivated ambiguities, nostalgia, and romance.[3]

Stories about community revitalization and policing reform intersect in ways that affect both community life and the possibility of a more democratic social order. This intersection is most commonly treated from the perspective of the police bureaucracy under the heading police-community relations, where stories about community focus on how police departments can use or appease communities.[4] This work attempts to treat this same intersection from the perspective of communities. For both of these reasons—the logic of community policing and the privileging of state-centered stories—understanding community policing requires a close examination of stories about community.

The logic of community policing assumes communities to be a form of association capable of informal social control. But the meaning of this claim has not been explicitly worked out by advocates.[5] This failure is apparent when stories celebrating community exceed practices enabling communities with the desired capacities. Prevailing stories praise communities capable of coproducing public order through their unique capacities for informal social control. Neither these stories nor the practices of community policing, however, focus on what it is about communities that makes informal social controls possible or on the resources needed to revitalize communities *with these capacities.*

Making these implicit stories explicit has four implications for how we understand the emerging relationship between communities and police departments. First, without a sense of the concrete social relationships that constitute communities with these capacities, calls for a return to community are significantly less constrained and *become* merely rhetorical. That is, the range of potential meanings for such calls would then be much less related to anything we would associate with a collective aspiration for democratic community or a form of association with specific informal social control capacities and much more likely to reflect a "collective rhetoric that encourages and supports an essentially individualizing practice."[6] With communities as a free-floating signifier, community-based policing brings persuasive stories and coercive practices into partnerships that reinforce state agency and (further) fragment competing forms of collective identity, such as communities.[7]

Second, the forms of association that constitute communities may be the social foundation for the type of political culture essential to the possibility of more democratic forms of social control.[8] Following the republican visions of our founders, where virtuous citizens were seen as the foundation of good government, citizens become virtuous living in ways that constituted communities as self-governing schools of liberty and concrete reproductions of the possibility of cooperation.[9]

Third, if strong communities are a more effective long-term crime control policy, as advocates of community policing imply, then the question changes from what the police can do to what can be done about crime and violence in the short term (by any of a variety of political actors) that is the least inconsistent with the long-term resilience of communities. Advocates implicitly recognize this when they praise the importance of revitalizing informal mechanisms of community-based social control. Skeptics recognize this when they highlight the gap between this rhetorical recognition and the concrete practices of community policing.[10] This gap may provide some discursive space for community groups intent on holding leaders accountable to the stories about community used to generate support for community policing.[11] Or this gap between the rhetorical appeal of stories about community and the empirical decline of communities may also manifest the disorganization and incorporation of communities through partnerships that decentralize responsibilities for crime while centralizing this broader range of social control resources in state agency.[12]

Fourth, community, in the sense discussed here, links crime control to other social and political struggles. As one of the leading activists in Seattle told me, "Many of those who were initially just law-and-order types have come to see that we cannot control crime until we address drugs, education, poverty, and homelessness."[13] Failing to link crime to other urban struggles, as it is in the stories and activities of communities leaves each issue to be addressed separately by functionally separated state agents. When the forces meeting in neighborhood space are treated as separate issues, addressing root causes *becomes* an impractical guide to political action. However, these bureaucratically separated problems are also the multiple facets of the experiences of those living in the neighborhood, integrated in their stories about community. As Skogan argues, and the logic of community policing affirms, root causes are likely beyond the scope of government alone to address.[14] While the police can assist in the development of what Skogan calls root solutions, the effectiveness of these also depends on the capacities of communities to address these as they integrate their multifaceted concerns in the stories that they tell about community and policing.

This chapter will proceed in the following manner. First, I will place community policing within a larger political discourse about community to show how the general ambiguity of a term like *community* makes it necessary to focus on those concrete social relations that constitute community life. This highlights the political utility of a failure to make the meanings of community in stories about community policing explicit. Second, I make explicit the stories about community central to the logic of community policing. Finally, I connect these explicit stories to larger political and economic struggles to control urban social space.

II. Stories about Community

Stories about community are not unique to policing. Stanley Cohen documents a similar turn in the decarceration movement.[15] American city planners are turning to the community in their discovery of European-style urban villages as a response to the conflicting needs for cities to grow and avoid sprawl. And other social service providers have long shown a capacity to intervene more often and more effectively into previously nonstate spheres through their gradual incorporation of initially independent, alternative, community-based service providers.[16] These current stories, too, are not without precedent in American history. Puritans actively sought to establish a sacred community as a city on a hill.[17] Progressive reformers mobilized a discourse about good government and professional ethics to defend their visions of community.[18] Today the stories about community in community policing draw discursive support from the general ambiguity associated with terms like *community,* an ambiguity that favors more disciplinary forms of social control, as manifest in the antidemocratic thrust of communitarian criticisms of liberalism.[19] Placing stories about community into this larger discursive context demonstrates the ambiguity of the term and highlights the political utility of a failure to make explicit the meanings of community.

Communitarians, Liberalism, and Community. Like Progressive Era stories about community, communitarian stories have emerged, in part, as a response to urban disorder.[20] These stories, like those implicit in community policing, argue that the violence and anomie characteristic of modern industrial cities are a consequence of liberal inattention to the traditional civic virtues of prudence, discipline, and family central to a strong community life.[21] While communitarians do not focus on the activities of the police per se, their emphasis is on mechanisms of social control. By strengthening formal and informal mechanisms of social control, through revitalizing community, communitarians argue that we can reverse the moral decay and disorder generated by the failures of the social welfare state and the excesses of liberal individualism.[22] This critique of liberalism contributes to the appeal of stories about a return to community in community policing.[23]

Communitarians are critical of an excessive rights consciousness in liberal society, one that undermines family and community by attempting to subject these relationships to public scrutiny with liberal notions like justice and privacy rights. Okin contends that communitarians obscure the ways that traditional communities have been obstacles to the achievement of equality for women. Okin argues that communitarians assert that which ought to be discovered (shared meaning), thereby narrowing liberal values, like justice and privacy, by excluding their capacity to structure the achieving of shared meanings that support democratic communities.[24] Without attention to the power relations embedded within stories about community, communitarians draw our attention to an overly simplified duality: individual liberty (anomie) or traditional community. However, for many, stories about communities constituted by white men with wives at home remain unappealing and appear to be more disciplinary than democratic.[25]

Others also argue that the communitarian critique depends on a misreading of liberalism.[26] Communitarians observe the tendency of community to atrophy in liberal society and conflate this into a claim that liberalism has no account of community. But it is not that liberalism has no account of community; it is that liberalism does not determine the shape and values of communities a priori. Kymlicka argues that within a liberal account of community the proper question is not about individual liberty or traditional community but of achieving forms of community that more or less support individual and collective capacities.[27] Community is not a given form of situatedness. It is a set of social relations forged by individual and collective choices over time as we discover our shared values by observing the consequences of our actions. Just as our situations constrain our life options, so do the choices we make regarding life projects contribute to our collective understanding of the good, to our definition of self and community.[28]

Liberal thinkers like Mill defended the importance of individual liberty *because* the social conditions within which individuals acquire their values, goals, and pursuits matter.[29] This is not a conception of individual liberty that *must* weaken community and lead to anomie. Nor does this mean that a liberal emphasis on individual rights has been sufficient to successfully subject public and private power to the constraints of critical public scrutiny necessary to protect resilient and resourceful communities.[30] However, it does show that some communitarian stories may rest "on a romanticized view of how legitimacy was created in earlier days, and a naive view of how our dominant practices have been defined."[31] Thus, it is important to make explicit the implicit and ambiguous stories about community and any tendency to assert rather than achieve community.

Communitarians highlight how liberal politics has become thin and one sided in its commitment to those social relations that constitute community life. At the same time, the failure to account for power relations within families and communities by communitarians highlights the importance of focusing on *achieving* the shared meanings and reciprocal forms of association constitutive of communities.[32] "If legitimacy is to be earned, it won't be by strengthening communal practices and sentiments that have been defined by and for others. It will require empowering the oppressed and dominated to define their own practices and ends."[33] Attention to power and community in a liberal polity, then, means attention to competing stories and the conditions necessary for achieving community, including the capacities of citizens to subject power relations within and across communities as well as between citizens and state agents to public scrutiny.

Privacy and Public Scrutiny. Some of the ambiguity surrounding stories about community can be traced to larger ambiguities associated with privacy. The public, at least since Hobbes, is often reduced to the state.[34] Weber's definition of the state as that social organization that is granted a monopoly on the legitimate use of force is often conflated to mean that state power and state agency are the only legitimate forms of public power and the only source of social order.[35] This construction limits our understanding of public scrutiny, as it limits privacy to a right to remain free from public scrutiny in particular spheres of social life.

The private sphere and privacy express liberal commitments to protecting areas of life—such as family, community, and the market—from state intervention. But marxists and feminists have argued persuasively that private arenas like the market and the family are as permeated with unequal power relations as more traditional public spheres and thus are no less appropriate for the public scrutiny constitutive of a democratic society. Private spheres can protect social space for community life just as they can operate to constrain reciprocity (and narrow or preempt critical public scrutiny) by privileging traditional stories about community.

Ackelsberg and Okin both highlight the confusion surrounding privacy rights and the political paradox involved in asserting such rights.[36] Ackelsberg concludes that the indeterminacy of concepts like public and private indicate that stories about them are a locus of political struggle over the configuration of power and the distribution of resources.[37] The meanings of such terms shift in changing political situations, and to understand their meanings one must focus on the social relations envisioned and justified by particular stories. This, according to Ackelsberg, requires analysts to challenge the assumed existence of a single coherent meaning of these terms (challenge the terms of liberal discourse) and to insist on particular meanings in practice that are likely to empower women (challenge power imbalances justified within liberal discourse).

Okin identifies the paradox of privacy claims in that these are both a foundation for institutions and practices that have been instrumental in perpetuating the subordination of women (by insulating unreciprocal power relations in the home from public scrutiny) and a foundation for women's successful assertion of their right to make decisions concerning their own bodies.[38] Thus, while the terrain marked out by privacy claims is slippery and involves real political risks, the denial of the importance of privacy may also impose unacceptable costs. This is because some find in privacy the expression of aspirations they hold, just as privacy also expresses aspirations central to competing stories about family, community, and agency.

Community is a similar concept. It expresses diverse, sometimes conflicting aspirations and is best understood by seeing how it plays out within concrete social relations. Community, like privacy, is also made more difficult to achieve when either is contrasted with an understanding of the public as simply the state. One reason many feel torn about both privacy and community is that both claims are often pursued through appeals for state action. When state agents, such as police officers, act, it is not always experienced as public in the sense of it being in the public interest or open to public scrutiny. It may be experienced as being drawn into another's movie, as the imposition of some other private actor's stories about privacy or community.[39]

This relates to community policing in the sense that the particular treatment of community, like the treatment of privacy rights, reveals a concept capable of carrying contradictory political claims and thus representing a promise and a risk to those who choose to mobilize it as political discourse. This contradictory nature of privacy and community reveals them to be both appealing, if contested, values and powerful symbols indeterminate enough to serve a variety of political interests.[40] This requires analysts to challenge the assumption of a single community (challenging the terms of prevailing stories) and make competing and implicit stories explicit to highlight the social relations they justify (challenging the power relations supported by prevailing stories). This means two things for understanding community policing.

First, when community is seen as private, it is assumed by some that the power relations within communities are not a proper subject for public scrutiny. While I do not contest the claim that community life is constituted by forms of association that are potentially unlike those of state agencies, this claim neither implies that community life *cannot* be beneficially subjected to standards of justice and public scrutiny nor that it is *only* through the state that such scrutiny can be applied as public scrutiny. This means that one part of understanding the meaning of community is to examine intracommunity relations and relations among competing communities. Caution is called for because, as soccer hooliganism, Governor Ross Barnett's Citizen Councils, Nazi Brown Shirts, and Bonaparte's Society of December 10, among others, show, stories about community can become a potent force for political action that is anathema to a democratic society.[41] Further, each of these and community policing depend on stories that tease out the fear of disorder in certain communities and channel this energy into social control practices targeting other communities.

Second, this particular construction of privateness makes it difficult to think about police accountability. When one thinks about community policing as a private-public partnership, the question of public accountability becomes hidden. It becomes less clear to which public, if any, police ought to be held accountable.[42] When stories about community portray potential publics as private (special interests), they weaken the social foundation for the power of these citizens to provide legitimate public scrutiny of police activity. Conversely, the police may simply recognize the most cooperative private citizens group and publicize it through a police-community partnership to insulate the police from more critical public scrutiny with a partnership lacking the incentive or resources to criticize the police department.

This confusion surrounding public and private is manifest in our contradictory approach to community and community revitalization. From Tocqueville, to the Progressive Era, to Community Action Programs and the Community Control Movement, to community policing today, the meaning of community in American politics has been ripe with promise and risk. What these varied experiences teach us is that stories about a return to community draw considerable power from support for community as an ideal *and* as a concrete foundation for political mobilization. But, like privacy, the political utility of stories about community cannot be fully determined in the abstract. It is critical to focus on power relations and the social contexts for mobilizing communities as a mechanism for social change.

Community and State-Centered Stories. The debate over public and private, while instructive, still leaves out consideration of state agency and how this affects the power of communities. With all the attention placed on evaluating the relative strategic value of employing privacy rights or stories about community to mobilize state agents, there is insufficient treatment given to the questions of *how* and *in what form* these agents ought to assist.

These questions have led to some of the more interesting work in the study of politics today. Social movement literature addresses this, with particular attention to the costs and benefits of state financial assistance and the utilization of legal strategies for social change.[43] The alternative dispute resolution literature has shown that it is the particular mix of both formal and informal forms of association—given meaning in specific social contexts—that determines when either (or both) forms contribute to a more disciplinary or democratic social order.[44] And work in collective action theory, which treats state agency as only one possible solution to collective action problems, highlights the otherwise obscured fact that there are alternatives to state action that may still constitute public action.[45]

The cost of not reexamining our concepts of privacy and community may be the channeling of democratic energies into the creation of more effective disciplinary mechanisms of social control. It was in part the failure of early-twentieth-century activists to challenge statist assumptions within social service agencies that led to the use of community at that time as "a polite label for the subordination of indigenous neighborhood forces to the requirements of the human services apparatus."[46] When state tutelage is the only means for public action, this narrows the possibilities for future innovation by dampening the vitality of community life as a valuable and perhaps irreplaceable social resource.[47]

State-centered stories, packaged within a liberal-democratic discourse, can undermine the social conditions for effective political participation and community life.[48] Early-twentieth-century activists encouraged only those forms of participation consistent with state agency, subverting "an important precondition for the self-constitution of community."[49] This attempt by state agents to "sanitize collective action" was premised on stories about community that are incompatible with the sometimes disorderly, indeterminate, and often passionate interactions of community members themselves. Much of the modern state-centered impulse to sanitize public life is anathema to the way people live in communities and to the development of the communications skills and social relations necessary to make community life self-sustaining and empowering.[50]

The lesson to be learned from this, and applied to understanding stories about community in community policing, is that community-based social change is indeterminate because appeals to community carry both promises and risks that are not evenly distributed. Will the structure and practice of community policing support communities capable of holding private power and state agencies accountable? Will the local leaders responsible for community policing attend to questions of power and clarify which forms of state-citizen interaction and community best vest excluded interests? Considering the meaning of community this way means seeing community as a democratic aspiration to forms of association unlike bureaucratic client-patron relations, which is consistent with the notion of community appealed to by the advocates of community policing: a form of association with specific capacities to subject unaccountable power in their neighborhoods to critical public scrutiny.

III. Making Explicit Implicit Stories about Community

The term *community* is both difficult to use and difficult to avoid using. I use it because it expresses aspirations and reflects power relations central to prevailing and competing stories about community policing. In this section, I make explicit the implicit stories about community central to the logic of community policing. The implicit stories draw discursive power and political utility from the traditional ambiguity associated with the meaning of community. Making these stories explicit embraces the indeterminacy of social change, illuminating how contingency is reflected in discursive struggles. It also exposes empirically groundless assumptions about a single, coherent, and given community to the possibility of critical examination. To do this, I make explicit the assumption, implicit and central to all stories about community policing, that police activity can enable communities with specific capacities, that is, communities capable of the informal social controls characteristic of traditional community life.

To do this without myself romanticizing community, I begin with a definition that grounds community in concrete social relations. Throughout this study I use the term *community* in this open-ended yet concrete manner. In this way, the term can refer to neighborhoods, professional associations, women's groups, garden clubs, or even (however unlikely) nation-states that demonstrate the identified characteristics.[51] The term simultaneously refers to a concrete social phenomenon, which can exist in varying degrees, and to aspirations directed toward achieving these particular types of social interaction. Let me begin with Taylor's definition of community and then proceed directly to using this definition to make explicit the implicit stories about community in community policing.

> It is clear that "community" is an *open-textured* concept; that is to say, there cannot be an exhaustive specification of the conditions for the correct use of the concept. . . . There are, however, three attributes or characteristics possessed in *some* degree by *all* communities. . . . The first and most basic of these "core" characteristics is that set of persons who compose a community have beliefs and values in common. . . . The second characteristic is that relations between members should be *direct* and they should be *many-sided.* Relations are direct to the extent that they are unmediated—by representatives, leaders, bureaucrats, institutions such as those of the state, or by codes, abstractions and reifications. . . . The third and final characteristic of community is that of reciprocity.[52]

When direct, multifaceted, reciprocal interactions are characteristic of a community, this creates a network of social relations within which informal social control is possible. As a set of concrete social relations, community can then become a resource for members to establish and maintain order collectively.[53] It is in these routine interactions and collective problem solving efforts that participants can achieve a sense of shared values, which can make their community stronger. Such a form of association might be more readily mobilized for effective and sustained political action, including political action in defense of their community.[54] An association defined by this type of interaction constitutes a community that itself *can* be mobilized as a collective resource, including its capacity to contribute informal social controls to the provision of social order.

But the story of communities capable of contributing informal social controls does not end with a recognition of the social resources that constitute community life. While the story highlights social resources, it also assumes that communities have the political and economic resources they need to define and defend themselves. It is important to recognize the different ways that stronger and weaker communities participate in politics as a sign of the types of resources they can mobilize.[55] From a community policing perspective, others have observed that stronger communities participate and weaker communities complain.[56] Fraser argues that the participation of weaker communities is often structurally limited to ratifying state action and intensifying their dependence on state agency. Stronger communities can more actively interact with state agencies and are able, if necessary, to act independently. An important component of these stronger communities is that they have the resources to seek redress effectively against state agencies with which they have a grievance. Weaker communities may lack internal resources, like reciprocity, and the capacity to seek redress externally. Further, they may also lack the ability to substitute private financial or political resources for their lack of reciprocity and redress.[57]

This definition of community highlights the fact that communities can exist without geographical referents and with very different degrees of political influence. Communities may have shared a neighborhood space in the past, and it may be easier to sustain the types of social relations that constitute strong communities when members live and work in proximity. But it is not inconceivable that groups could enjoy direct, multisided, and reciprocal social relations without living in the same neighborhood. This definition also highlights, by focusing on the social relations that make up communities, how particular forms of interaction, personal and collective histories built upon these interactions, and the shared values that may be a consequence of these can become a collective resource, or social capital, for members. Finally, this definition points to the importance of both reciprocal intracommunity relations and reciprocal intercommunity relations, as these may contribute to the strength of particular communities and their capacity for informal social control.

Social Capital. The stories about community in community policing are stories about traditional communities capable of informal forms of social control on the basis of their unique form of association. While Taylor's definition is useful because it highlights the social relations that constituted traditional community life, it is important to keep in mind that the growth of modern state and corporate bureaucracies has contributed to the atrophy of traditional communities.[58] Thus, the stories about community made explicit here rely heavily on nostalgia for their political appeal. For this reason, my first level of inquiry examines the connections between these stories and the power relations they justify to see if they enable communities with specified capacities. Since I argue that this enabling is largely absent, my second level of inquiry becomes an examination of the system of social control that is being created to link social capital to state-centered social control networks.

Social capital, unlike physical or financial capital, does not exist in a form that can be separated from the concrete social relations it grew out of, and the value of social capital increases as it is consumed. Social capital is not manifest in currency or land; rather, it "inheres in the structure of relations between actors and among actors."[59] It is found in the kind of civic leadership Roger Sales praises in Seattle's founders, what Robert Putnam calls the networks of civic engagement, which are a key factor in distinguishing those forms of government (or social control) that will succeed from those that fail.[60] Social capital is one way of thinking about the resources advocates of community policing are referring to when they seek to mobilize community-based mechanisms of informal social control. And this resource, to be available at all, requires attention to implicit stories about reciprocity in community policing.

The resources that inhere in communities (social capital) are targeted in prevailing stories about community policing. The police department wants information and resources from the community to improve its capacity to maintain order in a cost-effective manner. Communities also seek less costly forms of social control but place different cost structures into the calculation, including police harassment and other decisions by public and private decision makers that impact their quality of life. Thus, the most basic reciprocal exchange at the heart of stories about community policing is a police/state commitment to perform their duties in a way that enhances the generation of social capital in communities and a community commitment to invest a portion of that capital in cooperative efforts with the police to improve public safety. This clearly requires attention to the capacities of communities to generate social capital and subject unaccountable forms of power in their neighborhoods to critical public scrutiny.

IV. Taking Community Seriously: Reciprocity and Community (Policing)

The story about community made explicit here highlights the importance of attention to the concrete social relations that constitute communities capable of mobilizing mechanisms of informal social control. In traditional communities, these capacities inhered within networks of face-to-face, crosscutting, and reciprocal relationships. Reciprocity is an intersubjective precondition for the generation and investment of social capital, which is a form of stored reciprocity and, as such, a collective resource. The reciprocity that underlies community-based informal social controls (horizontal social capital) can also be supported by manifestly reciprocal relations between citizens and state agencies (vertical social capital). Like horizontal social capital, vertical social capital is embedded within indeterminate and contingent relational networks that depend on the level of reciprocity inhering within them to nurture and mobilize this resource. Vertical social capital, then, is nurtured by effective, open, and manifestly democratic channels of redress. Reciprocity within and among communities and redress in relations with state agents both strengthen the capacities of communities to contribute unique resources to social control. Reciprocity (horizontal and vertical social capital) will be used as an analytical tool to locate how stories and practices constitutive of this reform encourage relationships capable of sustaining the informal mechanisms of social control central to the logic of community policing.

Reciprocity is a structural precondition for the generation of social capital. The structures and agency supported by community policing, to take community seriously, must take into account the importance of intracommunity reciprocity for the effective operation of the informal social controls police seek to mobilize. The nature of social capital, especially the ways in which a lack of vertical social capital can weaken a community's capacity to mobilize horizontal social capital, means that the stories and practices constitutive of community policing must also protect the capacities of communities to criticize public and private power. Intercommunity reciprocity must, therefore, include manifestly democratic mechanisms for holding state agents (most immediately, police departments) accountable for the impact of their decisions on communities.[61] These criteria run contrary to the current focus on order in the stories and practices of community policing because these will involve the encouragement of those forms of disorder constitutive of democratic communities such as the disorder inherent in citizens directly and reciprocally integrating the competing concerns within their diverse communities.[62]

Reciprocity and Critical Public Scrutiny. The order maintenance component of community policing resonates with the need to reverse the disorder and decay of public spaces. But it is important to examine whether the way disorder is contained and public space defended frees up social space for the more democratic—and often disorderly—interactions constitutive of communities. Stories about strengthening community life, then, support an understanding of policing as inescapably part of larger (beyond crime control) struggles to control urban social space and the local resources embedded in the relationships that bring to life these spaces. Social spaces—like the pubs and sidewalks where people congregate, work, or play—are the locations where social capital is generated and invested. Evans and Boyte argue that it is the direct, face-to-face communication in these places that reveals the ways that community life can both constrain and encourage progressive social change.

> People live in communal worlds of daily activity and draw strength from the cultural resources and traditions embedded in such specific contexts. Structures and ideological themes that, at least potentially, nourish dissent and democratic values coexist with forms of accommodation and submission that are also woven into the fabric of communities.[63]

Thinking about community policing this way returns us to our earlier discussion of the distinction between public and private. Free social spaces are public in the sense that they are collective terrain, defined by direct, routine, and (potentially) reciprocal interactions. As public space, there is clearly a role for state agencies and communities in the provision of public order. And our tradition supports an expectation (if not always the actuality) that the relationships supported and resources applied to policy in public spaces will be subject to democratic constraints, including manifestly open forms of redress and accountability. These spaces are, however, also private in that they are relatively insulated from formal state penetration and control, which does not mean that these spaces are beyond constraints; it means that both state-centered and more decentered forms of constraint operate in these spaces, and each can still be expected to support more (rather than less) reciprocal relationships.[64]

The actual character of these spaces (and how they are controlled) remains stubbornly contingent on the indeterminate relationships among the individuals and groups who live and work there. Freeing social space, then, is an intersubjective process of enabling relationships where private persons can voluntarily join as equal associates to subject less accountable forms of power in these spaces to critical public scrutiny.[65] As such, it is clear that the role of police departments will be consistent with stories about community in community policing to the degree that policing policy does not damage the reciprocity central to the public or private nature of free social spaces. The nature of these spaces makes explicit the deeper democratic aspirations implicit in community policing. Stories about communities deliberating to solve problems rather than simply providing input into existing bureaucratic problem solving initiatives are stories that assume a capacity to solve problems, a capacity drawn from concrete reciprocal relationships that develop and deploy social capital.

Without reciprocity, *community* is more likely to signify a sense of political impotence created by an appealing but meaningless symbol, freely floating between an arena of unchecked bureaucratic power and individual isolation.[66] This perspective on the struggle to control urban social space provides a basis for seeing both the potentially empowering and repressive aspects of the stories about community in community policing—and the importance of seeing both. Where reciprocity exists, the democratic empowerment of communities becomes possible, though not automatic. This indeterminacy, while often a source of disorder, is also a component of democratic community life. Boyte argues that the creation of

> a serious foundation for democratic power to transform the large-scale structures and dynamics of the society . . . [requires] a politics of empowerment, for which the emphasis always remains squarely on the capacity building within the citizenry. Empowerment politics does not try to mobilize people towards pre-decided goals. Instead, it utilizes every struggle, every protest, every community conflict as an opportunity to strengthen character, develop community skills, acquire greater voice and power. . . . [The key is the] nature of public interaction.[67]

In the more reciprocal forms of association captured in concepts like free social space, individuals communicate directly and learn the skills required to be effective political actors.[68] A key issue in evaluating prevailing stories about community, then, is the nature of the public interaction they encourage. And the key to understanding the nature of the interactions is to focus on reciprocity (horizontal and vertical social capital). To what extent do the stories and practices constitutive of community policing encourage reciprocal interactions among citizens themselves, making them more capable of coordinating formal and less formal resources, directing problem-solving efforts, and subjecting unaccountable power in their neighborhoods to critical public scrutiny?[69] Reciprocity is the critical analytical starting point, just as it is central to the logic of both prevailing and competing stories about community in community policing.

Reciprocity and Power. While stories about community may highlight an imperative that community (policing) must empower communities by encouraging reciprocity if it is to revitalize latent community-based mechanisms of social control, social capital is only one investment at stake in this struggle to control urban social space. "To nurture the seeds of social progress," according to Spitzer, "we must have some concrete conception of the soil in which it is intended to grow. . . . [I]t is here that our visions of community come to the fore."[70] And the soil mixture is more than simply stories about social capital; the possibility of more reciprocal everyday interactions is often stillborn in soil that lacks the diverse nutrients needed to support healthy intra- and intercommunity relationships and reflects the domination of urban social space by a single organism: corporate capital. Even this rich fertilizer has not been able to secure prosperity without fragmenting contemporary communities, harming those Americans who are already the least advantaged, and aligning financial capital as an obstacle to the community revitalization envisioned in stories about community central to community policing.[71] By promoting the generation of these forms of capital at the expense of social capital, corporate leadership has weakened the resilience of our local communities. Capital flight, corporate downsizing, redlining, and various other routine corporate practices weaken our capacity to respond to changes in our environment with resources like social capital—resources that allow responses to crime that also preserve and protect our children, families, and communities from various unaccountable powers plaguing urban social space.

Katznelson argues that structural changes rooted in the Industrial Revolution have steadily undermined traditional urban communities. In these communities, precapitalist forms of social control centered on the routine social interactions of private individuals and groups working out conflicts within and as communities.[72] As industrialization broke up cross-class neighborhoods, new forms of social control emerged that have been hostile to the relational basis of social capital. Instead of "people sharing an identity . . . [by] fashion[ing] the units of conflict," state agents replaced these private forms of social control with an externally imposed social order structured to support the agency of corporate individuals and the value of commercial and financial capital.[73] Conflicts and their resolution became less constitutive elements of community life and more matters of state (police).

> An urban mosaic, whose parts were distinguished by class and function, had begun to emerge, altering the meaning of place, and the nature of "community." One result was a new kind of political conflict about urban space, as members of the dominant class sought to capture the benefits of city life without having to deal with the consequences.[74]

State-centered social control redefined traditional community-building interactions as resistance to state action in the public interest, justifying deeper state intervention and further weakening communities.[75] Deprived of the concrete social relations that made up traditional communities, citizens are left more dependent on state agents and vulnerable to romantic promises of community revitalization, even when these do not seek to reestablish the capacity of citizens to coordinate resources or subject unaccountable power to critical public scrutiny. "What is new in the current informalization and community justice programs," Boaventura de Sousa Santos warns, "is that whereas the oppressed classes have hitherto been disorganized at the individual level, as citizens, voters, or welfare recipients, in the future they will be disorganized at the community level. I suggest that state-sponsored community organizations will be the specific form of disorganization in late capitalism."[76] Seen this way, reciprocity is not only central to the logic of community policing; it is also a critical analytical tool for examining the power relationships justified by the stories and practices of community policing.

Chapter 3

(Community) Policing

Rather than assume that the contemporary location of police and police regulation in the context of state power is part of what police has always meant . . . this location is a historically contingent consequence of the process of state formation and the separation of state and society. Indeed, the history of police *prior to the term's modernization shows that police regulation was in many historical instances a vehicle for the expression of a communitarian rather than a statist consciousness, providing expression for an institutionally inchoate sense of collective responsibility for the reproduction of the well-ordered community.*

—Tomlins (1993)

I. *Introduction*

In their National Institute of Justice study, Skolnick and Bayley survey policing reform efforts around the world and conclude that the core of community policing is four general principles: community-based crime prevention, reorientation of patrol, increased police accountability, and decentralization of command.[1] These principles are, however, more policy prescription than empirical observation. As their study shows, in each country studied the salience of these stories about community policing was exceeded by the failure of police departments to act on any of these principles and reorient police operations.[2]

In Australia, Great Britain, and the United States, neighborhood block watch organizations have emerged, with little organizational impact on police departments. What change has occurred has been an incoherent patchwork. In England, the neighborhood organizations are dominated by the police. In Canada, Norway, Sweden, Denmark, and Finland, there has been some discussion of decentralization, but since community groups lack the resources to challenge police control of the reform process there has been little actual decentralization.[3] And in the United States Skolnick and Bayley conclude that community policing remains "more aspiration than implementation."[4] Thus, understanding community policing means focusing on competing and prevailing stories about community and policing.

Prevailing stories about community and policing advanced by advocates can be seen as efforts to (re)construct history to support state-centered stories about social control.[5] Prevailing stories about policing draw discursive resources from references to empowering communities with specific informal social control capacities while at the same time narrowing the possibility that policing in those communities most victimized by crime and disorder will receive resources beyond those strengthening state agency. Stories about community revitalization are central to the political appeal and coherence of prevailing stories about policing reform, but the logic of these assumptions is left to wither as prevailing stories narrow their meaning to reducing fear and problem solving, both police led activities that tap community partnerships only insofar as they are a resource for the police department, reversing the power flow from empowering communities to empowering the police.

Competing stories have less to do with a coherent reform agenda than with resistance to state-centered reform efforts in general. These stories are grounded in diffuse, ad hoc, and indeterminate relational networks and can be seen as an attempt by communities to repoliticize the narrow contemporary location of policing in law enforcement agencies and reassert a more decentered understanding of policing from an alternative tradition in American political thought. Tomlins argues that the current "institutional bias of modern analyses of police" obscures the fact that this broader notion of policing as a collective responsibility to contribute to self-governance has deep roots in the American political experience.[6] The broader notion of policing still survives in the American constitutional doctrine of police powers, in which the Supreme Court explicitly treats policing as encompassing the tasks of governance or, as Tomlins later says, "the community's capacity to ensure good order."[7]

Policing Is Inherently Political. Tomlins argues that eighteenth and early-nineteenth-century policing referred to an explicitly political strategy of governance based on a collective responsibility for achieving social order. This empirical situation remains unchanged. Policing is inherently political because social control is a core and contested task of governance. What has changed is the way we talk about policing.

With the formal, bureaucratic organization of municipal police departments, this more decentered discourse and its essentially communitarian vision were colonized by a state-centered vision of policing as professional law enforcement. Rather than expressing a collective responsibility to participate in democratic politics, stories about professional policing encouraged deference to state authority and passive acquiescence to state agency. To justify shifting the grounds for legitimation from politics to law, the professional discourse described policing as an apolitical and scientific profession appropriate for insulation from critical public scrutiny. These stories exclude more explicitly political stories about street-level policing and struggles within police bureaucracies.[8] Thinking of policing as an apolitical activity is in sharp contrast to empirical reality and normalizes deference to police expertise on law and order issues.

These Progressive Era policing reforms ushered in a paramilitary structure, civil service protection, random preventative patrol, rapid response, and regular rotation to avoid corrupting contact with citizens. Each of these insulated police officers from neighborhood-based political leaders. The trouble in paradise was rooted in the fact that professional policing also insulated officers from the citizens they served and alienated even law-abiding communities. The resulting distrust insulated officers from critical crime-related information and the social capital that inheres within the relational networks that constitute communities. Tomlins argues that this transformation reflects a tension between two stories about American democracy, one based on law and the other based on politics.

> In the last quarter of the eighteenth century, *law* and *police* constituted distinct conceptual bases upon which paradigms of republican socioeconomic order might be erected. The police paradigm was that of distributive justice politically managed—in other words, purposefully administrative activity by a democratic state for the promotion of human happiness and the maximization of individual and collective creative energies. . . . [T]he police paradigm offered an opportunity to express in a new form the communitarian ethos of the colonial past.
>
> What Jeffersonians saw as the promise inherent in the dynamic interplay of a broad-based democracy and the newly legitimated authority of the state, however, others interpreted as presaging a

> majoritarian assault on vested interests. Americans ended up choosing a different paradigm—that of *law*—which elevated the maintenance of order above mere politics, and which simultaneously labeled economic activity a private realm and segregated it from purposeful public direction. In this paradigm, the social order was constituted principally by protecting property rights from the expanded political nation through constitutional confinement of the scope of democratic politics. Indeed, by the early nineteenth century, property rights had effectively been removed from the realm of politics altogether. Thus, in the *law* paradigm, the administrative capacities of the state—the police power—became the subject of judicial, not political determination, and their use an issue in constitutional law, not democratic politics. As a strategy of ordering, police became, as in England, a matter of security rather than of happiness, an instrument for the facilitation of individual transactions among absolute proprietors and for suppressing alternative modes of conducting human affairs.[9]

In this quote, Tomlins "has located a road not taken by mapping the history of the concept of the police," transforming prevailing stories into efforts to construct history for state-centered purposes.[10] This provides a historical basis for seeing the discursive struggle to define policing as a political struggle between stories about collective responsibilities (manifestly recognizing that police work is embedded within complex, contingent, and indeterminate social relationships), and stories about state agency (organized to shield police departments from political influence). Seeing these competing discourses and the privileging of stories about state-centered law enforcement helps us to understand how the atrophy of community contributes to the meanings of community policing.[11] Understanding the competing stories and power relations that intersect in community policing are essential parts of evaluating the extent to which it maps a path toward freedom or servitude, to a more democratic or more disciplinary society.[12] And seeing community policing as a state-centered policing effort reveals how prevailing stories construct history to make more decentered stories about policing either less visible or only visible to the extent that these reinforce state agency. Like Progressive Era reforms, prevailing stories about policing and community here are inescapably political;

and the political utility of these reforms serves to extend state control over a widening range of social control resources.

A core assumption in the logic of community policing is that innovative police practices can mobilize now latent informal mechanisms of social control embedded within community life. Advocates argue that community policing will be more effective because it revitalizes communities with these specific capacities. Police-community partnerships are expected to empower citizens to overcome their fears and contribute to the coproduction of social order. This discursive overlap highlights potential resources for resistance that are delivered within prevailing stories and given force by their position at the intersection of stories that advertise social order through state agency and stories envisioning the possibility of social order through more decentered policing techniques. In the current practice of community policing, these concrete capacities are simply (and mistakenly) assumed, because prevailing stories depend on romantic tales about traditional community, without attention to the specific resources and relational networks that constitute communities and their social control capacities.

The argument proceeds as follows. First, I examine a concrete illustration of prevailing stories about policing reform to identify how three implicit stories about professionalism, fear reduction, and problem solving partnerships construct a particular history and present for policing. Second, I introduce explicitly political, competing stories about policing to highlight the ways that prevailing stories expand upon, rather than break with, state-centered stories about professional control and insulation from critical public scrutiny constructed to legitimate police power. Finally, I make explicit competing stories about decentered policing. This, like the analytical approach to the concept of community, provides a theoretical perspective capable of illuminating the broader discursive struggle to define community policing.

II. Prevailing Stories about (Community) Policing

Perhaps the most unavoidable conclusion one can draw from a study of community policing is that it means different things to different people. While many speak about community policing as beat cops on foot patrol, that has rarely been a major component of community policing initiatives.[13] Community policing is seen by some as an effort by the police to combine crime-fighting and community service strategies for improving organizational performance.[14] It can also be seen as the notion, presented by Herman Goldstein, that "a community must police itself [and] the police can, at best, only assist in that task."[15] Thus, the conceptual foundations for community policing range from nostalgic images, to management strategies, to visions of communities strong enough to police themselves. Prevailing stories construct each of these to support a state-centered vision of policing: professional beat cops, with the coaching and support of reform-minded police administrators, can effectively partner with communities to combine order maintenance and law enforcement, leading us all from anomie back to the safety and prosperity of traditional community life. This nostalgic story has the political utility of reinforcing state-centered stories, despite the fact that there is ample empirical evidence that decentered stories more closely map onto actual police work.[16]

State-Centered Law Enforcement. Prevailing stories about contemporary policing reform see community policing as the latest installment in a linear progression toward effective professional law enforcement. In 1994, John Eck and Dennis Rosenbaum, in an introductory essay to a volume of community policing studies largely funded by the Department of Justice, presented just this kind of prevailing story. This section will use their piece to illustrate prevailing stories because it explicitly builds on the three most important stories about policing reform: professionalism, fear reduction, and problem solving partnerships.

Eck and Rosenbaum argue that community policing is the latest attempt by police professionals to respond to long-standing public expectations: effectiveness, equity, and efficiency. This story about community policing identifies these expectations as a continuous thread within policing reforms to demonstrate that community policing retains a focus on the four core activities of professional policing: crime control, response times, arrest and clearance rates, and order maintenance.[17] Community policing provides additional tools for police professionals to meet these expectations, requiring only three minor adjustments. First, the priority of these four activities are rearranged, increasing police attention to nonemergency calls.

Second, community policing encourages police departments to reduce fear. "A fundamental objective of this community policing perspective is to help create self-regulating, self-sufficient communities where levels of crime and disorder are contained by the efforts of local residents and institutions."[18] Research has shown that the police cannot fight crime alone, encouraging police departments to look increasingly to communities for additional crime-fighting resources. But weak communities, those most in need of effective policing, lack many kinds of resources. They will be better able to participate in the provision of public safety, including participation in neighborhood problem solving with police officers, when they are less afraid. Police efforts to reduce fear will contribute to the capacity of communities to police themselves, thereby improving the effectiveness of policing.[19]

Third, problem solving "reorganizes the police role. Emergency aid [response times] and justice [arrest and clearance rates] are still important functions, but crime and nonemergency services [order maintenance] are now seen as two broad classes of problems, as are fear of crime and quality of life concerns. The problem [becomes] the primary unit of police work."[20] A focus on problem solving provides coherence to the adjustments of police function. From these three changes, Eck and Rosenbaum conclude that community policing adds two critical questions to existing measures of police performance: "Do the police detect problems that are important to most members of the community and do the problems the police handle decline in magnitude or seriousness as a result?"[21]

Problem solving proves to be the key element of Eck and Rosenbaum's discussions of equity and efficiency as well. The authors argue that efforts to reduce inequity will only be consistent with more effective policing if these focus on community empowerment to solve problems rather than forging partnerships per se. Efficiency can be increased in a way that will also increase police effectiveness only when problem solving enhances the department's ability to tap communities as an additional resource and cost-cutting efforts focus on improving the problem-solving capacities of police officers by making better use of their experience and local knowledge.

For equity and efficiency, Eck and Rosenbaum also argue that a community policing regime will supplement existing policing standards. For equity, they argue, "the most relevant measures are the perceptions of the various publics served by the police." Two standards are appropriate for efficiency. Given two equally effective community policing agencies, the agency that makes the greatest use of resources beyond its direct control and with a flatter organizational structure should be viewed as the most efficient. Eck and Rosenbaum argue that this should include integration of resources from "other government and private organizations and citizens' groups."[22]

There are three analytically separable stories about policing reform within this larger story. First, Eck and Rosenbaum depend on a story about the history of policing reform as linear and progressively more professional that is best represented by the work of Kelling and Moore. Second, the prevailing story outlined above depends on popularized speculation about the relationship between the fear of crime, crime control, and community that is best represented by the work of Wilson and Kelling. Finally, the story presented by Eck and Rosenbaum depends on the claim that problem solving will be more effective than officers employing only existing professional policing techniques. This claim is best represented by the work of Herman Goldstein. I will consider each of these to complete this deconstruction of prevailing stories about policing reform.

Professionally Managed Order Maintenance. Kelling and Moore divide American policing history into three periods that they call political, reform, and community. The political era (1840s to the early twentieth century) was characterized by "struggles between various interest groups to govern the police."[23] The organization of policing was decentralized. Its function was broadly defined to include services beyond law enforcement as these contributed to public order. The police force was integrated into the neighborhoods they served, and they were seen as a collective tool against disorder and a viable avenue of social mobility for new immigrants.

The reform era (1920s to 1970s) created the professional model and is characterized by Kelling and Moore as a "remarkable construction—internally consistent, rigorous, and based on the most advanced organizational and tactical thinking of the time."[24] Reform era policing became a state-centered, hierarchical, law enforcement activity, designed to be insulated from political influence. The core activities (rapid response, random preventative patrol, and investigative follow-up), however, failed to fulfill its new and narrower mission of fighting crime.

The community era is characterized by Kelling and Moore as a combination of political and reform policing, taking only the best from both approaches. Political policing drew its authority from the community, and reform policing shifted to authority based on law and professionalism. Community policing is authorized by the community, law, and professionalism. Similarly, the function of community policing combines an earlier service orientation with professional crime control. It combines centralized and decentralized forms of organization, combines political era tactics such as foot patrol with reform era tactics such as motor patrol, and strengthens a state-centered command and control hierarchy that focuses on law enforcement with professionally managed order maintenance and problem solving.[25]

This story about community policing promises more intensive police-citizen contacts without returning to the corrupt policing of the political era. Policing will improve because professionally managed order maintenance will "invite and channel" latent mechanisms of social control from the community as well as increase the department's access to information.[26] Increased officer contact with citizens and discretion will not produce corruption because "the bureaucratization, unionization, and professionalization that characterize contemporary policing seem more than ample bulwarks against the inappropriate influence of any single neighborhood or interest."[27]

Disorder, Fear Reduction, and Informal Social Controls. In "Broken Windows" (1982) Wilson and Kelling argue that to the extent that policing manages disorder and reduces fear it is an efficient allocation of department resources: "The essence of the police role in maintaining order is to reinforce informal control mechanisms of the community itself. The police cannot, without committing extraordinary resources, provide a substitute for that informal control."[28] Fear of disorder paralyzes communities. This stifles informal mechanisms of social control, which in turn amplifies the consequences of disorder. Left untended, this spiral of disorder, fear, and decay invites more serious crime and requires costly, often futile, police intervention. Wilson and Kelling argue, therefore, that the effective response is early intervention. This kind of proactive policing is more efficient when the department already has access to information and support from the community.

To stop the cycle of decay, make neighborhoods safer, and reduce the cost of providing public safety, the police need to strengthen those informal mechanisms of social control weakened by the decline of community life. These mechanisms are weakened when residents see disorder going untended and thus modify their behavior—by using the streets less and refraining from the neighborly interaction that is the social basis of informal social control. Wilson and Kelling argue that central to low-cost policing is the reduction of community-paralyzing fear. Community policing attacks disorder—it responds to community concerns by fixing broken windows—and thereby reduces fear. No longer paralyzed by fear, communities can cooperate with the police department and contribute social capital and other resources to the effort.[29]

Problem Solving Partnerships. Herman Goldstein argues that patrol officers should be encouraged to solve problems rather than simply respond to 911. Community policing will improve the crime-fighting effectiveness of a police department to the degree that it also improves police effectiveness on a broader range of community problems such as managing disorder and reducing fear. The logic of "Broken Windows" is also important here because it provides a discursive link (the cycle of neighborhood decline, which begins with an untended broken window) between effective crime-fighting, fear reduction, and order maintenance to justify problem solving as an effective crime-fighting tool. Departments will be more effective if they tap the knowledge and experience of the community and rank-and-file officers and invest in more proactive initiatives to prevent or reduce community problems.

Goldstein contends that a problem-oriented approach provides coherence to otherwise piecemeal policing reforms. Reforms that simply seek to establish a more congenial relationship with the community lack focus and risk encouraging a diffuse, uncontrolled form of citizen participation.

> If one is concerned about *both* the need to make fuller use of the community in seeking to control behavior and the need to focus on substantive problems rather than the organizational and institutional arrangements for providing police service . . . involving the community as needed in dealing with specific problems is preferred.[30]

This means avoiding broad, ambitious organizational reforms designed to develop a new relationship with the community in favor of an incremental focus on specific, concrete problem solving partnerships designed to improve the effectiveness of police officer activities.[31]

III. Competing Stories: Urban Politics and Police Power

It would be difficult—and unwise—to separate the story of policing in America from the larger story of American politics. Policing in America has changed significantly since the eighteenth century, when locally elected night watchmen—such as Paul Revere—served their communities as an informal duty of citizenship.[32] American politics has changed at least as much. As an eighteenth-century agrarian society moved into the nineteenth century, the promise of a seemingly unlimited frontier began to push up against its limits and populations swelled in large industrial cities. Industrialization produced high standards of living, while urbanization concentrated racial and class conflict. By the late nineteenth century, middle- and upper-class white Protestants—fearing that urban disorder would destroy public morality and economic security—succeeded in outlawing gambling, regulating saloons, and passing Sunday blue laws. In the early twentieth century, these same reformers outlawed alcohol and undermined the voting power of working-class immigrants with the Progressive promise of government without politics. Middle- and upper-class support for these laws was matched by working-class opposition.

> To the dismay of the reformers, many immigrants continued to gamble, drink, and do business on Sunday; and so, for that matter, did many native Americans. By the turn of the century the issue was clearly drawn. Whether or not these laws were enforced would henceforth shape the prevailing life-styles and underlying morality in urban America and thereby influence the relative standing of its social classes and ethnic groups.[33]

Industrialization and the associated problems of governing big cities required new ways of securing social order.[34] Nineteenth-century policing was decentralized and controlled by working-class ward leaders according to the political needs of their local communities.[35] The wards were loosely organized into personalized political machines that provided public employment, public safety, and public services in exchange for electoral support. Policing contributed to the stability of this system by getting out the vote, defending neighborhoods against outsiders, and providing a steady pool of secure jobs for new immigrants.[36] The function of the police was to maintain order and respond to the needs of the decentralized social system they served. "Whoever controlled the police possessed an enviable flexibility to respond to confrontations and crises in ways consistent with their own political objectives, which was a tremendous advantage in a society so prone to group conflict."[37]

Machine politics and the tradition of politically responsive policing encountered opposition in the early twentieth century from Progressive reformers. Reformers argued that decentralization left officers open to partisan influence. And corruption was inevitable as long as officers were merely expected to regulate crime, tacitly licensing vice.[38] "Committed to the concepts of an underlying social harmony and an overriding public interest, [the Progressives] labored to replace wards with at-large councils, strengthen the mayor's office, and thereby eliminate the pervasive localism of urban politics."[39] This included efforts to separate policing from politics. The prevailing story about policing *became* a story about centralized professional law enforcement.[40] Control of policing became more insulated from the networks of electoral support in the working-class neighborhoods and was relocated in the professionalized city, state, and federal bureaucracies dominated by white, upper middle class, educated Protestants.

These stories about professional policing and good government, which have dominated since World War I, have been interwoven with technological advances into what Lawrence Sherman calls a single-complaint crime-fighting strategy.[41] Recent research suggests that professional policing has also been characterized by wasteful resource allocation, a less than effective impact on crime, and deteriorating community relations.

> Ironically, the justification for moving to single-complaint policing was to focus the police role on crime-fighting. The abandonment of proactive order maintenance and intelligence gathering was the price of this emphasis on crime control. But recent research has supported the theory that single-complaint policing is less effective in controlling crime than *was* community policing.[42]

Since the late 1960s and early 1970s, following what many perceived to be police mismanagement of urban unrest, a series of studies criticizing professional policing practices created discursive space and resources for the revival of alternative stories about policing. Professional policing alienated the community, including the law-abiding community. The studies showed that random preventative patrol and an emphasis on reducing response times did not reduce crime; nor did they make residents feel safer. The 911 single-call response system, overloaded with emergency and nonemergency calls, was criticized for failing to provide officers with the on-site information needed to investigate criminal activity and for giving many callers the impression that the department did not have time to respond to their immediate needs.

Ironically, August Vollmer and O. W. Wilson, the police reformers who created the professional model, believed that this approach would be *more* responsive to citizen concerns (by responding to each call for service), a *more* efficient allocation of resources (fewer officers covering a larger area), and a *more* effective crime-fighting strategy (because random patrol gave an appearance of saturation and improved response times). However, research has shown that random motor patrol put officers at cold crime scenes, where essential information remained unavailable because officers insulated from political influences are not invested in the networks of local relationships where this essential information is located.[43] Assigning motor patrols to neighborhoods where the officers had no local connections reduced opportunities for corruption. It also reduced the department's access to crime-related information and community support.

Police work remains embedded within these networks, but when police officers do spend time managing disorder, working on the kinds of activities that can—over time—build strong relations with community members, they have not been encouraged or supported by police administrators.[44] Without extended beat integrity, this bureaucratic bias inflates the police officer's role as state agent and deflates the officer's role as a local insider empowered and constrained by the complex social relationships that constitute the communities that they work (and live?) within.

Police Discretion, Corruption, and Community. While, as Goldstein and Tomlins observe, a bureaucratic bias has been characteristic of professional policing, police work has remained largely decentered. Studies show that police officers, even in the professional era, still spend between 60 and 70 percent of their patrol time on order maintenance, despite professional stories about their focus on crime fighting.[45] Police work has remained embedded within the complex and indeterminate social relationships that constitute urban communities.[46] This more decentered view of policing leads to stories less about strengthening police managers than about strengthening in communities the capacities to subject various forms of unaccountable power in their neighborhoods to critical public scrutiny.

In previous reforms, each time the police improved their capacity to insulate themselves they also undercut their political support. Stories about community policing that preserve the empirically unfounded image of police work as professional law enforcement and combine it with the assumption of communities with the specified capacities constitute a discourse of free-floating signifiers, allowing the police to reestablish a political base in shadow communities, which can be used to further insulate themselves from political oversight by elected officials. And a base in weaker and more fragmented communities may provide police with a net gain in insulation *and* political support compared to oversight by a city council or mayor's office.[47]

While police do not work independent of formal constraints, the order maintenance activities encouraged by community policing are to some degree defined by their additional distance from formal law enforcement.[48] Klockars concludes that policing reform can best improve order maintenance by opening "channels for complaints to those with limited access to them."[49] Rather than increase administrative control of discretion, as in prevailing stories about policing reform, Klockars argues that restructuring formal institutions to encourage more reciprocal relations between citizens and the police will support innovative, community friendly, and effective policing. Policing that increases the accountability of officers and police departments can provide community groups with formal and informal resources they can use to subject less accountable forms of power in their neighborhoods to critical public scrutiny.

Within this story, to the degree that it recognizes the inherently political nature of policing, community policing may support effective networks of relationships for constraining the added discretion that patrol officers will enjoy as a result of a problem solving focus. Farrell suggests that a problem solving focus increases officer accountability by making it easier for the community and the department to evaluate the results of an officer's efforts.[50] Officer discretion can be rewarded when it contributes to problem solving and punished when it wastes resources or fails to address community concerns, as was suggested by Eck and Rosenbaum. Oversight and evaluation of officer performance will require the police chief and precinct commanders to become much more publicly political figures, but this interaction with community leaders can have very positive side effects for the career of individual captains and for the department when it can mobilize supporters for city council meetings at budget time. And the community can serve as eyes and ears for the chief. "An officer who is known to the community is easier to report for either good or poor conduct than one who is not known."[51] The style of monitoring may also be more to the liking of police officers, since it is unlikely to be as legalistic and more likely to be results oriented, focusing on particular neighborhood problems. It would also explicitly recognize the embeddedness of police work, providing discursive resources in the practice of police work for the sustenance of decentered stories about community policing.

Controlling police discretion is not simply a bureaucratic problem. What the survival of order maintenance activities teaches us about improving policing is that even a highly centralized, paramilitary public bureaucracy must interact—as individuals—with competing groups and other individuals on the street if it is to be effective.[52] Negotiating within the relationships that constitute community life has been and remains a core component of policing. With this insight, it becomes clear that formal, bureaucratic, and legal mechanisms are only one in a larger menu of ways that police behavior is currently constrained. The problem of police discretion has not simply been a bureaucratic question of command and control. It has not simply been an issue for judicial oversight. It has also been a form of power—not without constraints that inhere in the relationships that surround its deployment—that can serve or destroy.

The Catalysts behind Community Policing. There is one common element found in nearly all documented experiments with community policing in the United States: none report that the reform initiative began as a citizen-sponsored effort.[53] This is true of community policing efforts in New York City, Houston, Baltimore, Portland, Minneapolis, St. Louis, Los Angeles, and Savannah.[54] The police perception, then, that the community was not satisfied with their work can probably be traced to the insulation and isolation of the police subculture, growing public concern about violence and disorder, and the effects of urban fiscal stress on police budgets, forcing police managers back into more visible political battles for funding.[55] As a result, a primary catalyst behind current forms of community policing has been reform-conscious police managers, not communities. One important consequence of this has been the dominance of state-centered stories about policing among reformers.

While it may not be inherently troublesome for policing reform to initiate in the chief's office, it is something to think about when this control extends to all stages in the development of community policing. As Oettmeier and Brown explain in the Houston case, and not unlike other experiments in community policing, the programs that came to constitute this new approach to policing often existed prior to the reform and were devised by department managers with little substantive input from either the communities targeted or the patrol officers responsible for implementing the new practices.[56]

This kind of police control over the reform process raises doubts about realizing the role of communities implicit in Wilson and Kelling's "Broken Windows" argument. As Mastrofski puts it, "community policing has attempted to strengthen some direct citizen-department linkages, but it has studiously avoided any attempt to revitalize traditional channels of political input, which, in fact, have formal responsibility for the police—local elected officials, such as mayors and legislators. Community policing reforms appear to thrust these officials even further to the periphery of meaningful policy making and operational oversight."[57] It may be in the interest of police managers to pursue this style of policing reform, since links with less powerful community groups, which can be played off against each other, can be used to keep more powerful elected officials at arm's length. But the tendency of police managers to keep a tight grip on the development of community policing, justified with reference to their particular professional expertise, raises questions about the openness of police managers to external oversight.

Police control of the initiation and development of policing reforms that claim to be community based may also indicate that community policing has emerged as a new style of policing that is actually more responsive to the social control and legitimation needs of the police bureaucracy than to the concerns of the communities the police serve.[58] Studies on the impact of community policing to date show little or no impact on crime, disorder, or fear reduction.[59] What they do show is a positive impact on citizen attitudes toward the police and patrol officer attitudes toward their jobs.[60] It is possible, then, that this reform, while mobilizing a rhetoric of democratic responsiveness to community concerns, is more accurately described as responsive to the needs of the police bureaucracy to manage public opinion.[61]

Wilson and Kelling expect community policing to be more responsive to community concerns because they assume that communities want more intensive police-citizen contacts.[62] This conclusion may not be warranted. Research on police professionalism shows that deep mutual suspicion often exists between professional police officers and the communities they serve.[63] Other research shows that minority communities have good reasons to fear both crime and the police.[64] Even in communities with no history of conflict with the police, Manning's research suggests that it is not clear whether an increased police presence makes residents feel safer or increases their awareness of the presence of danger.[65]

Greene and Taylor argue that the logic of community policing as it is presented by Wilson and Kelling assumes rather than explicates the core concepts of community and fear. Fear can be measured in a variety of ways (perceptions of crime, perceived vulnerability, estimates of risk), but "Broken Windows" provides no justification for one measure or another. This encourages the kind of mismeasurement of fear and community that characterizes many community policing programs.[66] The confusion surrounding these key terms may contribute to the unexamined nature of the assumptions about community revitalization and informal social controls in prevailing stories about community policing and the political utility of this failure—unquestionable police control of policing reform.

IV. Democracy, Discipline, and Decentered Policing

Prevailing stories about policing are state centered. In this section, I return to Eck and Rosenbaum, using an explicitly decentered approach to policing to draw out potentially democratic and disciplinary characteristics in stories about community policing. First, I challenge the usage in prevailing stories of the labels "traditional" and "professional" as inaccurate and misleading. Second, I applaud the efforts of Eck and Rosenbaum to redefine the core elements of professional policing in a way that will separate out those principles it can be argued the police ought to continue to pursue from the particular policies and tactics that research has shown have not effectively pursued them. But I also contend that they have failed to complete this task. And, finally, I consider the democratic and disciplinary implications of this discursive struggle.

Eck and Rosenbaum studiously avoid claiming that professional policing has failed by mistakenly inserting "existing forms of policing, earlier forms of policing or traditional policing" in statements where they are clearly referring to research that has specifically found professional forms of policing (random preventative patrol, rapid response, and investigative follow-up) to be ineffective. These linguistic gymnastics allow the authors to assert, without defending, the claim that whatever community policing brings to policing is simply building on established police practices. This selective reading of policing research is a common component of prevailing stories about policing reform.[67] In this case, I suspect that the preservation of stories about professionalism is expected to help police managers overcome the internal resistance of police officers who perceive community policing to be social work. What it also does, however, is provide an inaccurate basis for analysis that directly contributes to an incomplete and misleading discussion of police effectiveness, the politics of policing reform, and the range of potential roles for communities in community policing.

It is inaccurate because traditional policing generally refers to preprofessional era policing.[68] The confused discussion of police effectiveness that is based on this usage would be far less tortured had the authors simply asserted that professionalism has come under attack for specified reasons but the principles that professional tactics failed to achieve ought to remain an important part of police functions. In this way, terms like emergency aid could be contrasted with rapid response as currently practiced; the importance of "serving justice" could be contrasted with the overemphasis on arrests in police work, as currently practiced and evaluated; and nonemergency services could be explicitly connected to the long and honorable tradition in police work of effective order maintenance—a tradition that survives despite professional policing's efforts to degrade it, failure to reward officers for engaging in it, and refusal to administratively support it. This refusal to see the problems in policing as, in large part, failures of the professional model also makes the authors' marginalization of community less visible.

"The public asks a number of things of the police."[69] This is how the authors start, but their analysis is not based on any articulated concerns of specified publics; rather it is based on what police already do (the basic tenets of the professional model). In discussing effectiveness, the authors assert that effective policing begins with crime control, rapid response, arrest and clearance rates, and order maintenance. Then, with a distinctly skeptical tone, the authors indicate that some police chiefs believe there is a role for communities in preventing crime. This role is then reduced to a police obligation to reduce fear and serves as the logical transition to the discussion of problem-oriented policing. This analytical slippage is unfortunate because problem solving is an important development in policing for precisely the reasons the authors present. It is also unfortunate that it serves the rhetorical function of removing consideration of a role for communities from the discussion of effective policing, despite the prominent place such a role plays implicitly in prevailing and competing stories about community policing.

If the reader will recall the discussion of prevailing stories, it will become clear how these stories both draw discursive resources from references to community revitalization and also narrow the possibility of effectively achieving this. Prevailing stories often begin with the way fear denies the community a critical constitutive resource (informal social controls) and the assertion that problem solving can reduce fear and empower communities to reclaim these capacities. In doing so, prevailing stories point to common sense expectations of a community role in crime prevention and assumptions about the necessary resources for fulfilling this role. These expectations are central to the coherence and political appeal of these narratives, but the logic of the assumed resources gets reversed: community capacities are not enhanced, and communities are constructed, in stories about problem solving partnerships and citizens' academies, as additional resources for police departments.

In discussing equity, the authors again start from current police practice rather than public concerns, allowing them to conclude without evidence that "community policing is an attempt to forge links between police and previously excluded communities."[70] Such claims appear in stories about community policing but rarely in police practice. Further, the category itself—equity—as a surrogate for police-community relations, also limits the potential roles of communities to those already consistent with professional policing. As the authors indicate, police departments routinely respond to a wide range of community concerns with evidence of fidelity to the professional policing ethic of equity even when it is unclear that equally distributed patrol strength is the most effective or fair approach to crime control. Finally, in discussing efficiency the authors reverse the logic of democratic government. Instead of presenting the police as public servants who need to ensure that the public resources they mobilize and embody are made available to communities, they argue that the police need to see communities as an additional resource for the department—a resource that can surveil, patrol, target harden, lobby for the police, and "authorize the police to act on their behalf."[71]

The same story, told with a more sober view of professionalism, emphasizes the critical and constitutive role of nonstate actors in policing. Research shows that professional policing has alienated the police from even the law-abiding communities they serve because rapid response, separating patrol from investigations, and random preventative patrol have been administrative initiatives that discourage patrol officers from developing the long-term relationships with citizens and the local knowledge necessary for effective problem solving.[72] These administrative failures have constructed a style of policing that, like professional governance generally, has contributed to the decline of community by making state agents less available as a resource for citizens.

For these reasons, police began to seek partnerships with communities only to find that those communities most in need of more effective crime control were too weak to provide additional resources and too suspicious of police departments to be interested in the coproduction of social order. Police attempts to organize these communities, when they have occurred at all, have been less than successful. What this effort has amounted to in practice is police departments partnering with communities that are already resource rich, often to target the activities of other, weaker communities.[73] When prevailing stories make the range of roles for communities invisible, they also make the marginalization of weak and distrusting communities inevitable.

A more modest, sober, and radical role for police in this regard would reexamine current police practices to eliminate the ways in which these contribute to weakening already weak communities.[74] Then police-community partnerships in the neighborhoods most victimized by crime might become possible and, to the degree that they are relatively reciprocal relationships, more effective. To sustain these gains, police could then go beyond policing that no longer weakens communities to experiment with policing that might contribute to strengthening them.[75] This broader understanding of policing is not new, nor is it simply an extension of professional policing. It is a competing, decentered story about policing that depends on attention to the concrete resources and relational networks that empower communities with the sought-after informal social control capacities.

Chapter 4

Communities and Crime on the South Side of Skid Road

The Valley is different from the rest of the Seattle. Once it was a thriving, heavily Italian farm community, and Columbia City was its center. But huge government housing projects built in the area to handle the influx of workers at Boeing and the shipyards during World War II were converted to low income housing when the war was over. The decision made a ghetto of the Valley.

—*Seattle Post-Intelligencer*, January 10, 1988

I. Introduction

Rainier Valley has had a sometimes difficult relationship with the rest of Seattle. This relationship has contributed to decline and a wide range of citizen activism in the valley around issues of crime and community revitalization—the community component of what the National Institute of Justice later called a model police-community partnership. In this chapter, I argue that the declining capacity of communities in Rainier Valley to control crime was a foreseeable consequence of choices made by Seattle's public and private leadership in the postwar era.

While individuals are the victims and the perpetrators of criminal violence, crime is a community concern because crime rates vary by geographical location and the socioeconomic composition of a city's communities.[1] Differently located communities have dissimilar capacities to control crime. The cumulative effects of legislation, public housing, freeway construction, zoning enforcement, investment patterns, and job opportunities "can ultimately destroy the integrity of communities as viable collectivities."[2] Reiss argues that public and private decisions can and do adversely affect the capacity of communities to mobilize and promote social order through informal social controls, as advocates of community policing expect.

> When there is reason to conclude that the mobilization of a community to control conduct affects its crime rates, then one may want to intervene in whatever causes a diminished capacity. When public programs or laws destabilize a local population and hence its capacity to control conduct locally, one may question the soundness of such policies.[3]

Decisions about land use, demographic changes, and changes in the socioeconomic status of the population all contribute to a neighborhood's capacity to address crime.[4] In Southeast Seattle, community stories about a more effective and accountable police presence were interwoven with calls for a more "vigorous local political control of zoning, planning, and building code requirements."[5] Residents in Rainier Valley were active in these areas and in seeking other political reforms aimed at enhancing community control: district-based city council elections, local control over Seattle Housing Authority decisions and school administration, and a police-community partnership.[6]

Seattle is a middle-class city with the highest rate of home ownership in the United States.[7] In 1989, *Money* magazine rated Seattle the best place to live in the United States. In 1993, the *Seattle Times* reported that crime had "pushed Seattle to #2."[8] The entire city was concerned about crime, as shown by the prominence of the issue in the mayor's race, but Rainier Valley had the worst reputation for high crime. According to the *Seattle Weekly*, this perception was partly deserved (crime was a problem in the valley), but it was no more deserved than parts of Capitol Hill, the Central District, Greenwood, Aurora, the University District, Northgate, or Wallingford. In 1990–91, these areas had more than twice the rate of serious crime as Rainier Valley. And lower Queen Anne, Westlake, Pioneer Square, and First Hill had rates 50 percent higher than the valley.[9] Valley residents have long struggled against the way "smug North End residents mix the geographically and culturally distinct Rainier Valley and Central Area into a single lawless stereotype."[10]

From the time of the first white pioneers through the early nineteenth century, Seattle prospered because it encouraged commercial development in a way that was designed to support family and community life.[11] But the boom of the late nineteenth century marked the beginning of the withdrawal of the wealthy from civic leadership, the rise of class and racial divisions, and the decline of a vision of Seattle based on commercial diversity.[12] "[P]ublic values evolved into a private vision of individual and family well-being, and the possibility of politics as the expression of something more than personal desires was lost."[13]

When the decisions of civic leaders create an urban regime that looks like a single-cell organism, dependent upon a single industrial employer, the result is a limited city, like the one Peterson is resigned to in *City Limits* or Katznelson is critical of in *City Trenches.* When Seattle's civic leaders moved from a community-based vision, they laid the foundation for a new type of regime—one with different limits and possibilities, as Clarence Stone found in his work on regime change in Dallas.[14] When Seattle's civic leaders retired from public life after World War I to pour their energies into a different kind of commercial development, they weakened stories about Seattle as a city where prosperity was built on the resilience of diverse communities. Seattle communities became less resilient, less able to manage economic development or the consequences of unmanaged development for social order in communities.

When Seattle rejected the Bogue Plan in 1912, it broke with its own tradition of planning for the future. Sale argues that this amounted to a re-creation of Seattle's political culture.[15] Seattle had been built to encourage resilient communities that provided stability and innovation in times of rapid social change. But complacence captured the wealthy and impoverished Seattle's leadership, while fear captured the middle class, as both, in different ways, sought "an abrogation of the essential urban ideal of tolerance of variety in favor of a suburban commandment: be like me."[16] This trend left Seattle vulnerable. New growth came but in a less diverse form. Seattle became a single-cell organism vulnerable to the slightest changes in the market conditions of a single industry: aerospace.

Seattle's dependence on Boeing brought good fortune until 1970, when the company laid off two-thirds of its work force. This left Rainier Valley, where many of the Boeing engineers hired during the boom years had settled, with newly financed empty homes and apartment buildings. Rents fell dramatically, and the demographics of Rainier Valley changed with an influx of minorities from the Central Area replacing the primarily white Boeing engineers.[17]

What is most remarkable about the bust, however, is not that lower-income residents moved into the parts of the city that had fallen upon the hardest times but that only 15 percent of those laid off actually left the city.[18] For Sale, this speaks volumes about the continued power of earlier stories about Seattle as a city of resilient communities. Buzz Anderson, owner of a family hardware store in the valley, expressed his resilience this way: "I am an old timer and I refuse to leave. My grandfather came here in the late 1880s before Columbia City was part of Seattle. I was born and raised a block from this store."[19] Speaking of old stories as a source of inspiration for the future, Sale concludes that the hope is in the "public actions of private citizens either ignoring government or making it suit their immediate needs."[20]

This chapter examines these stories, told by citizens in the valley about policing and community. In the next section, I will outline how the intersection of various historical forces—public policy decisions, the decisions of Boeing executives, and demographic changes—contributed to the current perception of Rainier Valley as a dangerous place to live. In section III, I will begin the discussion of community revitalization where it started, with two important community groups, the Southeast Seattle Community Organization (SESCO) and Southeast Effective Development (SEED).

II. The Political Geography of the Rainier Valley

The problems in Rainier Valley today were not inevitable but resulted in fairly foreseeable ways from decisions made by Seattle's public and private leadership, especially in the decades following World War II. This position is best developed in Sale's *Seattle: Past to Present.* A 1991 article in the *Seattle Weekly* presents a brief account of politics in the Rainier Valley, which is also consistent with the account presented here.[21]

Physical Landscape. Rainier Valley is located in Southeast Seattle and makes up about 15 percent of the land area of the city. Prior to the industrial era, the valley was heavily forested. Once the area was cleared of timber, Italian farmers moved into what became known as Garlic Gulch. Railroad tracks were laid through the valley in the late nineteenth century to service Seattle's emerging timber industry.[22] The railroad also made settlement possible farther from the city core and led to the settlements that have since become the neighborhoods that make up Rainier Valley (see fig. 2).

These neighborhoods enclosed a set of economically diverse com-

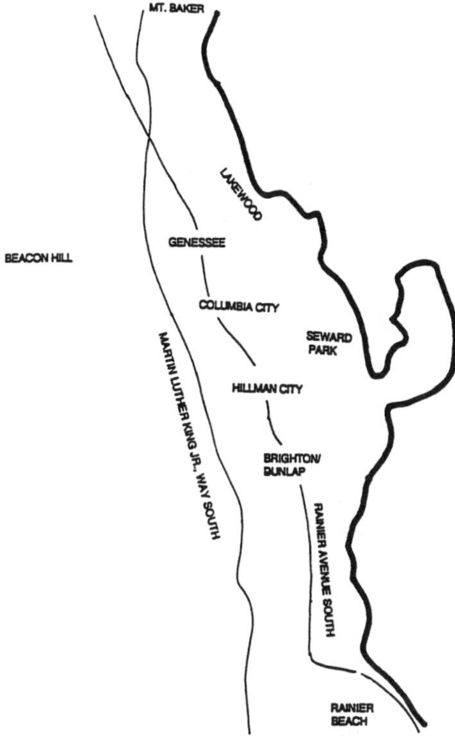

Fig. 2. Rainier Valley neighborhoods, 1990

munities. This may have been a fortunate consequence of the peculiar geography of Rainier Valley. Its long north-south orientation, with expensive lakeshore properties from Mt. Baker to Rainier Beach along the east side, kept its upper-middle-class neighborhoods intact through hard times. The working-class neighborhoods lower in the valley, while suffering from the economic uncertainty that came with the Boeing collapse, were able to weather the storms, in part because of the close proximity of more stable neighbors.

The valley is geographically defined by the north-south ridges that enclose it. To the east of one ridge is Lake Washington. To the west of the other is a freeway, I–5, and the Duwamish River. The result is that Rainier Valley is geographically isolated from the rest of the city. The primary forms of transportation in, out, and through the valley are the north-south corridors marked by Martin Luther King Jr. Way and Rainier Avenue South. Surrounding these streets are commercial properties and working-class neighborhoods (Genessee, Columbia City, Hillman City, Brighton-Dunlap, and Rainier Beach). Farther from the commercial strip at the center of the valley there are middle-class and upper-middle-class neighborhoods (Mt. Baker, Lakewood, Seward Park on the east, and Beacon Hill on the west). "By and large, social and economic conditions vary according to topography with the lowest incomes and poorest conditions occurring in the valley, and the highest incomes and best conditions occurring along the two ridges"[23] (see table 1).

Fleissner, Fedan, and Stotland describe the situation in Rainier Valley as steadily worsening in the decade leading up to the formation of the South Seattle Crime Prevention Council in 1989. Business growth was slower than in the city as a whole. New construction was declining, and, while the rest of Seattle was experiencing rapid increases in real estate values, home values in Rainier Valley were not increasing as quickly.[24] According to a report prepared by Southeast Effective Development, home prices were well below the city average. The mean sales price in the Mt. Baker, Lakewood, and Seward Park areas declined from 1984–89 by 13.2 percent. In the same period, the mean price in the city as a whole increased by 7.5 percent.[25]

TABLE 1. Valley Income by Topographic Community, 1989

Area	Median Household Income	City Median (%)	Below Poverty (%)
Rainier Valley			
Northern 1/3	$13,226	81	21.8
Central 1/3	$17,203	105	11.2
Southern 1/3	$13,167	83	21.3
Total	$14,167	87	19.3
Beacon Hill			
Northern 1/3	$15,897	97	11.9
Central 1/3	$19,318	118	3.6
Southern 1/3	$21,578	132	8.2
Total	$17,873	109	8.9
Lakeshore			
Northern 1/3	$26,220	161	6.5
Central 1/3	$21,531	132	9.2
Southern 1/3	$22,383	137	7.0
Total	$24,100	148	7.5

Source: Southeast Seattle Background Report.

Seattle has four large public housing projects. All were built with federal funding in the 1940s by the Seattle Housing Authority (SHA) to house Boeing and shipyard workers during the war. Three of the projects are in South Seattle; two of those are in Rainier Valley. The SHA also has four town houses (none in Rainier Valley) and several high-rises. The two high-rises in Rainier Valley, Holly Court and Beacon Tower, surround the large Holly Park project, concentrating Rainier Valley's public housing units into one neighborhood. According to an SHA administrator, 118 of 121 census tracts in the city have some section eights, but the bulk of these are concentrated along the Central–Rainier Valley corridor.[26]

Vacancy rates in multiunit apartments concentrated along the corridor carved out by Martin Luther King Jr. Way and Rainier Avenue were 16 percent in 1989 compared to a city average of 4 percent. This made it difficult for current property owners and the area as a whole to attract new construction. In the 1960s, almost 14 percent of Seattle's multiunit construction occurred in Rainier Valley. By the 1970s, the figure had fallen to 6.7 percent, and in 1980s it was less than 3 percent.[27]

Human Capital. Demographic changes in the Rainier Valley contributed to its image as a high-crime area. African Americans are concentrated in the Central Area and Rainier Valley. Even after Seattle's African American population increased by 70 percent from 1950 to 1960, however, African Americans still accounted for only 5 percent of the city's population. Sale argues that African Americans have never been very welcome in the Pacific Northwest, except when they were brought in as strike breakers.[28] And then they have only been a welcome sight to a particular segment of the community and only for a very limited amount of time.

The African American communities in Seattle have, despite racism, contributed to stories about Seattle as a city built on diverse and resilient communities. In the 1950s and 1960s, Seattle African Americans created a preschool program that later became the model for the now highly regarded national Head Start program. And the Central Area Motivation Project (CAMP) is still one of the city's most active and innovative community organizations dealing with youth issues.

In the summer of 1968, Boeing still employed over 100,000 local workers, the Black Panthers were active, and urban unrest had moved from the television to the streets of Seattle.[29] The imminent layoffs at Boeing and the fear of street protests contributed to a pushing and pulling of Seattle's most vulnerable groups. The pull of lower rents, especially around the two large public housing projects in the valley, combined with the push of gentrification in the Central Area (which is adjacent to downtown).[30] For many African Americans, weakened job prospects and a strengthened police presence in Central Area neighborhoods made the lower rents in Rainier Valley an attractive alternative.

> Three-fourths of the blacks in the 1960s lived in 9 of the city's 121 census tracts, half within four of these, and most of the elementary schools within what is called the Central Area were more than 90% black. . . . Almost surrounding the ghetto, and effectively walling it off, were some of the best neighborhoods of earlier days. . . . Only to the south, toward Rainier Valley and Beacon Hill, could the ghetto easily expand without running into full-scale opposition.[31]

The displacement of lower income residents from other parts of the city shifted the racial and class balance of the valley. The region had always been Seattle's most diverse, economically and ethnically, but in the 1970s and 1980s the white population of Rainier Valley became a minority population (see table 2). In the 1970s and 1980s, the total population of the valley declined, the white population declined most rapidly, and real estate values dropped while values in the city as a whole were rising.[32]

African Americans have lived in the valley since the late nineteenth century but in very small numbers. In fact, the population of African Americans in 1940 had dropped to about 150. "Growth pressures in the Central Area and the 'Boeing Bust' of the early 1970s encouraged African American migration to the Rainier Valley, with the

TABLE 2. Racial Composition of Southeast Seattle, 1960–90 (in percentages)

Year	White	Black	Other
1960	88	4	9
1970	69	14	17
1980	44	29	27
1990	33	30	36

Source: Southeast Seattle Report.

result that, as of the 1990 census, the area population was 34% African-American."[33] Perhaps more important, the rising African American population was also experiencing disproportionately high unemployment. In 1990, African American youth (ages 16–25) had an unemployment rate of 23 percent, twice the rate for white youth. In 1974, 14 percent of all African American men in Seattle were not working. In 1984, that number was 43 percent and in 1990 it reached 47 percent.[34]

Civic Leadership. The Boeing boom started when the British Royal Air Force placed orders for Boeing B–17s in 1940, and it picked up pace with American orders for B–29s.[35] Boeing's work force grew from 4,000 employees in 1939 to more than 50,000 in 1944. While employment fell from 1946 until the early 1950s, the Korean War demand for B–47s and B–52s provided Boeing with the profits to develop the 707.[36] The problem for Seattle was that even as Boeing boomed the rest of the city's economic resources stagnated. Seattle began to look like a company town. And, Sale argues, it was a company town turning inward, away from a concern about public life. Seattle's new, postwar neighborhoods "embraced house and lot and rejected almost everything else."[37]

The Boeing bust, like its boom, can be traced to two sources: the market and the state. The decline of commercial air travel reduced the demand for planes. Then, when the U.S. government decided to discontinue work on the SuperSonic Transport, Boeing cut its work force by two-thirds. Seventy-five thousand residents lost their jobs between January 1970 and December 1971.[38] Seattle's unemployment rate jumped from below the national average to the highest in the country. Boeing executives had failed to anticipate a significant turn in the market, failed to encourage local suppliers to diversify, and failed to assume an active role in civic leadership and encourage corporate and state policies more consistent with stories about a Seattle built upon resilient communities. Instead, Boeing encouraged Seattle to become dependent on it. As a result, the Boeing bust hit Seattle harder than it might have, and recovery was slower than it could have been. Rainier Valley was hit hardest because this was where most of the Boeing boom workers had settled with their families.

The Boeing bust is representative of other choices that contributed to the current difficulties in Rainier Valley. Compared to the rest of the city, the valley has the fewest supermarkets, with the poorest quality produce, the fewest pharmacies, and not a single movie theater.[39] Referring to the Columbia City business district in 1990, which lies at the heart of the valley, a local activist noted that "it's no longer a vibrant retail core. It's a nationwide phenomenon, as the malls get more and more popular the neighborhood business centers close down. Wherever you have empty storefronts, you don't have as many eyes looking out for the area."[40] Rainier Valley struggled, and continues to struggle, against bank redlining. A two-year community study (done by SESCO) found that in 1988, 25 percent fewer home loans were made in Rainier Valley compared to the rest of the city.[41] A 1991 study based on Federal Reserve data indicated that in Seattle mortgages were denied to minority applicants 13.1 percent of the time and to white applicants only 8.6 percent of the time.[42]

The effects of these private choices on Rainier Valley have not yet been fully overcome. The average income in Rainier Valley has been steadily declining in relation to the rest of the city. In 1950, 35 percent of Southeast Seattle residents had incomes below the city median; in 1980, almost 55 percent fell below the median. In 1989, 18.7 percent of all Southeast households received public assistance, double the rate for the city as a whole.[43] As table 1 indicates, the 1989 mean income in Rainier Valley was $14,167, with almost 20 percent of the population living below the poverty level.

The business sector certainly did not conspire to hurt the city or the valley. The point is that, just as their foresight is celebrated in stories about the Boeing boom, their lack of foresight is remembered in stories about crime and community decline in Rainier Valley. According to the *Southeast Seattle Action Plan,* "The rush to develop inexpensive housing in the 1960s, when housing demand was strong, left Southeast Seattle with the majority of its apartment stock in aging and deteriorating condition."[44] As a result, today 35 percent of the rental units in Rainier Valley are subsidized, compared to a city average of only 17 percent. And these subsidized units are concentrated in the Holly Park (898 units) and Rainier Vista (496 units) projects, built for Boeing and shipyard workers by the federal government in the 1940s and later converted to low-income public housing. The SHA reports that (through 1991) 41.5 percent of Seattle's 4,474 section eight housing certificates were concentrated in Rainier Valley. This contributed to the concentration of less desirable social service providers in the region.[45]

Decisions made by public actors also contributed to the area's difficulties: concentrated (rather than scattered) subsidized public housing blocked attempts to improve the housing market; general commercial zoning contributed to blight along the Rainier Avenue and Martin Luther King Jr. Way corridors; complaint-driven (rather than proactive) zoning and building code enforcement was preferred by the Department of Construction and Land Use; the move to at-large elections hurt the electoral chances of minority candidates further hurt by 1992 redistricting; recreational facilities were of poor quality in the area of the city with the highest and fastest growing under-18 population; city attempts to direct commercial development to meet downtown rather than neighborhood needs (such as the siting of CX Corporation at the old Sicks Stadium, over SEED opposition, which closed two years later); and the neighborhood destruction resulting from the ongoing I-90 freeway expansion struggle.[46]

Public choices impact the development (or underdevelopment) of an area. The Department of Community Development identified 81 vacant and unused city-owned properties in the Rainier Valley appropriate for improved uses. These city-owned properties include abandoned power substations, vacant lots, and land purchased for utility rights-of-way and highway construction, and "this aspect sets the area apart from many urban districts where pockets of redevelopment are often restricted by the quantity of available space."[47]

Following the Boeing bust, the weakened southeast was politically vulnerable to other public and private actions, such as the disproportionate siting of undesirable city facilities in the area and the partial loss of both small businesses and larger employers.[48] Residents had to work hard to dissuade the city from siting a large garbage incinerator and later a new jail in the valley. Perhaps most devastating to the area was the neighborhood destruction and population displacement resulting from the city's decision to construct a freeway interchange at the north end of the valley. Building the highway ramp caused residents of the Judkins neighborhood to change the name of their community council to Judkins-Rejected.[49] Before that section of the freeway was built, the areas around Jackson and Atlantic Streets were thriving business districts surrounded by stable middle- and working-class neighborhoods. Now the area is best known for the success of the Atlantic Street Center, a community-run program for at-risk youth.[50]

Of course, these events and policy choices can leave an area like the Rainier Valley vulnerable to crime as well. Though this has been the case, residents argue that this image of the valley is grossly exaggerated, adding further obstacles to community revitalization. At the same time, residents complain that the city has failed to respond to the real crime problems in Rainier Valley. The following statement by a city official provides a snapshot of these competing stories. Assuring residents that Columbia City was as safe as anywhere in the city, this official concluded with the comment that in Columbia City "drug dealers co-exist peacefully with law-abiding neighborhood residents."[51] Such a comment might reassure an official who has long considered the valley to be Seattle's no-go area, but it is unlikely to reassure residents who know differently and experience the consequences of such official misperceptions all too regularly.

Citizens have tried to fight back by pressuring the Seattle Housing Authority to implement a scattered housing policy, opposing the continued siting of undesirable city facilities in the valley, pressuring local employers to hire local workers, pressuring landowners to clean up their properties, working to attract new businesses, and attempting to combat crime and the image of the region as dangerous. SEED lobbied for more proactive zoning enforcement and a southeast zoning overlay that would put development choices into the hands of Southeast Seattle residents. Mayor Rice refused to "sacrifice product for process" with a zoning overlay to increase community control.[52]

The Judkins-Rejected neighborhood was beginning to recover in 1994. But the point is that their plight was not inevitable or unavoidable; it has a history. What was once a neighborhood of mixed race and class with a thriving business district had suffered at the hands of city planners. "Bureaucrats began tearing down homes in the 1960s, first for the once-planned RH Thompson Expressway and then for the I–90 clover leaf that never got built."[53]

> The state purchased nearly 40 homes and other properties more than 20 years ago to make way for the proposed 14 lane I–90 highway. In the interim, the homes were rented to low-income families, in some instances the original owners. When the highway was scaled back to 10 lanes, the homes no longer were needed.[54]

The city, rather than act to check the worst instincts of the market and protect community life, chose to act as an agent of the market and demolish neighborhoods, transforming stable, homeowning taxpayers into displaced populations or dependent tenants of public housing. But these residents did not give up because their stories about Seattle as a place for resilient communities remained important enough to them *not* to leave.

III. Fighting Back

In response to these and other trends in Southeast Seattle, citizens began to organize on a variety of issues, including crime and the perception that high crime made Rainier Valley an undesirable place to live. Southeast Effective Development and the Southeast Seattle Community Organization were two early catalysts. The Rainier Chamber of Commerce organized a Court Watch Program, resulting in the removal of two judges.[55] The Crime Prevention League, a private crime prevention organization, was formed in 1981 in response to an increase in burglaries.[56] Safeway and Eagle Hardware were persuaded to build large commercial outlets in the valley, while less desirable businesses (such as two after-hours clubs, the Neighborhood Gathering Place and The Monastery) were closed through civil abatements initiated by southeast residents.[57] As the city created block watches, merchants in Rainier Valley established what Fleissner, Fedan, and Stotland believe was the first Business Watch Program in the country.[58] This program improved the organization of the business community and may have contributed to the later success of the Criminal Trespass Program, which was implemented through the police-community partnership. Citizens, with leverage created by the federal Community Reinvestment Act, successfully pressured local banks to address redlining and reinvest deposits in Rainier Valley communities.

SESCO and SEED were the first groups to successfully focus public attention on conditions in the valley. While the two organizations shared an office for the first six months and eventually cooperated on several projects, they each had a very different identity, used different tactics, and appealed to different segments of the Rainier Valley population. SESCO was an activist group, SEED's "more rabble-rousing counterpart."[59] SESCO marched and petitioned, demanding that banks and city agencies respond to valley needs. After nearly 17 years of fighting City Hall, the older members began to retire and those hired to replace them decided to reorganize SESCO as the Brighton Community Council, primarily to attract more government funding.

Oscar Hearde, an elder statesman of the SESCO activists, explained at their final meeting as SESCO that Rainier Valley had been a "dumping ground for the whole city [and] the more we complained the less we got until SESCO."[60] While the final meeting at times felt funereal, Hearde asserted that SESCO was "not dead, just retired, [waiting] for some younger people to carry on."[61] SESCO took on the issues no one else would—issues that were either not glamorous (repairing a Holly Park bus stop) or required a long-term commitment (such as five years of meetings with a local bank to iron out redlining problems and get a commitment to reinvestment in the community).

In 1981, SESCO held its first convention. More than 600 residents of Rainier Valley attended, and they decided to focus their efforts on the following agenda: getting a one to one exchange policy in the city's voluntary busing program;[62] saving the Holly Park Library; opposing attempts to rezone the Rainier Beach and Beacon Hill areas to reduce the number of single-family units; lobbying the city for capital improvements, including additional bus stops in the valley; and converting Kaboda Gardens into a public park. Success with this agenda inspired the 400 residents attending SESCO's second convention in 1982 to build their own bus shelters, publicly embarrassing Metro; persuade a Group Health Clinic to stay in the valley; and raise more than $40,000 for neighborhood improvements, mostly from membership dues.

In 1983, SESCO's main objectives were to achieve financial independence, pressure the city to build a new South Precinct Police Station, and promote animal control. In 1984, SESCO led the successful opposition to a proposed garbage incinerator and also focused on crime prevention, traffic problems, and job training. These issues would come to define SESCO's activities for the remainder of its tenure. The job program became a five-year effort called the Community Economic Campaign, which included the negotiations with Rainier Bank referred to earlier as well as health care for the poor and fundraising. SESCO's opposition to the incinerator pushed the city to accept recycling and other policy changes as part of a city solid waste plan, which was later put in place and remains a model for cities across the country.

The other important citizens' group to form in the early days of community revitalization in Rainier Valley was Southeast Effective Development (SEED). From 1975 to 1992, SEED managed development projects totaling more than $5 million and an annual budget in excess of $800,000, which included funding from six government agencies (three city, two federal, and one state) and four private foundations.[63]

SEED was originally created as a coalition of 35 different community groups, chambers, merchants' associations, and service clubs. According to executive director Tom Lattimore, SEED "was formed because in the mid-seventies the city was getting a lot of money from the feds, like community block grants, that type of thing. That money was given to the city based on a formula, taking a census of people in poverty. They were taking the money—at one time it was $20 million a year—and essentially using it to fund downtown stuff. This community said 'Hey, you're getting this money based on people here in this community, and you're spending it down there for nice, glitzy projects. We want the money that's entitled to this community. . . .' That's how it started."[64]

SEED operated as an umbrella agency and fiscal agent for a shifting coalition of smaller community groups. They provided staff for ongoing or ad hoc community organizations. In 1982, SEED became a licensed general contractor, cutting out the funds-absorbing government bureaucracies that would otherwise sit between federal dollars and the construction of neighborhood projects. This construction expertise allowed SEED to act as a broker for community development. They were a catalyst in brokering projects like the new Eagle Hardware complex, the new Safeway at Genessee and Rainier, and a new shopping center that includes Olson's, Food Pavilion, Drug Emporium, Hollywood Video, and smaller shops. SEED owns 25 percent of the shopping center project and plans to use its profits to fund other operations.[65]

SEED literature lists an impressive array of services. The organization is involved in zoning analysis and the review and design of development projects. They provide a training program for local youth interested in construction. SEED has produced an annual community arts program since 1979 and founded (and provides staff for) the Rainier Valley Seattle Arts Council, which has installed 20 murals at area bus shelters. SEED also acquires and rehabilitates housing units. They own and manage 33 units. They sponsor the Mutual Housing Cooperative of Southeast Seattle, which manages another 36 units of rehabilitated housing in the area. SEED helped create the Mt. Baker Housing Association, which renovated a 144-unit complex, and HomeSight, which acquires and renovates single-family homes for sale to first-time buyers.[66] In 1986, SEED joined with SESCO in challenging Rainier Bank's lending practices under the Community Reinvestment Act.[67] Perhaps the best known of SEED's efforts was the creation of the *Southeast Seat-*

tle Action Plan (1991). The *Action Plan,* according to the *Seattle Weekly,* was

> at once sweeping and fine-toothed, for fixing almost everything that ails Southeast Seattle, from missing gutters to mis-zoning, from disinvestment to crime. . . . Rather than hitching itself to big, solitary gambles such as the CX Plant, it amounts to dozens of incremental attacks on the central problem of community decay. Its housing, reinvestment, public safety, recreation, public works, and other strategies are complementary but each is, to the some degree, self-sufficient.[68]

At a time when federal, state, and city money was tight, SEED's *Action Plan* represented a community-generated resource. SEED's credibility, inclusive consensus building, and long-term assistance to neighborhood businesses all combined to pressure the city to take this *Action Plan,* and citizen concerns in the valley, seriously.[69] The *Action Plan* was a monumental citizen effort to gather information and make a case to public and private investors to revisit Rainier Valley. The plan recommended a multipronged effort because the citizens surveyed agreed that the problems in Rainier Valley were interrelated. The report's recommendations were based on the priorities listed in table 3.

The preferences summarized in table 3 indicate that the residents of Rainier Valley were very concerned about crime and the image of the valley as dangerous. When citizens were asked to evaluate the conditions of private and public facilities and services in the valley they expressed broad dissatisfaction (see figs. 3–5). This indicates that citi-

TABLE 3. Community Survey Priorities, 1991 (in percentages)

Citizen Responses to Preexisting List of Categories	
Improve public safety	80
Improve the image of the valley as a place to work	72
Improve neighborhood appearance	65
Improve housing conditions	55
Increase employment opportunities	50
Increase retail variety and services	46
Improve traffic movement and access	27

Source: Southeast Seattle Action Plan 1991: app. A.

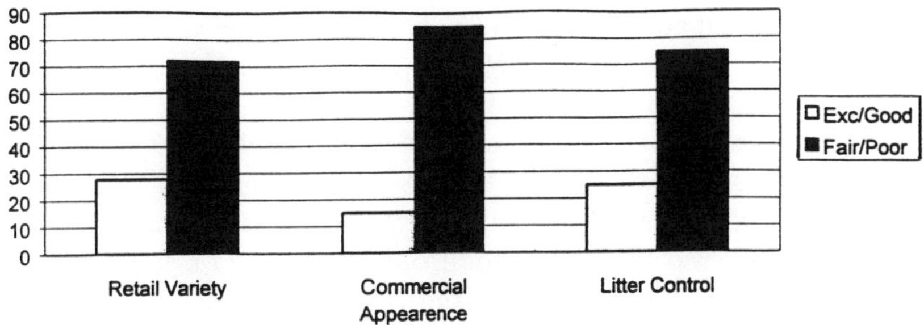

Fig. 3. Rating of privately owned facilities, 1991. (From SEED Background Report.)

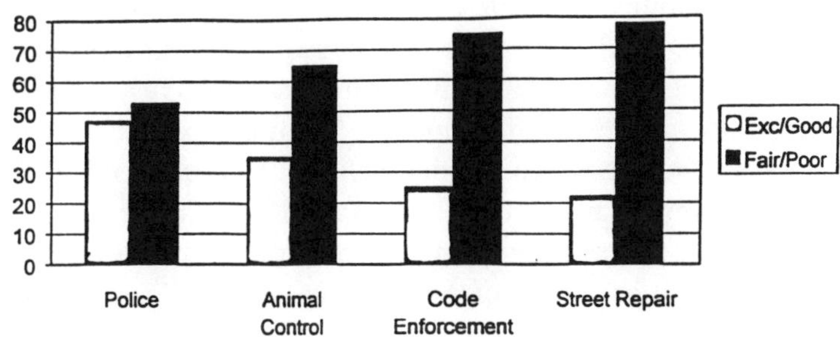

Fig. 4. Rating of public services, 1991. (From SEED Background Report.)

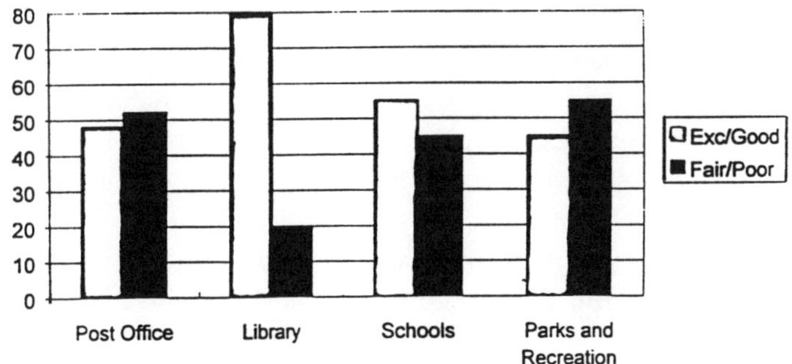

Fig. 5. Rating of publicly owned facilities, 1991. (From SEED Background Report.)

zen stories about community and policing in Rainier Valley integrate concerns about public safety, housing, employment, image problems, and unresponsive public and private leadership.

New Civic Leadership. The activities of both SEED and SESCO are important because both groups emerged after the Boeing bust with broad-based agendas for community revitalization in Rainier Valley. Their activism also reaped electoral dividends. Mayor Norm Rice is from Rainier Valley and was one of the founders of SEED. Three of nine city council members (Jane Noland, Margaret Pageler, and Cheryl Chow) are from Rainier Valley, and Cheryl Chow was a member of the SSCPC. Jane Noland was the chair of the Public Safety Committee when the SSCPC was founded. Before her, Norm Rice was the chair.

Mayor Rice campaigned on a promise to take a multipronged approach to revitalizing Seattle communities.[70] Rice added 80 officers to the SPD in 1989 and another 45 in 1993; supported Initiative 593, the controversial Drug Traffic Loitering Ordinance, and Weed and Seed.[71] Beyond public safety, Rice coordinated a $5 million two-year loan program for small businesses in Rainier Valley.[72] His urban villages plan promises investments in commercial and residential construction along the Rainier and Martin Luther King Jr. corridors.[73] He has targeted an extra $60,000 for the training of African American child-care workers, in response to a study that showed that African American day care centers have far fewer resources than white day care centers.

Rice also directed a Housing and Urban Development (HUD) grant of $600,000 to Rainier Valley to set up the Rainier Community Development Corporation as a wholly owned subsidiary of SEED. This corporation plans to buy up blighted real estate along the Rainier and Martin Luther King corridors and coordinate redevelopment with local investors to maximize local control.[74] Two other HUD grants went to Holly Park for drug intervention work. Rice established a citywide Partnership for Homeless People in 1991 and, in 1992, challenged Seattle business leaders to add 500 new mentors to existing mentorship programs.[75]

In addition to his own initiatives, Rice supported the Late Night Recreational Program, the SEED *Action Plan,* and the efforts of local banks to comply with the Community Reinvestment Act.[76] The response to Rice's efforts was cautious. Gladys Jordan, a Southeast Seattle activist, said: "If they follow through, it will meet a lot of our needs."[77] Rice was retelling stories about a city built on partnerships between strong communities, businesses, and government. His vision draws power from older stories about Seattle communities. It was born in the neighborhoods of Rainier Valley, forged in citizen activism around revitalizing the valley, and provided a resource for communities interested in directing development.

This vision was not entirely his own. The city council's award-winning Neighborhood Matching Funds Program[78] was another manifestation of a renewal of stories about a city built on strong, stable, and safe communities. Decisions in the private sector to make capital available to the area or to invest directly in Rainier Valley (Glant Textiles, CX Corporation, Eagle Hardware, and Safeway) were also components of this new vision. As a result of these public and private choices—and the citizen activism that guided the process—stories about Seattle as a place where families, communities, and commerce can support each other have been given new life in Rainier Valley.

Chapter 5

The Emergence of the South Seattle Crime Prevention Council

We said we know what the problems are. We've proven we can solve some of them ourselves. You have to work with us. It was a real gunfight. And we stared 'em down. And they finally said, okay we will work with you. We actually hammered out a contract, an agreement to work in partnership for 1988, and now the police department is taking full credit for doing this wonderful thing for the community.

—SSCPC activist

I. *Introduction*

The challenge to the possibility of community in modern society is posed starkly around questions of social order. The logic of community policing assumes that contemporary communities can still contribute to the provision of social order. But it is precisely on issues like social order that these modern community organizations have proven most difficult to sustain. As Skogan has shown, citizen crime prevention organizations have difficulties expanding their agendas and resources to maintain their organizations.[1] Skogan distinguishes between preservationist (mobilized in defense of the status quo) and insurgent (mobilized to change the status quo) crime prevention groups, highlighting the importance of a group's relationship to state agencies.[2] Given the atrophy of communities, growth of state agencies, and related power imbalances, this relationship proves critical to understanding the discursive struggles to define community policing, and the possibility of community-friendly forms of social order in modern (or postmodern) society.

Long-term, multifaceted, reciprocal citizen activism accounted for the emergence of community policing in Rainier Valley. The character of this activism indicates the resilience of stories about self-governing communities and decentered policing. In this chapter, I argue that the relatively reciprocal character of citizen activism in Rainier Valley contributed to the emergence of three different crime prevention organizations, which were able to cooperate despite differences in background, tactics, and resources. Their cooperation centered on efforts to coordinate formal and informal resources and direct these toward addressing neighborhood concerns. The resilience of competing stories about community and policing contributed to strengthening the capacity of communities to subject unaccountable forms of power in their neighborhoods to critical public scrutiny.

In the previous chapter, we saw that SEED and SESCO coordinated resources like public meetings, demonstrations, building bus stops, and monitoring judges with resources like state and federal funding, Seattle Housing Authority policy, zoning changes, and private investment patterns. Crime prevention organizations coordinated a similarly diverse set of resources for community revitalization and social control. They collected crime-related information, cleaned up vacant lots, painted out graffiti, planted trees, provided schools with metal detectors, pressured property owners to clean up blighted areas, pressured the police and other city agencies to be more proactive, pursued civil abatements, demonstrated on neighbors' front lawns, photographed crack houses, testified at city council meetings, and lobbied for new crime control legislation.

The efforts of citizens' groups to coordinate formal and informal resources indicated that the distinction between formal and informal organizations obscured the importance of both to democratic politics by drawing attention away from who was empowered by particular forms of association. Thus, by focusing on relationships and resources—such as reciprocity—I argue that this analysis provides a useful standpoint for evaluating the costs and benefits of both more and less formal organizations. Those that provide resources that empower communities ought to be preferred over those that provide services that encourage fragmentation and dependence on state agency. In Southeast Seattle, the mixture of formal and informal resources evolved from citizens subjecting unaccountable power to critical public scrutiny into a state-dominated, but more decentered, partnership. By the end of the second year of the partnership, power was mobilized less by citizens as scrutiny and more by citizens and state officials as surveillance.

The crime prevention organizations in Rainier Valley were able to combine formal and informal resources because they grew out of a long tradition of multifaceted community activism. Their success required the moderation of conflicting demands made among various community groups. Scheingold argues that our political culture privileges punitive approaches to crime control but that moderating urban political forces tend to balance radical law and order demands against other city interests, muting the potential impact of law and order politics.[3] The early cooperation among the three crime control groups discussed here was consistent with this punitive yet moderated thesis.

What this work can add to this thesis is an understanding of the dynamics within and across citizens' groups that encourage moderation. The forces of moderation, it turns out, not only muted more radical law and order demands, but they marginalized concerns about community control and official accountability. Moderation was a result of citizens facing other citizens and forging a more integrated understanding of their collective concerns. Many of the activists studied here moderated their perspectives over time, but the dynamics of the moderating process cut in several directions. Groups that resisted moderation were more easily marginalized and criticism of the police was screened out, revealing a dialectical relationship between democratic moderation and disciplinary normalization.

Three crime prevention organizations—Operation Results, Neighbors Against Drugs, and the South Seattle Crime Prevention Council (SSCPC)—within the larger context of citizen activism and despite their differences, cooperated in coordinating resources, and moderating and integrating competing concerns, to have a positive impact on both public safety and community revitalization in the valley. They expressed concern about the physical (vacant lots, abandoned cars, broken windows) and behavioral (public drunkenness, noise, youth violence) dimensions of neighborhood disorder.[4] They were also concerned about the social and political dimensions of disorder (unaccountable public and private power) in their communities.

II. Three Citizen Crime Prevention Groups in Rainier Valley

All three groups attempted to expose some form of less accountable power in their neighborhoods to critical public scrutiny. All three criticized the police administration and praised the patrol officers in their neighborhoods. All three sought more proactive forms of policing and geographic integrity in patrol allocation. All three told stories about what policing is that were extensions of stories about their communities. And all three enjoyed some success, though the most impressive achievements were a consequence of their loose prepartnership cooperation and then their combined pressure on the department, which led to the creation of the partnership, a dynamic force only in its initial period.

The Operation Results story about community and policing focused on reorienting patrol to avoid political constraints on policing. The Neighbors Against Drugs story about community and policing highlighted the importance of citizens holding drug dealers and police administrators accountable. The South Seattle Crime Prevention Council story centered on targeted policing to better protect property along the Rainier Valley's commercial strip. Each of these exposed unaccountable power, criticized police administrators, praised the proactivity of patrol officers, and opposed department policy that administratively rotated officers out of their neighborhoods just when they became effective. But, just as their stories intersected, so did they diverge in the details.

Operation Results: A Discourse on Reorienting Patrol

When the founder of Operation Results discovered a crack house on his block, he called the South Precinct. Then he called the Narcotics Division downtown. Being a strong supporter of the police, and a special operations veteran with an advanced degree and graduate work in criminology, Jon Daykin was not satisfied to sit and wait for his neighborhood to turn around.[5] Operation Results could provide a type of resource for crime control not available to the police.

Daykin argued that Seattle could be gang and drug free in two years at little cost if it were not for political pressures constraining the police. He noted pressure on the police department to rotate officers out of neighborhoods to avoid the appearance of corruption, pressure from property owners benefiting from secondary drug money, and pressure from middle- and upper-middle-class residents who patronized the drug and sex markets but preferred to keep them and their violence out of their own neighborhoods.[6] This story about policing and communities led Operation Results to develop citizen mobile watches to circumvent political constraints.

According to this story, crack dealers are in a business that requires darkness, isolation, and secrecy. Operation Results attacked these market conditions, driving dealers out of neighborhoods.[7] To do this, citizens conspicuously observed and photographed activity around a suspected crack house. Neighbors kept their porch lights on or installed floodlights that shone through the rear windows of approaching cars. By denying dealers the darkness, isolation, and secrecy they needed to market their goods, Operation Results forced them to close up shop and relocate. A citizen mobile watch scared off potential customers with mechanical substitutes for the gaze of a traditional community.

This is a story about displacing criminal activity, forcing dealers to internalize externalities, and sending a message about power in the neighborhood. As Daykin told it, forcing dealers to move destroyed the perception that gangs were invincible or that this neighborhood was their turf. Moving on was a clear sign that they did not own the neighborhood. And Daykin argued that this sent a message to the children in the neighborhood to seek out different role models. A citizen mobile watch forced dealers to accept additional costs by mobilizing publicity as a sanctioning system. A form of unaccountable private power in the neighborhood was forced to weigh the costs of private profiteering in a public place against the costs of public scrutiny.

Subjecting Crack Houses to Public Scrutiny. Operation Results operated a 24-hour hot line to determine the location of new crack houses. Operation Results did some community outreach, helping landlords to evict dealers, persuading businesses to place their lots and phones off limits to dealers, and pressuring uncooperative property owners to accept the fact that there was a dealer on their premises. But their primary tactic was the citizen mobile watch.[8]

A citizen mobile watch generally involved two neighbors in one car with a camera and a note pad. They took pictures, recorded license plate numbers, and observed traffic patterns. Then they passed this information on to the police. According to Daykin, this nonviolent form of citizen surveillance closed a crack house on his block in four days—after the police had been unable to do so for nine weeks.[9] That block remained quiet four years later; the house had been demolished, and the lot was vacant.

The use of cameras became a source of some discomfort, however, in both the community and the police department. When a neighborhood association in the valley asked Daykin to stop using the cameras to avoid provoking an incident, he refused, arguing that the cameras kept citizen mobile watches safe and effective.[10] As a result, the president of the association fired Daykin three months after inviting him to chair their Crime Prevention Committee because the police had informed him that citizen mobile watches were too dangerous. The South Precinct commander confirmed this, saying, "I fear for their safety. We don't want citizens doing things that are police in nature. If they are inferring that they are police, they are violating the law."[11]

Composition. According to Daykin, the membership of Operation Results was approximately one-third Asian, one-third white, and one-third African American, with income levels ranging from welfare recipient to upper middle class. It was difficult to verify this; news stories about Operation Results focused almost exclusively on Daykin, only occasionally mentioning two assistants—a white woman and a black man.[12] Daykin claimed to be able to mobilize 150 to 300 active members in the Rainier Valley.[13] But he kept no membership lists.

Daykin insists that Operation Results is not based on any traditional community organization model. "Those means are fruitless. They get everybody there and the actual purpose of the meeting changes from the goal that they had to begin with to getting the number of people out to make the meeting. This never worked for me. What has worked for me in the past is selecting people you need to get the job done. So I hand-pick people."[14] A National Institute of Justice (NIJ) study described this structure as a unique combination of effective citizen action and a special forces command structure.[15]

Crime Prevention and Community. Despite controversy, the story mobilized by Operation Results was persuasive enough to attract the attention of Seattle neighborhood associations, government agencies like Drugs Draw the Line, the National Institute of Justice, and the president of the United States. After Daykin and a handful of his neighbors closed a crack house on their block in June 1989, neighbors on adjoining blocks sought their assistance. In June 1990, Operation Results received $20,000 from Drugs Draw the Line to sweep the Rainier Valley of crack houses from Dearborn on the north to the city limits on the south.[16] In 1989, before the Operation Results sweep, the Seattle Police Department estimated that there were approximately 1,400 crack houses operating in the valley.[17] In February 1994, according to Daykin, it would be difficult to find five.[18]

Praise for Operation Results came from the police, city council, and two members of the SSCPC. Jean Veldwyk and the South Precinct commander helped Operation Results get started.[19] A Seattle police officer working with the South Precinct Community Police Team praised Operation Results for "helping people take back their community."[20] City council member (and chair of the Public Safety Committee) Margaret Pageler, in a letter to Operation Results, praised the group as proving "that citizens can come up with innovative solutions to the problems that plague our neighborhoods."[21]

In 1992—as Daykin was preparing to receive a Point of Light Award in a White House ceremony with President Bush—the *Seattle Post-Intelligencer* and the Points of Light Foundation president, Richard Shubert, expressed reservations about the choice.[22] According to the *Seattle Post-Intelligencer,* some members of the Rainier Valley community held a "dim view" of Jon Daykin. This sentiment apparently accounts for Shubert's attempt to deny Daykin the award.[23]

Citizen mobile watches were criticized as unsafe, insensitive to the broader concerns of other communities in the area, and simply a vehicle for the advancement of Jon Daykin. Larry Montgomery, chair of the Rainier Valley Neighborhood District Council, said: "A lot of people in the community feel their short-term approaches [displacement] don't get at the root of the causes—they don't help these kids find some other way to survive."[24]

Daykin believes that political considerations conspired to reduce the effectiveness of Operation Results, the SSCPC, and the Seattle Police Department. He believes the neighborhood association fired him under pressure from merchants and landlords living off secondary drug money.[25] The SSCPC, Daykin argued, had begun as a great organization because of citizens who were willing to get things done, but "it got to the point where every time I would go to a meeting and I would count the people sitting at the table, everybody sitting there was being paid to be there." Daykin proudly asserted that his organization was "not politically beholden to anybody."[26]

Perhaps the success of Operation Results was a source of the controversy surrounding it. The claim that Seattle could be gang and drug free within two years at very little cost might ruffle a few feathers if a 1994 SPD reverse sting was any indication of the type of clientele frequenting Seattle drug markets.[27] Chambliss, writing about the corruption scandal that hit the Seattle Police Department in the late 1960s, argued that many people fail to understand that "shared interests are at the root of the forces of social control" and that these interests are not necessarily interested in controlling all crime. As long as the citywide demand for drugs, prostitution, and gambling is met in a way that keeps these services (and associated violence) invisible to more affluent neighborhoods, there is a shared interest in ignoring claims like Daykin's and opposing the use of cameras by citizens.[28]

It is also possible that citizen mobile watches alienated members of other Rainier Valley communities. The success of the citizen mobile watch did reveal one low-cost way to regain control of public spaces. If taking photographs was enough to close a crack house, this indicates that the power of public scrutiny is a vastly underdeveloped resource to fight crime, and, as Daykin put it, "just a mere presence can have an effect."[29]

But Daykin was the target of bad feelings from others in the community for acting without community support. This may be one cost of Operation Results' success: their extreme individualism alienated them from others in the community, insulating them from the moderating influences of reciprocal social relations and in turn preventing their crime prevention work from contributing to the strengthening of community life in the valley.

As a citizen action that disregards reciprocity, citizen patrols contributed less to building community. Citizen patrols generated suspicion among the community and in the police department precisely because they were "politically beholden to nobody." Citizen patrols highlight the importance of intracommunity accountability and reciprocity. Even though Operation Results cooperated with other crime prevention groups in Rainier Valley and photos were a potent tool linking community-based sanctioning with potential court sanctions, a group that is "beholden to no one" raises accountability concerns, especially when their activities may circumvent due process and violate the rights of other residents in the community.

An NIJ study found Operations Results to be a success because it "focused on enhancing the efficacy of residents to fight back against drugs rather than emphasizing their vulnerability and previous failures to prevent crime. The over-riding message was: 'Citizens can make a difference if they decide to take action.'"[30] The small investment in community embodied in such an effort reaped rewards, but Operation Results achieved this freedom of action by eschewing intracommunity reciprocity and the informal constraints that inhere in these relational networks. The stories about policing and community mobilized by Operation Results reveal that an individualistic disdain for intracommunity reciprocity prevents even effective crime prevention activities from contributing to community revitalization. Some crack houses were closed, but Operation Results' members and their model of citizen action were increasingly marginalized in Rainier Valley. Their failure to link up with a broader vision of community and to integrate their concerns with others in the community transformed their stories about policing and community into yet another form of unaccountable power.

Neighbors Against Drugs: A Discourse on Accountable Policing

Neighbors Against Drugs enjoyed, even sought out, a high public profile in the Seattle media. Unlike Operation Results, they were frequently covered in the *Seattle Times*.[31] Also unlike both Operation Results and the SSCPC, Neighbors Against Drugs was not selected by the White House to receive a Point of Light Award. Perhaps the single most significant difference between Neighbors Against Drugs and the other two organizations, however, was its very acrimonious relationship with then chief of police Patrick Fitzsimons. Neighbors Against Drugs placed the blame for the crack and gang situation in Rainier Valley squarely on the chief's desk, just as Saul Alinsky would recommend.[32] And they did this loudly and publicly, organizing rallies and a petition drive to remove the chief.[33]

Neighbors Against Drugs was established to address the problem of police nonresponse to crack houses. According to LaChance, in 1985 there were five crack houses in a six-block radius of Rainier Beach, the southernmost neighborhood in Rainier Valley. Neighbors noticed that car prowls, burglaries, and traffic were all rising. Neighbors repeatedly called the police, but the police failed to respond. In a local Presbyterian church, a group that later became Neighbors Against Drugs called a public meeting. City council member Norm Rice was there; so was the chief. LaChance described the scene to me the following way:

> You can imagine. If you were a councilperson or the chief of police and 350 pissed off neighbors show up at this church. And they're saying we want something done and we want it done now. Well

> things started to happen. I'll never forget, the guy they're touting to be the next chief of police, he stood up in front of 350 people and he said he couldn't find any 911 records of anybody calling. And I said wait a minute, I called 35 times myself, and here's a list of all the times and days of when I called, and a woman who kind of spearheads that Rainier Beach Community Club up there said the same thing: we've documented all the times we've called. So something's wrong, and she flat said it: either you're grossly mistaken, or you're a liar. She just said that. They're not used to having people really challenge the system and say something is wrong. So a pretty good core group got together after that meeting. That was on a Wednesday night, and that Sunday morning we put about 150 people on the front yard of the rock house there on Waters Avenue and we sent out a press release, and that was pretty much the first time anybody had really marched on a rock house. Of course, the media ate it up; they just couldn't believe it. Monday morning the commander was out there with a couple of sergeants and that place was gone, they were history. . . . So we just continued to do those kinds of things. Every weekend we picked a different neighborhood, and finally they got the message and the cops started raiding those places.[34]

The story about policing and community animating Neighbors Against Drugs focused on a lack of department accountability. According to the *Seattle Times,* the story Frank LaChance told to other citizens' groups was to assist the police by documenting drug activity in their neighborhoods and then follow up to make sure the police acted on this information in a way that was consistent with the communities' concerns and priorities.[35]

Exposing Police Management to Public Scrutiny. The failure of the police to respond to citizen concerns expressed through the 911 system contributed to the critical attitude these citizens had toward the police administration. LaChance told me, and this was confirmed in other interviews, that the members of Neighbors Against Drugs had a good relationship with the street cops in their neighborhoods. They criticized police management for failing to properly utilize the knowledge and skills of street cops and community members.[36] This is one lesson the group learned in its struggle against crack houses in their neighborhood. The police *can* be a valuable resource for citizens. But police managers are reluctant to share control of state resources.

LaChance argued that the chief was reluctant to let the community get involved and reluctant to have officers walk beats. The chief's reluctance was consistent with the professional policing model, which holds that citizen involvement with street cops walking the beat is a primary source of police corruption. The Seattle Police Department was embarrassed by a corruption scandal in the late 1960s. Fitzsimons, brought in from the outside to reestablish department credibility, sought to avoid such problems under his administration. But public pressure from citizens and elected officials forced the chief to consider some form of police-community partnership.

Composition. While Neighbors Against Drugs made enemies in the chief's office and failed to get any recognition from the White House, it mobilized a significant number of citizens in Rainier Valley. According to Neighbors Against Drugs, its members included former hippies turned homeowners, a multiracial mix of lower- to middle-class residents of the Rainier Beach neighborhood. No membership lists were available, but press reports of hundreds of residents participating in Neighbors Against Drugs protests indicated a large and broad-based mobilization.

The Neighbors Against Drugs hot line identified an after-hours club, the Neighborhood Gathering Place, as a source of disorder. Drug dealing and fighting were taking place on and around the premises, there were reports of shots fired, and the properties of nearby residents were being used for public urination. LaChance described the events that followed this way:

> They were out there dealing dope, firing pistols; neighbors were installing alarms, scared to death. [We] couldn't get the city attorney's office, cops, anything. They just said there's nothing we can do about it; these guys have a business license; they have an after-hours club; we don't have anything to regulate this. And we're saying "bullshit." The civil abatement laws can be used to deal with these things. And the civil process has nothing to do with criminal activity. It's all the things that revolve around the place like the prostitution that went on, the public drinking, guys urinating, all those kinds of things. The loud noise, the fights, the cars

> racing up and down the street, all those things fall under the civil nuisance laws.
>
> We even gave them the example of . . . when Judge Dwyer . . . used those laws to close down The Monastery. The old monastery was a club downtown that claimed it was a church . . . [but] they were serving alcohol to kids in there. The place was a mess, outta control; open drug usage went on in there. I went in just a few times to look at the place, and usually took a kid outta there, usually a street kid . . . they used those same laws to close that place down. So we gave them the example, went back and showed them all these things and said, these are the things we can use to close the thing. We went to all the neighbors. We went to a guy who owned the apartment complex next door, whose manager had been beaten up running guys out of the carport area.
>
> We took all this stuff, 10 hours of videotape, and all the neighbors ponied up what little money they could put together; we filed a civil abatement on this thing, took it into court. The city attorney's office is saying you're never gonna win this thing. We go to court, the judge looks at a half-hour of videotape, hears testimony from all the neighbors on what went on there, we subpoena the watch commander, a guy by the name of Lt. Owen Burke, helluva guy, standup guy, he didn't even dodge the bullet one minute. He said, "I have to allocate a third of my manpower every night this place is open." We closed the thing down. [An acquaintance who] worked for the city attorney's office, called me the next day and said you rocked the city attorney's office and police department. Nobody ever believed citizens could file their own civil abatement and make it happen. You know, right after that, [city council member] Margaret Pageler would go on to rewrite the civil abatement laws so that they would use it.[37]

With public victories such as these, the pressure on the chief from Neighbors Against Drugs began to have some effect. While the chief was resistant to citizen involvement and slow to respond to the emergence of crack in Seattle, the South Precinct commanders were not. Beginning with Precinct Commander Tony Guston and continuing with Commander Romero Yumul and Sergeant Chuck Pillon, South Precinct police officers experimented with team policing and Anti-Crime Teams. These officers and their innovative approaches to policing provided an education in crime control alternatives for the citizens in Rainier Valley.

However, another consequence of these initiatives was that Guston, Yumul, and Pillon were transferred out of the precinct and the original Anti-Crime Teams (ACT I) were disbanded by the chief. Guston went to Records, Yumul to Juvenile. Pillon refused his transfer off the street and was fired, losing his pension after 26 years on the force. Citizens in Rainier Valley were outraged, and the pressure on the chief mounted. He created new Anti-Crime Teams (ACT II) with a strict law enforcement mandate more tightly controlled from downtown.

But the chief's new Anti-Crime Teams ran into trouble. In response to pressure from Neighbors Against Drugs, the new Anti-Crime Teams targeted crack houses, and the number of drug raids increased. First William Tucker, a 44-year-old black resident of the Central Area, and then Erdman Bascomb, a 41-year-old black resident of Rainier Valley, were killed in Anti-Crime Team drug raids.[38] Bascomb was killed as his door was broken down and he stood up with a TV remote control in his hand. In a previous raid on Bascomb's apartment on December 18, a small amount of "suspected flake, rock cocaine, and marijuana" was found. This time, however, no weapons or drugs were found in the apartment.

According to a report in the *Seattle Times,* "Police acknowledge that no weapons were found inside the apartment but stressed that guns usually are found in rock-house raids. . . . Wednesday night's raid netted only a white powder usually used to cut cocaine, and a scale, the type often used for weighing narcotics."[39] Neighbors Against Drugs, in the same article, promised to lobby the city council and the mayor to postpone the raids because they were putting officers and residents at risk. Fitzsimons announced he would not suspend the raids, saying, "We have to keep the pressure up. These places are near schools and the complaints are pouring in."[40]

Crime Prevention and Community. Neighbors Against Drugs had learned the importance of the second piece of advice LaChance gave to other neighborhoods: Follow up and be sure that the police are using the information you give them in a way that is consistent with your concerns and values. These deaths made the group question whether ACT II was the way to go. Before ACT II, Neighbors Against Drugs had tried to talk to neighbors with drug dealers working out of their homes, with little success. They found that dealers paid rents otherwise unimaginable in the area.[41] The tragic outcome of the chief's new Anti-Crime Teams, however, gave Neighbors Against Drugs reason to reconsider the value of a neighborly chat. Even if it was sure to be a slower approach, it would be safer for all involved.

Neighbors talking to neighbors was more consistent with the approach used by the first Anti-Crime Team. That approach was called "knock and talk." The teams did not seek arrests or batter down doors with search warrants; they tried to disrupt normal operations by talking their way into crack houses or parking outside until toilets flushed, proactive techniques consistent with community policing's deemphasis on traditional law enforcement (arrests). Following the deaths of the two residents, Neighbors Against Drugs revisited the citizen compliment of this approach.

> I started figuring out that we could do those kind of things if we went out and started knocking on doors and saying to those people, hey listen, what you're doing here is not conducive to a family neighborhood. We're gonna camp out on you here. We're gonna write down license plate numbers, that kind of stuff, and we're gonna turn it over to the police. It's time to talk. Let's negotiate some kind of truce here so we can all live together. Well, there were people in the department that said I was crazy, but we proved that curiosity took over before any kind of aggression, that anybody treated with honesty and respect responded.[42]

Neighbors Against Drugs combined citizen surveillance and direct action with a commitment to monitoring police performance and a critical attitude toward the chief. Their success, like Operation Results, was a consequence of subjecting less accountable agents in the community to increased public scrutiny, and, unlike Operation Results, it contributed to the strength of community because it involved face-to-face conversations rather than a high-tech gaze and large numbers of citizens cooperating with each other and with the police.

At least five groups in other parts of Seattle or Washington state have tried to emulate the success of Neighbors Against Drugs.[43] LaChance told me that in October 1993 he received one of many calls from citizens seeking assistance. He was invited to a Burien neighborhood that was trying to deal with two crack houses. For the past 18 months, residents had been calling the police with nothing to show for it. After sharing his experiences in Rainier Valley, LaChance was invited back in the first week of November and awarded a 1993 Neighborhood Block Watch Hero plaque.[44]

LaChance worked with the SSCPC, serving as a committee chair.[45] He also worked with Operation Results on closing the Neighborhood Gathering Place. Gladys Jordan was a key member of the SSCPC, representing both the African American community and Neighbors Against Drugs. LaChance indicated that these groups were able to work together despite differences.[46]

Despite a more critical posture, Neighbors Against Drugs was able to cooperate with other groups, and as it observed the consequences of this cooperation it moderated its position and encouraged other groups to moderate theirs. This respect for the reciprocity that constitutes communities paid off in the survival of the stories about policing and community mobilized by Neighbors Against Drugs as others imitated their approach to crime prevention. Neighbors Against Drugs contributed to ongoing citizen efforts to revitalize community life in the valley by bringing together community-based and police department resources.

> Well, even though we disagreed on some things, we were all determined to make the thing work. So things smoothed out, got better. We started targeting different things; we set realistic goals. We picked specific rock houses. We set up a hot line where people could call in anonymously and say this is what's going on. We'd make a priority if we got, say, 25 calls on one particular residence, and a lot of times we would go out and watch this thing and look at it, and yeah, they're dealing dope outta here all right. So we would meet the following week with the precinct commander; they would come back the following week and talk about these targets, and as we eliminated problems we would add another target on. And we would only pick like three or four a week to deal with so we could achieve some kind of goal. So it worked.[47]

Neighbors Against Drugs combined various resources—local time and organization, publicity, and cooperation with street cops—and brought these to bear on community concerns. As LaChance put it, communities have to be the watchdog.[48] Communities have to be empowered to challenge police bureaucrats who show up at meetings armed with statistics to show that there have not been an unusual number of 911 calls or that crime is down or arrests are up or that calls for service are up and department funding is not keeping pace.[49] "I don't care if crime is down 150 percent. What's the true gauge? The true gauge is how safe you feel in your neighborhood, how safe you feel in your home. That's what counts."[50]

The Neighbors Against Drugs story about community and policing focused on accountability, more so than was initially intended. Protesting to expose unaccountable police management and unaccountable drug dealers led Neighbors Against Drugs to pressure for more proactive policing of crack houses. After the two deaths, Neighbors Against Drugs learned that all actors, including community pressure groups that stop short of a genuine coproduction of public safety, need to be held accountable for their decisions. They had pushed hard for a state-centered solution, without considering the costs of this choice, rather than a mobilization of police and community resources under the close supervision of the citizens themselves.

SSCPC: A Discourse on Partnerships to Target Policing

The South Seattle Crime Prevention Council (SSCPC) was set up as a police-community partnership in 1988. It adopted the corporate shell of an earlier private crime prevention organization, the Crime Prevention League. Several core members of the SSCPC had been active in the Crime Prevention League and others in the Court Watch Program. The defining characteristics of the SSCPC were its long history of activism and support from the local business community.

The early efforts of the community activists who formed the SSCPC were described by the *Seattle Times:* "Some good citizens go to church on Wednesday night. Others go to the PTA. These people—salt of the earth, as ordinary as the Cleavers—track reports of narcotics arrests and drive-by shootings. Under a map of the Southeast filled with push pins—blue for drugs, red for prostitution—sits a former PTA president, a real estate saleswoman, a bank vice president, a carpet salesman, and a Boeing worker. They have poured hundreds of hours into tracking crime in the area, and hundreds more lighting fires under the local police to get them to do something about it."[51] That real estate saleswoman estimated that she put in at least 20 hours of volunteer labor each week working for the council. She argued: "Nothing will work if you're not willing to put in hundreds of hours."[52]

The former PTA president and then director of the Rainier Chamber of Commerce, Kay Godefroy, was the only paid staff member of the fledgling SSCPC. Godefroy later became the executive director of the Neighborhood Crime and Justice Center (NCJC).[53] She initially got involved in crime prevention in 1987 to support the business community's response to crack. When asked in 1992 if she felt the effort was worth it, she said: "No question. I still live in the Southeast, and it's a different community entirely than it was five years ago. Much better. Much safer."[54]

Property owners and business leaders in Rainier Valley told a story about policing as one part of a larger civic responsibility to contribute to safe, stable, and strong communities. They were able to mobilize the vertical social capital inhering in their relationships with city officials to pressure the police department to support activities in the community that contributed to building horizontal social capital across community groups. These included graffiti paint-outs, beautification, and the development of innovative programs like the Criminal Trespass Program, Anti-Crime Teams, and the Drug Trafficking Civil Abatement Program.

Prior to the establishment of the SSCPC, the activities of this group, in cooperation with other groups in the valley, contributed to strengthening communities because they integrated and moderated competing concerns, brought competing groups together in concrete and visible problem solving activities, and as such contributed to building relationships across communities. Thus, it was the chamber group that was best able to mobilize vertical and horizontal social capital to bring formal and community resources to bear on crime prevention and community revitalization in the valley.

Social Capital and Critical Public Scrutiny. In Southeast Seattle, there is a tradition of citizen activism. The activists who founded the SSCPC had long records of accomplishment and reputations in the community and downtown as serious and responsible civic leaders in the Rainier Valley.[55] It was this long-term commitment to civic responsibility that constituted a form of social capital, which, when they announced they were holding a press conference without the chief, provided the leverage that turned that into a credible threat of critical public scrutiny, forcing the chief to accept a police-community partnership. But it is necessary to look backward before looking forward to understand how this social capital developed into a potent form of collective political capital, one that inhered in the structure of relationships within the community and between community leaders and city officials.

The first significant effort by the citizens who later became involved with the SSCPC was a Court Watch Program. A local real estate agent, Jean Veldwyk, and the owner of a local hardware store, Buzz Anderson, spearheaded a campaign to monitor King County Superior Court judges who they felt were soft on crime. Buzz Anderson said that this group "felt the police were doing everything they could, but they kept telling us the courts weren't backing them up. The community should have a part in sentencing. Judges are elected officials."[56]

The Court Watch Program sent citizen volunteers to observe in courtrooms and monitor judicial performance. The group even registered as a research organization to gain access to the prosecutors' files. With support from the chamber, the county prosecutor, and Police Chief Hanson (who added that he thought the police should also take part in sentencing), this small group eventually joined with others to form the Rainier Community Action Center in 1974.[57] This group of more than 100 citizens formalized the court watch as a 30-month study of 23 judges. After reviewing 485 cases through June of 1976, they issued a report critical of eight judges. Two of these were defeated in the next election.[58]

Following its success in ousting two judges, the court watch effort dwindled, but the citizens remained active in response to a rise in residential burglaries in the valley. Buzz Anderson and others formed the Crime Prevention League in 1981, funded primarily with the approximately $2,400 per month generated at the Columbia City Lions Club bingo games.[59] The league focused on residential and commercial burglaries by encouraging target hardening and organizing a loosely coordinated business watch.

Before crack hit Seattle in the mid-1980s, league members had begun to think they had worked themselves out of business. While the image of Rainier Valley as dangerous lingered in the minds of some, serious crime was down. From February 1981 to February 1982, Part I offenses in Rainier Valley fell 10.6 percent while increasing 14.1 percent in the rest of the city.[60] The emergence less than three years later of gangs, graffiti, guns, and crack houses changed the situation in the valley again. While citizens were making progress in the struggle to revitalize their communities, recovery remained slow and crime prevention was but one small part of the larger multifaceted efforts. The arrival of crack was a first step in the rising salience of crime prevention within citizen stories about policing and community. Fighting crack further united the residents of Rainier Valley as the drug problem moved deeper into their neighborhoods. Crack dealing was linked to burglaries, drive-by shootings, and gangs, as the Crips settled in the Central Area and the Bloods in Rainier Valley. A homegrown street gang also emerged, the Black Gangster Disciples.[61]

The chamber group began to meet sporadically with the South Precinct command staff in 1987. Progress was slow. "These people were there because the chief supported a good discussion," Veldwyk said. "But at all levels . . . they explained why things didn't work better, not how they could be better. . . . We hadn't found any bending on the part of the department."[62] Godefroy felt the police were trying to protect their power to say what policing was, which included a limited role for communities. "We could report crime, but we couldn't solve problems."[63]

It was at this stage that the citizens acted on their own to show the police and the city they were serious. Gang activity led to an increase in graffiti and vandalism in Rainier Valley. In response to this and SPD resistance, the first community mobilizations directly linked to the SSCPC began to emerge. Initially spontaneous, and then sponsored first by the chamber and later by the city Department of Engineering, these citizens organized a graffiti hot line, paint-outs, and cleanup programs. Participants included citizens from a variety of community groups. These same citizens, in coordination with the South Precinct commander, developed the Criminal Trespass Program to improve the policing of gang and drug activity on private commercial property.[64]

Both Veldwyk and Godefroy remember that Chief Fitzsimons was initially very resistant to the idea of changing police practices. In 1991, Godefroy claimed that the resistance was continuing.

> I'm not convinced that the command staff clearly understands what the community wants is police that are part of the community. I get little glimmers now and then that it's coming, but I'm not certain that it's sold. Part of it is the resistance from the chief himself, who was brought here so we could get our department cleaned up and insure that we have a spanking clean department with no corruption whatsoever. And his strong belief is, you have

> to have a centralized police department that is not connected to the community to achieve that.[65]

This track record of political successes, community mobilization, and a willingness to work with the police made it possible for the chamber group to arrange a meeting with the mayor to pressure the SPD to sign a partnership agreement. In the next several months, the group met with the police at least 34 times. By the end of September, the group was again frustrated and presented the SPD, in a meeting that included the mayor, with their own 15 Point Plan (see fig. 6). On October 7, 1987, after still getting no response from the chief, the group informed the city that it would hold a press conference in one week to announce the partnership. The chief showed up, announced, and took credit for, the new partnership at the press conference two days later.[66]

This agreement created the SSCPC. In May 1988, the chief proposed to the National Institute of Justice that a study be done to evaluate the partnership. This study produced the Fleissner, Fedan, and Stotland report (1991). One community group built resources and respect through small victories and persuaded the SPD to cooperate. As Godefroy put it:

> Our first success was with the criminal trespass enforcement, that was a community/police partnership in 1987. We had problems in private parking lots, and the police had no way to address it, so the ordinance was on the books. We looked at it, we looked at how we could implement a program so that it could be enforced even if the owner wasn't there to call. Tremendous success. It would not have happened without the community component. . . . So as soon as we got everything in place and went back to the police and said, "OK, we did our part, now you do yours. . . ." Well, once you have a success, you're confident to try something else. The graffiti was just incredible. The Southeast was beginning to look like Los Angeles looks now because people weren't doing anything about it. They just assumed, well they're going to come back and do it again, so they'd just leave it. So we started our paint-out project. And proved to the community that it worked. . . . We said we know what the problems are. We've proven we can solve some of them ourselves. You have to work with us. It was a real gunfight. And

RAINIER CHAMBER OF COMMERCE
15 POINT PLAN FOR SOUTH SEATTLE

1. The South Precinct Commander shall head the project. This person must be proactive and community oriented, a motivator, creative, and committed to community participation in the program. He/she must have total support from the Chief of Police, the Mayor, and the Community Advisory Committee to effectively implement the Program.
2. A Community Advisory Committee shall be established to work directly with the South Precinct to develop community support and monitor the program and establish guidelines. This Advisory Committee shall work closely with the Precinct Commander on all aspects relative to the reduction of crime in Southeast Seattle, understanding, of course, the confidential nature of police work. Members of the committee shall be selected from a cross section of Southeast residents and business people. The committee shall be representative of the socio-economic diversity of the area.
3. Three lieutenants (watch commanders) shall be assigned to the Project at the South Precinct. These lieutenants must have a working knowledge of the Program, must be able to work closely with the community, and must be committed to the basic concepts of the Program. Six patrol sergeants (three Robert and three Sam sector sergeants for three shifts) shall be assigned. The sergeant should have the ability to motivate and aggressively lead officers in a pro-active effort.
4. These sectors shall be staffed with officers dedicated to the spirit of the Program.
5. Staffing: Eight patrol officers shall be reallocated from other police functions. This assignment is intended to increase the number of two-officer patrol units, directly accountable to the South Precinct Commander.
6. The staffing level of the anti-crime team shall be maintained. A clerk shall be assigned to the team.
7. The following staff shall be assigned to the South Precinct: Two detectives from the Narcotics Unit, one detective from the Commercial Unit, two juvenile detectives, two officers from the Special Patrol Unit (SPU), and an officer from the Crime Prevention Unit. All of these individuals shall be accountable to the Precinct Commander, to be used as needed in this pilot project.
8. An incentive program shall be an option to be implemented at the South Precinct, at the discretion of the Captain.
9. Additional clerical assistance shall be provided from officers on limited duty, such as the CSO Unit, to free up as possible, professional staff time from clerical duties.
10. Reasonable funds shall be committed for confidential informants and control narcotics buys.
11. The community will assist in recruiting "loaned" clerical workers, in purchasing equipment, and in locating space where the Police Department budget will not provide needed resources. This support activity will further include, but not be limited to, enlisting community support to work in and organize trouble areas as identified by police, secure office space if needed and be available, as needed, to coordinate with the Seattle Public Schools and local social services agencies.
12. Precinct personnel shall be trained to deal with selected problem areas in cooperation with the Community Advisory Committee to provide liaison between the community, the Committee, and the South Precinct.
13. A computer and software for tracking data from the two sectors, plus approximately $2,000 for miscellaneous equipment such as surveillance gear, shall be provided to the Program. If the Department has insufficient funds, the community shall undertake a fund-raising campaign to pay for this equipment.
14. A total commitment to this Program from the Mayor and the Chief of Police is <u>CRITICAL</u> to the Program's success.
15. A total commitment from the Southeast community throughout the term of the Program is <u>also</u> essential to the Program's success.

Fig. 6. SSCPC 15-point plan. (From various SSCPC meeting minutes.)

> we stared 'em down. And they finally said, "okay, we will work with you." We actually hammered out a contract, an agreement to work in partnership for 1988, and now the police department is taking full credit for doing this wonderful thing for the community.[67]

Composition. The chamber group was, not surprisingly, dominated by small business owners. It also included several prominent Seattle civic leaders. Cheryl Chow later served on the city council. Denis Law was an influential founder and publisher of local neighborhood newspapers. Jean Veldwyk, Norm Chamberlain, Buzz Anderson, and others had been active leaders in the valley for decades. Most members were upper middle class and white. The Neighbors Against Drugs member, Gladys Jordan, was only one of two active minority members in the founding period.[68]

Resources and Community. The official story of community policing in Seattle began with the South Seattle Crime Prevention Council. But this story had grown out of a decade of citizen efforts to reclaim their neighborhoods. These activists can be credited with making an important contribution to revitalizing the Rainier Valley. Their activism and early successes demonstrated to some city officials the potential value of a police-community partnership. According to a 1989 feature article in the *Seattle Times,* they can be proud of "phenomenal results for a neighborhood that, a year ago, was considered the chief combat zone in the war on drugs. In the last year [1988], major crimes have been reduced by 7% in the South Precinct," which contrasts sharply with a 1.3 percent increase in the rest of Seattle for the same period.[69] This police-community partnership was so successful that it was awarded the thirteenth point of light from President George Bush.[70]

The valley corresponds to six police beats (R3, R4, R5, S3, S4, S5; see figs. 7 and 8) in two of three sectors that make up the South Precinct. Crime fell in 14 of the 15 beats in Robert and Sam sectors in 1987–88. In 1988–89, crime continued to fall in four of five Robert beats (R1, R3, R4, R5) and one of five William beats (W5) but rose in all five beats of Sam sector. So, while Fleissner, Fedan, and Stotland were very sensitive to the difficulties involved in evaluating community policing, they still concluded that the initial phase of this police-community partnership had a positive impact on the target areas.[71]

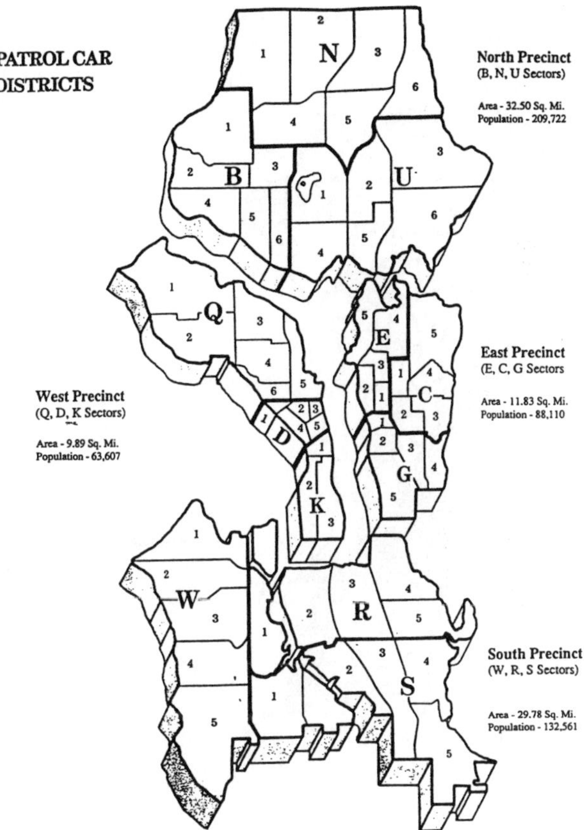

Fig. 7. Police precinct map of Seattle, 1990. (Courtesy of the Seattle Police Department.)

III. Conclusion

While decisions made by powerful public and private leaders have not always boded well for the valley, unlike the fate of some other inner city neighborhoods in the United States, residents did not leave when times were hardest. The valley remains Seattle's most economically and ethnically diverse region, and, as one activist told me, this has been a source of strength and resilience. In this context, three crime prevention groups emerged within and contributed to the reciprocal networks that constituted the communities of Southeast Seattle.

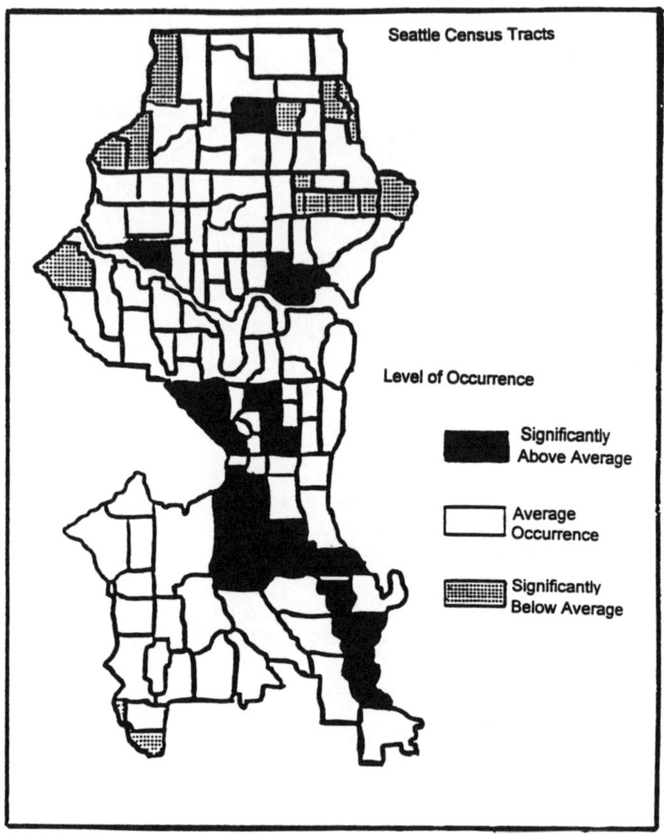

Fig. 8. Geographical distribution of Part I Offenses, 1988. (From Seattle Police Department 1988c.)

The myriad activities in Rainier Valley began long before the SSCPC persuaded the SPD to agree to the police-community partnership that the National Institute of Justice has called a model for community policing. Thus, much of the community revitalization that has occurred in the valley can be traced to the long-term activism of its residents, beginning with SESCO, SEED, and the Court Watch Program. Operation Results added tactics to reclaim residential streets. Neighbors Against Drugs brought concerned neighbors together in front yards, used the courts for civil abatement, and monitored the police as a public resource that ought to be available to help neighbors clean up their shared public spaces.

All these groups were participating in the struggle to control urban public space. Their stories about policing and community demanded that their streets be safe social spaces for the multifaceted, routine, reciprocal interactions that constitute communities. They objected to drug dealers treating these spaces as a private domain. They mobilized formal and informal resources to challenge the privatized forms of association that had come to colonize their own front yards. In this way, their activism built on their roots in the community and contributed to the strength of the community.

Operation Results forced crack houses out of the shadows and into the light of community surveillance. Neighbors Against Drugs and the SSCPC expanded scrutiny from dealers to the police and elected officials. Because the SSCPC leaders had the longest record of activism in the area, their accumulated social capital provided them with an additional resource, which separated their activism from Neighbors Against Drugs and Operation Results and contributed to the pressure on the police department to cooperate with them.

These three groups have grown weaker over time. Citizen crime prevention organizations do not endure by focusing exclusively on crime control issues.[72] Even as these organizations atrophy, however, the activists keep reappearing, sometimes in new issue areas, sometimes sharing their experience with other neighborhoods. Godefroy is now working citywide on crime control, homelessness, and social services for children. LaChance and Daykin are advising other citizens' groups. Norm Chamberlain is building a senior center in the valley and still participates in regular graffiti paint-outs. Buzz Anderson has become the president of the Rainier Valley Historical Preservation Society. Even as the organizations have changed, a legacy of citizen activism integrating diverse concerns has continued.

Perhaps the sustainability of organizations is a deceiving indicator of community and grassroots mobilization. In this case, from the Court Watch Program, to the Crime Prevention League, to the SSCPC and beyond, the organization has been an ephemeral snapshot of networks of social relations dancing along the border between formal and informal resource mobilization. The history of these citizens and their cooperation presented here shows them to be embedded within relatively reciprocal relational networks. These networks provided individuals and groups with an awareness that their ability to sustain episodes of cooperation was one of their most powerful tools for protecting their children, families, and property.

While the particular organizations came and went, activism remained. Citizen pressure ebbed and flowed in an ongoing attempt to coordinate the application of formal and informal resources to community concerns. This coordination function confirms Abel's observation that the boundaries between formal and informal are fluid, with both operating as modes of potential state or community power.[73] The tactics of Operation Results and Neighbors Against Drugs involved surveillance and neighbors speaking with neighbors as well as civil litigation. The SSCPC sponsored paint-outs and innovative legislation. As LaChance advised, citizens effectively assisted the police and then monitored them to ensure that they acted on their information in a way that was consistent with their values.

Neighbors Against Drugs, Operation Results, and the early efforts of SSCPC activists were all initially reacting to crack and police unresponsiveness. All were critical of crack houses and the police administration; each supported the officers in their neighborhoods and beat integrity to keep them there. What might have become just a reaction against perceived enemies, however, became a proactive discovery of the valuable resources present in the everyday social interactions that constitute community life. The SSCPC spoke for the local business community and, like Seattle's founders, provided a solid foundation of responsible civic leadership. They combined a track record with a deep concern for valley communities drawn from their own interests there. This allowed them to convince the city and the SPD that investing in Rainier Valley would reap rewards because many strong communities remained committed to the area and have shown that despite their differences they can cooperate.

A previous study of Seattle found that downtown business elites, while eager for order, wished to avoid an alarmist image of the city as disorderly. As Scheingold argued, this provided a powerful pressure to moderate the punitive edge of law and order politics. In the 1970s, when downtown civic leaders chose to support the creation of a citywide network of crime prevention councils, they were choosing to moderate more radical, competing stories about unleashing the police or constraining judges as well as stories from minorities demanding community control of the police.[74] This study's findings are generally consistent with this characterization of law and order politics as punitive yet moderated.

A network of crime prevention councils moderated citizen demands through direct interaction with other citizens. This created the possibility of deliberation, such that moderation supported innovative political action. This process of moderation, however, supported stories about resilient communities and democratization as well as stories about co-optation and more disciplinary mechanisms of social control.

It was clear in Rainier Valley that the steady increase in interaction between the police and citizens educated people about crime and politics. This was a mechanism of moderation. As the community learned more about policing, it became both more demanding and less critical of its precinct, and, as the precinct learned more about the value of community involvement, officers became more open to dialogue and more focused on how partnerships enhanced the resources available to the department. Each side became more open to cooperation even as the process filtered out demands that were inconsistent with prevailing institutional interests and the stories that justified them. Both Operation Results and Neighbors Against Drugs were moderated out of the emerging police-community partnership. The moderating out of two of three groups indicated a shrinking of the stories about policing and community to those components that sat at the intersection of chamber and SPD stories.

The key remains reciprocity. A lesson for community policing that can be drawn from Southeast Seattle ought to be that it worked because there were citizen groups rooted in relatively reciprocal relational networks, able to cooperate with each other, and capable of coordinating formal and informal resources into an ongoing, integrated, multifaceted approach to community revitalization. Their crime control efforts were one part of this larger mobilization. The SSCPC was recognized by the SPD; Operation Results and the SSCPC were recognized by the White House and the National Institute of Justice; and Neighbors Against Drugs was recognized by emulation in at least four other neighborhoods. Each of these three groups played a part in changing the way policing is done in Southeast Seattle. It is not the independence of a community group that makes it effective. Groups that are part of long-term, reciprocal, and interdependent networks of social relations have an advantage over other groups when they seek to mobilize.

But if social capital was key, so were other resources critical in the struggle to define community. The establishment of a police-community partnership was an achievement for a network of relatively reciprocal community groups. It was also an official recognition of the Chamber of Commerce group, compounding existing resource inequities in the community. Neither Operation Results nor Neighbors Against Drugs was able to successfully integrate its crime prevention activities with its work/investment activities in the way that members of the SSCPC could. All were able to defend property, but the chamber group was also able to defend and increase the value of their commercial property. This increased their incentive to volunteer labor and their capacity to contribute the kinds of private resources the police department found attractive. It also provided incentives to target crime in a particular manner and to concede to the department efforts to insulate the partnership from more critical stories about community policing.

Chapter 6

Policing Reform in Southeast Seattle

The methods we employ in the enforcement of our criminal law have aptly been called the measures by which the quality of our civilization may be judged.

—Earl Warren

I. Introduction

Community policing in Southeast Seattle is a meeting ground for at least two tracks of political reform, one in the police department and another within the communities of southeast Seattle. These two intersecting histories show a department that has always been a powerful local political institution and a long and checkered history of citizen involvement in the provision of social order. In this chapter, I examine how continuity and change in the organization and practice of policing in Seattle have contributed to the emergence of community policing. I argue that the structure of policing as both hierarchical (internally as well as linked to a national network of functional bureaucracies) and inescapably street level (part of indeterminate, routine, and potentially reciprocal relational networks in communities) created a prevailing story about policing that hindered the possibility of effective policing reform in this case. The influence of federal funding, studies from national institutes, and the managerial perspective of police administrators sometimes clashed and sometimes combined with the needs, experiences, and suspicions of the street cops who must implement policing reforms.

The Seattle Police Department has been consistently embroiled in partisan politics. This makes it hard to hear calls for police independence as expressing much more than a desire on the part of police managers to be free of these limited forms of accountability. Further, while Scheingold finds different periods with different forms of policing in Seattle, this chapter will argue that there is also significant continuity in policing reforms here. Policing reforms from 1861 through the end of the Fitzsimons regime (1994) have all involved a steady centralization of police organization and, with some minor exceptions, increases in the authority and independence of the chief.

II. A History of the Seattle Police Department

The Early Years

Since the first town marshal was appointed in 1861 and the office of the chief of police established by the city council in 1876, the Seattle Police Department has been a central actor on the local political stage. The city's law enforcement community played a leadership role in the lawless expulsion of 196 Chinese residents in 1886. In 1901, Chief of Police William Meredith was shot and killed by John Considine, a former business partner who was the major player in Seattle's booming vice industry. When Prohibition hit Seattle three years before the passage of the Volstead Act, the police formed a "dry squad" to enforce the impossible mandate against the speakeasies and bootlegging that flourished despite the new legislation. In 1932, then mayor John Dore ordered the police department to abolish the liquor and vice details and establish a "shotgun" squad, a bomb squad, and a bunco squad to combat organized crime. In 1941, a divided city council refused to reappoint the police chief and later split over Mayor Millikan's nomination. And in the late 1960s a corruption scandal crippled the Seattle Police Department.[1] Before turning to that episode, it is important to note that not only have the agents of law enforcement in Seattle been consistently embroiled in partisan politics but city residents have also had a long and checkered history of involvement in the provision of social order.

Citizen Input. Central to Seattle policing from the start has been the mixed blessing of citizen participation. In 1882, mobs stormed the city jail and lynched a murder suspect. In that decade, the population of Seattle would jump by more than 3,500 each year from 3,533 in 1880. The railroads accounted for much of the population increase, bringing in Irish and Chinese labor to lay tracks. Mary Kenworthy, a local member of the Woman's Suffrage Association, became a citizen leader in efforts to clean up the rapidly growing city. Morgan described her perspective as follows. "She saw her town grow in size and saw the property of those who had come early (including herself) rise in value. She saw the deserving and the undeserving make fortunes through blind luck, and she saw others just as deserving or undeserving go broke. She dreamed the old dream of a society in which this could not happen."[2] Mary Kenworthy spoke for women and labor against "the interests." She lived in Seattle when women were first given the franchise by the Territorial Legislature in 1883 and the Territorial Supreme Court found this to be unconstitutional in 1887.[3] Perhaps her most notorious activism, however, was her strident insistence (along with other labor and civic leaders in Seattle at the time) that Chinese residents be forcibly expelled from the city.

In 1886, Chief of Police William Murphy found himself a leader of a mob of anti-Chinese residents driven by their fear of unemployment to an irrational lust for popular justice. The Chinese had been popular when they first arrived in the Northwest, notorious for working long days on a handful of rice without complaint. After the final tracks were laid, however, "[t]he fact that the Chinese were accustomed to receiving less than the white men no longer seemed laughable to the white workers; with the construction boom over and business slow, there was competition for every job—and fear of economic competition always increases prejudice."[4] Violence against Chinese began in the small mill towns, chasing the Chinese into the cities, where they expected the police to protect them by enforcing the law. "The police sided with the mob, and the Chinese found themselves outside the law."[5] Labor seized upon the anti-Chinese sentiment, holding a Congress of Sinophobes and fielding its own candidates for local office. The law and order community was split.

Sheriff McGraw did not attend the congress and instead organized a Home Guard to defend the interests of the more moderate civic leaders opposed to expelling the Chinese immediately. (Though they did not support a Chinese presence; they had negotiated with Chinese leaders to work out a gradual departure without violence.) Mary Kenworthy argued that the conflict must be seen as a class war, with the McGraw faction defending the eastern financiers and monopoly capitalists who had stolen the timber land and coal mines from local hardworking citizens.[6] In January 1886, Chinese were forbidden by law to own property. In February, the Murphy faction, organized into citizen "order committees," began knocking on the doors of local Chinese homes to perform health inspections of the premises. Each Chinese resident was informed that his or her home was condemned and advised to leave town to avoid trouble.

"The steamer *Queen of the Pacific* was at the ocean dock, about to sail for San Francisco. Did they want to leave with her? The Chinese had no choice. With their doors open and hundreds of determined workingmen milling in the streets outside, they could only say yes. Once the Chinese had agreed to go, the chairman would tell the people waiting outside 'to help out the heathens.' The mob would rush in, carry out all the household goods and pile them in wagons, and hustle the Chinese off to the ocean dock."[7] According to a short history of the Seattle Police Department provided by the department, "Chief of Police William Murphy, a leader in the anti-Chinese movement, was busy organizing the hasty expulsion of the Chinese."[8] With tensions high and law enforcement at the center of a conflict involving actively mobilized citizens, it is surprising that when violence did erupt only one man was killed and five others wounded. One hundred and ninety-six Chinese were forced to board the ship and leave Seattle. Later that same year, Chief Murphy was elected mayor.

Professionalization. Perhaps as a result of incidents like the one described above, another trend in Seattle policing has been the steady upgrading of the communications and other hardware available to the police bureaucracy to control crime and the behavior of its officers. In 1891, the Gamewell Police Signal System installed call boxes in the city using telegraph technology to allow one-way communication from beat officers to headquarters.[9] In 1906, the city council approved the first automobile for the department, and the era of the horse and buggy patrol came to an end. A Detective Division was formed in 1908, which was where the department first began to collect information, including fingerprints. Radios were installed in 11 cars in 1930, about the time that the Detective Division established its first training program. By the 1930s, the department began to establish specialized units and close precinct offices in favor of centralization downtown, a trend that has remained characteristic of policing today. Despite a vigorous negative public reaction to the closing of neighborhood precincts, the department went ahead with the plan, arguing that the "slack in police protection was to be taken up by providing extra radio-equipped prowler cars."[10]

As far back as 1900, the SPD was already focusing on its law enforcement role as a crime fighter and shedding its organizational commitment to order maintenance.[11] As the police themselves described their mission: "Not only are the police compelled to encounter extraordinary dangers physically, but they are called upon to cope with brainy criminals, who must be met with on lines that bring forth skill and shrewdness."[12] The early years of the Seattle Police Department show a department dedicated to constructing its crime-fighting mission, centrally involved in political controversies around issues of law and order, and increasingly centralized around a downtown administration with an advanced communications system. These early trends in Seattle law enforcement and the history of citizen involvement continue to be crucial to understanding prevailing stories about policing within the Seattle Police Department today.

At the same time, decades before Earl Warren was to join the U.S. Supreme Court, the department was criticizing the courts for letting crooks escape punishment on technicalities and the public for blaming the resulting crime on the department.[13] In 1900, the department was arguing, as it does today, that "the force must be increased, and new police headquarters and substations erected, together with every modern improvement and equipment known to police circles."[14] In 1923, it was clear that the police were the target of criticism when Mayor Edwin Brown came to their defense, saying: "Despite criticism to the contrary, the records prove that Seattle's Police Department is improving every day."[15] Thus, in addition to centralization, the early years of the SPD show a tendency to favor law enforcement over order maintenance, blame other elements of the criminal justice system for rising crime, and, with the aid of prominent city residents, deflect criticism of the department. Reverend M. A. Matthews, in a 1923 essay entitled *Our Police,* did this in no uncertain terms but in language remarkably consonant with the rhetoric of community policing.

> The policemen are the agents of the people. They are the concrete mobilization of all the people. Every citizen is embodied in the police force. Every citizen is represented in a mobilized form in the patrolmen who control the beats, protect the city, and direct its law enforcement. They are the proxies of all law-abiding, God-fearing, honest citizens. . . . The public ought to recognize him as the indispensable friend of the home, the women and the children. . . . He is their friend, instructor, protector, and companion.[16]

In another 1923 essay on the role of the detective, the decline of community life and the rise of individualism are identified as primary obstacles to social order. "Our large floating population, drifting from city to city, without attachment to any spot, parasitic, predatory, considering themselves strangers wherever they be, *not feeling the restraints which affect citizens in fixed abodes* . . . makes the work of detectives an unremitting toil."[17] The restraints the author is referring to are much like those the advocates of community policing call the informal social controls that emerge when residents have a stake in their communities and thus an incentive to obey and enforce the law. What this voice from 1923 identifies, which the advocates of community policing do not, however, is how individualism and wage labor markets can undermine community life, while widespread property ownership and stable employment can make possible the operation of community-based informal social controls.

Finally, another similarity in discussions of law and order in the Seattle of 1923 and 1994 is the prominence of fear focused on substance abuse. Like today, those familiar with the drug problem saw it as a medical, social, and criminal problem with "only the latter aspect receiving adequate attention."[18] Also like today, there was a discernible racial and class prejudice associated with the drug war approach to crime control. In 1923, the dealers were described as "white, black, yellow, brown and red—the Indian, Filipino, Jap, Chink, and degenerate white. . . ."[19] All of these similarities help us to see that today's problems (and solutions) are not as new as many claim them to be, nor is this the first time the magnitude of these problems and their impact on community life have led citizens or officials to call the situation a crisis and demand more police protection.

The Scandal Years

In the late 1960s, a corruption and payoff scandal badly damaged the reputation and morale of the Seattle Police Department. While the officers were taking payoffs, corruption went far beyond the department. In some sense, the department was made to be the fall guy for a much larger criminal network. For our purposes, the important thing that comes out of this period is a department that continues to blame its problems on outside political influence, increasingly seeing departmental independence as the best response to crime. Another continuity highlighted by the corruption scandal (and found in stories about community policing) is the effectiveness of coordinating public and private agencies around the provision of social order.[20] The coordination of city agencies manifest in Seattle policing from World War II to 1968 is illustrated in the story of Seattle restaurant owner Charlie McDaniel. McDaniel bought a licensed restaurant only to discover after the deal was final that it included a bookmaking operation and a cardroom (which he had not purchased). Failing to close down these operations, he tried to keep them under his control. The pressure brought to bear on McDaniel included visits from the previous owner, police officers, Teamsters, the city and state liquor licensing boards, and fire and health inspectors. The fire inspector came during a lunch rush, closing the restaurant for the day. The health inspectors came during a dinner rush and insisted on inspecting each pot, empty, scaring off the evenings customers. The city council revoked his liquor license.

When vandals damaged his building, a police report simply stated that this was due to a memo the owner had put on his door claiming he was a victim of police harassment and shakedowns. After fighting for a while, McDaniel sold out, losing all of his investment. He held a news conference to expose the corrupt network of public officials, police officers, and union leaders, but no one showed up. The ability of this network of public and private agencies to coordinate their actions against this enemy of their community kept the media from covering the story, and McDaniel was forced to leave town.[21] While today, in a context in which city governments are in fiscal trouble, it is taken as unambiguously good to improve efficiency through greater interagency coordination, Seattle's experience in the three decades following the war indicates that coordination, especially involving law enforcement agencies, is anything but unambiguously good.

What the scandal shows, and the widespread coordination of city officials confirms, is that the demand for drugs, gambling, and prostitution includes a significant number of Seattle's respectable citizens.[22] In this context, when civic leaders call for more effective crime control, it puts the police in a difficult position. As a result, the police department exercises its discretion in a way that preserves its political position. This means allowing a vice industry to serve the needs (or meet the demands) of those with power but keeping it invisible to those with power opposed to it.

> Faced with such a dilemma and such an ambivalent situation, the law enforcers do what any well-managed bureaucracy would do under similar circumstances. They follow the line of least resistance. Using the discretion inherent in their positions, they resolve the problem by establishing procedures that minimize organizational strains and that provide the greatest promise of reward of the organization and the individuals involved. Typically, this means that law enforcers adopt a tolerance policy toward the vices, selectively enforcing the laws when it is to their advantage to do so. Since the persons demanding enforcement are generally middle-class and rarely venture into the less prosperous sections of the city, the enforcers can control visibility and minimize complaints merely by regulating the location of the vices.[23]

This is a political lesson learned from the corruption scandal that helps account for why it is that the Central Area and Rainier Valley have such a disproportionate amount of drug dealing and other vice-related criminal activities. The location of street crime in poor, minority neighborhoods is not an accident. It is a product of public and private choices. No one person made the choice, but a "series of individual decisions made by people who share the same interests" goes a long way toward accounting for the location.[24]

After the scandal broke, the police blamed the politicians for the tolerance policy that left them publicly embarrassed. They were partly correct. The city council, contrary to the state constitution, passed a Public Cardroom Ordinance in 1954 to allow for the licensing of cardrooms in Seattle. In 1969, the city council rescinded the tolerance policy, which is an interesting commentary since there never was an official statement of such a policy.[25] But the SPD, rather than enforcing the law and seeking to overturn the tolerance policy, sought to profit from it. Once exposed, the department tried to protect those involved and persecute the good cops who were attempting to clean up law enforcement in the city.[26] And, further, by pushing for police independence rather than increased accountability for all public officials, the department contributed to the impression that if it had not been for meddlesome politicians this could not have happened.

This scandal and the publicity surrounding a grand jury investigation signaled the end of an era in Seattle policing. All at once the police were charged with being unresponsive to the community, expected to deal with street protests in a divided society, and increasingly subjected to judicial supervision by the Warren Court. For the police, this was not just the exposure of an isolated scandal; it was the end of an era when police officers had the discretion to do whatever worked on the street and could count on the support of their superior officers when they did. According to one officer Scheingold interviewed, the departing era was one in which cops were "recognized for what you did, not by how many arrests" you made.[27] This indicates that policing in Seattle, despite prevailing stories about professionalism and fancy hardware, also included decentered stories about policing through the late 1960s. Perhaps this survival of competing stories about policing is partly responsible for the development of community policing in Seattle. Before we can explore that possibility, though, we must look more closely at the department's response to the scandal, especially in the South Precinct, which is the place within the SPD where community policing began over the resistance of the police chief brought in after the scandal, Patrick Fitzsimons.

Responding to the Scandal

Immediately after the scandal, the department invited the International Association of Chiefs of Police (IACP) to do a study of the SPD. This was followed by two other major studies conducted by outside agencies: the Buracker and Associates management study and the MM Bell study. While these studies did lead to some changes in the SPD, they did not alter the direction of change away from centralization, insulation, and managerial coordination of a police department functionally fragmented into specialized units.

Managerial Authority and Insulation. While the department continued to centralize and focus on managerial reforms, the rank-and-file organized to protect themselves from the political forces that they believed had led them to take the fall for the scandal. "[T]he rank-and-file re-grouped around an increasingly militant and politically assertive police guild."[28] While the more active guild could sometimes pressure the chief, stories about a larger enemy (political influence from outside the department) transformed the possibility of rank-and-file-ed policing reform into a battle between the mayor and the chief over public accountability and department independence.[29]

Scheingold argues that there were two consequences of this political posturing. First, those reforms the chief did initiate were half-hearted, "indirect consequences of power struggles" between the mayor and the chief and consistent with prevailing stories about policing. Second, since status quo reinforcing reforms were not designed to tap the local knowledge and experience of the street cop to improve police effectiveness, the direction of reform within the SPD proceeded independent of the nature of crime concerns in Seattle neighborhoods. As Scheingold puts it, the chief and guild "cultivated public images suggesting that crime control was a priority issue, but what really seemed to count was asserting police independence and improving the wages and working conditions of police officers."[30] A bureaucratic focus on managerial control treated the street officer as a bureaucratic problem rather than a community resource.

The focus of reforms on organizational independence and managerial control also expressed a profound contempt for community concerns and was manifest in reduced police efficiency and effectiveness despite increased funding. The chief was "unresponsive to the grievances of minorities," and the mayor was "willing to settle for ineffectual gestures to minorities." At the same time, with department funding at its highest levels in a 20-year period, the numbers of arrests per officer (efficiency) and arrests per reported crime (effectiveness) were at their lowest levels.[31] Scheingold found that the SPD had been most effective *in the scandal years,* under Chief Ramon, and that under Fitzsimons police effectiveness had declined. Scheingold attributes this to Fitzsimons's efforts to professionalize, aimed at improving the department's public image with "overtones of community policing."[32]

What Fitzsimons did was emphasize the affirmative action hiring of minority police officers. The number of blacks in the department increased from 1 percent (12) in 1969, to 2 percent (24) when Fitzsimons took office in 1977, to 4 percent (40) in 1980 and 10 percent in 1994, when Fitzsimons retired.[33] Those actions may have improved the department's image in the black community without altering the direction of policing reform from its path of centralization and insulation. Not surprisingly, then, Scheingold finds that Fitzsimons's style was more popular with downtown elites than with neighborhood activists and Rainier Valley small business leaders, where symbolic policing through administrative tinkering cannot erase its ineffectiveness on the street. But even the moderate reforms Fitzsimons did attempt were made possible by changes in the political landscape in the city, specifically the rising political power of minority communities in the Rainier

Valley.[34] While Fitzsimons would resist less moderate reforms, the pressure would continue to mount when this political transformation placed an African American from the valley in the mayor's office. That victory became more significant when Mayor Rice appointed Chief Norm Stamper to replace Fitzsimons.[35]

Early Policing Reforms. The first significant change was initiated by the department command staff. In 1943, on the basis of recommendations made by Chief H. D. Kimsey, the department was reorganized into four divisions and the assistant chief position eliminated. In 1945, the same chief commissioned an outside study of the department by V. A. Leonard, who recommended a shift to three divisions and reducing the number of patrol precincts from six to three. No action was taken on these recommendations until the next chief, George Eastman, conducted his own study, which favored a move to three precincts and the addition of a fifth division. This established the basic organizational structure that remained in place until 1968.[36]

Fitzsimons's Reorganization Project

In 1979, in response to a request from the city council, the SPD management did its own extensive reorganization study. They sought to establish a "new organization, based on modern police management principles, [to] provide efficient delivery of services, and at the same time provide the flexibility for change and expansion" in the future.[37] They recommended three changes. Field units were combined into an Operations Bureau to improve planning and rapid response capacities. This amounted to a return to the format recommended by the IACP in 1968. Investigative and detective units were restructured to improve coordination between juvenile and property crimes. An experimental use of detectives at the precinct level to avoid duplication in case assignments between adult and juvenile investigators was implemented in the South Juvenile and South Burglary/Theft Squads.

In a third change, citizen services were consolidated to improve efficiency. Prior to this change, citizen services were provided in an ad hoc manner within each division or section, often without any specific citizen services section. The consolidation of operations and patrol allowed for the creation of a Field Support Bureau, which absorbed the various citizen and community service functions. These were combined with Crime Prevention, Criminal Information, and Communications. The study argued, in language consistent with community policing, that this change would send a message that the department was ready to emphasize "the importance of police/citizen interaction and mutual participation in crime prevention." Not only would it send a message, but it would make the sending of messages more efficient. The study continued:

> In the future, the elements which gather crime prevention data, receive 9–1–1 calls for service, and which deliver prevention and security services will speak with one voice in recommending policies and procedures for effective crime prevention. This Bureau will complement the mission of the Operations and Investigations Bureaus by developing criminal information and a crime analysis system, sharing crime prevention data, and sensitizing operations and investigations to community needs. It will expedite the Department's mission by involving citizens in community projects designed to increase awareness of security measures and harden targets against crime. The Citizen Services Division will emphasize the importance the Department places on citizens participating and doing more for themselves and their city. . . . In the new Field Support Bureau, [the Communications Division's] importance as the key to citizen contact and operational efficiency is emphasized by making it one of the primary Divisions in the Bureau.[38]

The study was guided by a desire to improve planning, coordination, and centralization of decision making. These primary principles require, according to the study, improved flexibility, accountability, and citizen involvement "in order to meet the demand for change, without impeding service delivery or imposing unacceptable working conditions on the line staff."[39] While neither citizens nor line officers were involved in the study, citizens' concerns were "injected into the Reorganization Study by the timely conclusion of a series of telephone surveys conducted during 1978–79 by the Law and Justice Planning Division of the Office of Policy and Evaluation."[40] The study concluded that its recommendations were consistent with the mayor's focus on accountability. It seems this conclusion was based on the commitment to efficient service delivery and to "interface with the community to emphasize the mutual responsibility of citizens and police to ensure peace in this city."[41]

While there was language in this study to indicate the influence of community policing style thinking in the SPD, there was also evidence of resistance. The study identified three issues to be addressed. In each of these, the report adopted a professional approach to policing reform. The first issue was the control and allocation of resources. Here the study was unequivocally not walking the walk of community policing. "To provide these services the Department must be reactive, since the demands and needs of the citizens determine when and where police assistance is needed."[42] Thus, the department reforms in this area focused on improving response time.

The second issue was the lack of coordination between the Criminal Investigations Division and the Juvenile Division because cases were assigned according to two different criteria (age of suspect and crime type). Thus, it was not uncommon for there to be duplication or loss of information in such cases. The Juvenile Division was changed to a section and placed within the Criminal Investigations Division to improve coordination. However, the study also recommended an experiment that involved some decentralization to the precinct level. The South Precinct Juvenile and Burglary/Theft Squads were relocated to the South Precinct for one year.[43] Placed under the combined command of a single lieutenant, this experiment became known as the Decentralized Detective Squad.

The third issue involved citizen participation. The study argued that traditional police services were divided into field services or investigations. Over time, a third type of service, citizen service, emerged in the form of proactive efforts to assist citizens with crime prevention, fear reduction, information collection, and access to social services. These services were provided by Community Service Officers, but "these units were assigned to the traditional service branches of the agency. It is acknowledged that these services are sufficiently important that the organization should be restructured to try to coordinate and expand this area of policing."[44] The study goes on to discuss the importance of the community as a departmental resource that had not been fully utilized. Reorganization was designed to promote citizen participation through target hardening and the provision of information to the police in criminal investigations.

The Buracker Management Study. In 1989, a consulting firm managed by a former police officer with 22 years of experience at all levels of policing presented a detailed analysis of the SPD management structure in response to a request by the city council. According to its report, "most of the recommendations in this study relate to the continued expansion of nationally recognized progressive police programs" focusing on the need for additional officers, new technologies, decentralization, civilianization, and community-oriented policing.[45] The recommendations included, in order of suggested priority, adding 167 new positions (41 civilian and 126 officers), upgrading the management information system, and making several smaller modifications in division or section structure and operation. The most important component of the last recommendation included decentralization to precincts of some crime prevention personnel, establishment of precinct advisory councils, and various attempts to improve the department's capacity for strategic planning in coordination with the rest of the criminal justice system and other city agencies.

The report praised the SPD administration as a nationally recognized progressive department with an excellent affirmative action program and a very good relationship with the Police Guild. The problems came from outside the administration. The first problem was that the city used 911 for emergency and nonemergency calls, seriously overloading the system. The department's communications system needed upgrading, and new computer equipment was needed. The clerical staff was insufficient. Physical plant space was inadequate. The entire criminal justice system of the city was understaffed, which had a negative impact on the ability of the SPD to do its job. The departmental planning section was understaffed and as a result unable to devote the resources it should to analysis of calls for service, response times, or repeat offenders. The study suggested that to address each of these deficiencies would cost the city $6.7 million.[46]

The Buracker study identified the SSCPC, foot patrol, victim assistance, the business watch, commercial security, a repeat call project, and decentralization of some services as the key positive innovations of the SPD. The study's focus on alternative policing was specifically requested by the city council to determine whether it might improve policing in Seattle.[47] The study concluded this section with the statement that the SPD was effective in all areas of community policing. This conclusion was based largely on the South Seattle police-community partnership, which the study said ought to be expanded to each precinct with the addition of 24 officers and four sergeants.

However, the Buracker study's exclusive focus on justifying the need for additional officers led to some odd discussions of alternative policing. In addressing neighborhood policing, the study argued that this was "an interactive process between police officers assigned to specific beats and the citizens" who live there, which dated back to the 1960s, although the city of Houston provided the most recent model. Houston had introduced neighborhood policing on a very limited scale, which had required an increase of 1,100 officers over a four-year period, while the SPD had seen an increase of only 48 officers during the same period.

In discussing fear reduction, the study cited the Baltimore COPE experiment as successful because it added 45 new officers. Problem oriented policing was effective in Madison, Wisconsin, because the city had added 40 new officers who were concentrated in only a sixth of the city. Foot patrols had shown positive results, but because the primary model (in Flint, Michigan) had manned the patrols without increasing officer strength, the effectiveness likely came as a result of taxing other departmental resources such as motor patrol. While each of the programs cited from other cities could have been used to identify specific elements that might be transferable to Seattle, they were instead used to show that alternative policing is policing as usual, that is, effective policing can only be achieved through large increases in public spending to hire additional officers.

Since this study concluded that the SPD was a leader in community policing, and focused only on the need for additional department resources, one would expect that policing reform could be traced to the SPD. According to this study, however, the impetus for alternative policing came from city council and Southeast Seattle communities. In 1986, the council passed Resolution 27596, which became known as the *Public Safety Action Plan*. This plan specifically focused attention on the need to commit resources for proactive, community-oriented policing, including downtown foot patrols, increasing precinct-level staffing and authority, and community outreach. As a result, foot patrols increased from a daily average of 16.6 officers in 1983 to 39.6 officers in 1988.[48] This city council's action was the basis of the study's claim that Seattle was a leader in community crime prevention, reorienting patrol, and decentralizing authority to the precinct level.

The other catalyst behind alternative policing in Seattle, according to the Buracker study, was the communities of the southeast. While the operations of the SSCPC are examined in great detail in chapter 7, it is interesting to note the way that this study analyzed it. Citizen activism was identified as the initial impetus for reform. This led to the founding of the SSCPC and reduced crime in the southeast even while crime in other parts of the city increased. Perhaps the most revolutionary aspect of this effort was that "although the program has been successful, it was implemented by using existing resources."[49] The use of the qualifier *although* foreshadows the study's treatment of this phenomenon. Rather than concluding that this showed how the department could innovate and improve public safety without hiring additional officers, Buracker concluded that, despite its success,the partnership had hidden costs.

> In making more time available for more proactive patrol efforts, the South Precinct decreased the daily number of patrol cars deployed, increased the overall response time more than other precincts, and increased overtime significantly compared to the average of the other precincts. In addition, other City departments may have had additional costs or may have had to reallocate their resources. For example, the Department of Construction and Land Use used its resources to help eliminate abandoned premises identified by patrol officers. . . . Seattle is encouraged to continue and expand its program of decentralizing police services, working with the community to address the issue of fear and expanding its problem-solving program. The Police Department, however, needs additional personnel to accomplish this objective.[50]

The remarkable thing about this conclusion is not that a call for additional resources was unwarranted. It is that—despite empirical evidence to the contrary—hiring additional officers was the *only* serious recommendation to emerge from this review of alternative policing. Further, the study failed to separate police overtime, as a legitimate hidden cost (also identified by then council member Rice as a reason not to overpraise the partnership), from the decrease in motor patrols and response times (a concern reflecting Buracker's professional bias) as resource reallocations that contributed to reducing crime rates. For these reasons, the study concluded the section with recommendations it could have made without ever considering innovations in Seattle or any other city. The SPD needed many more officers if Seattle was to remain a safe place to live.

The MM Bell Study. Also conducted in 1989, this was not a study of the department's overall management structure. It focused on reforming the department's internal investigations of police misconduct. This study did not become part of the SPD success story. The Buracker study identified four components of alternative policing and concluded that the department was a leader in each. However, it would be more accurate to say that the city council and communities in the southeast were the leaders in policing reform. While city council and citizens were the catalysts for change, the department was responsive enough to implement limited reforms in each of these areas. This contributed to minor improvements in three of the four areas identified by the Buracker study: community crime prevention, reorientation of patrol, and decentralization of authority to the precinct level. It is the fourth component of community policing, the focus of the MM Bell study, that has yet to secure the departmental cooperation necessary for its implementation. That component is accountability.

The findings of this study focused on three issues. Many citizens interviewed indicated that they were frustrated with the lack of information available on how the process works or on their complaints once filed. Many citizens also expressed an interest in some form of external process for complaint handling. Finally, the study found that "independent of what kind of complaint handling process they have, most cities and most police departments make more effort than Seattle does to publicize its complaint handling procedures and their intake process."[51] In Seattle, other city agencies and community organizations interviewed for this study *"uniformly believe the SPD to be closed to citizen complainants,"* not objective, and excessively secretive.[52]

It is difficult to evaluate a department's Internal Investigations Section (IIS). The rate of complaints per 100,000 residents was lower in Seattle (56) than the average in 18 other cities (68). But the percentage of allegations that were sustained by the SPD (12 percent) was also lower than the percentage sustained in other cities, such as Phoenix at 29 percent (see table 4). The number of allegations of excessive use of force increased by 150 percent in the period from 1984 to 1988.[53] The SPD records both major and minor complaints (which is unusual), but the minor complaints are recorded only into a contact log, which was not reviewed by internal investigations or any department supervisor and was not noted in an officer's file. The rapid growth of complaints in the last 12 years has been largely in these uninvestigated contact log entries (see table 5).[54] Further, while the SPD opposed external review because the reviewers would not be "sufficiently familiar with police procedures and with investigative techniques to assess misconduct," the department does not require officers to have any training or special experience before being assigned to the internal investigations unit.[55] And, finally, the time required to investigate complaints increased to almost six months, a concern shared by both officers and complainants.

TABLE 4. Disposition of Complaints for Selected Cities, 1988 (in percentages)

City	Unfounded	Exonerated	Not Sustained	Sustained
	A. Internal Review Only			
Cincinnati	10.8	28.7	24.3	36.2
Columbus	49.9	14.9	16.5	18.7
Denver	22.8	33.5	22.6	21.0
Houston	18.0	6.4	58.6	17.0
Memphis	0.0	81.7	0.0	18.3
Phoenix	29.5	30.0	11.4	29.1
San Diego	43.9	19.6	16.5	20.0
Seattle	42.8	27.7	17.4	12.1
	B. Internal and External Review			
Atlanta	16.0	17.6	47.9	18.5
Hartford	30.0	20.0	30.0	20.0
Miami	42.0	0.0	32.0	26.0
Minneapolis	25.1	10.1	63.7	1.1

Source: Seattle Police Department 1989a.

TABLE 5. Seattle Police Department Complaints, Contact Log Entries, and Investigations 1978–88

Year	Complaints	Contact Log Entries (as % of complaints)	Investigations
1978	719	384 (53%)	204
1979	752	334 (44%)	435
1980	726	389 (54%)	358
1981	765	373 (49%)	392
1982	866	499 (58%)	367
1983	755	470 (62%)	285
1984	780	577 (74%)	223
1985	814	623 (77%)	191
1986	891	627 (70%)	264
1987	1,025	810 (79%)	215
1988	865	606 (70%)	259

Source: Seattle Police Department 1989a.

"Effective complaint handling processes, whatever their organizational structure or placement, *actively seek citizen input regarding police behavior*. Effective processes aggressively deal with officer misconduct. The study team believes that in Seattle an internal agency operating as part of the SPD can meet these objectives."[56] The MM Bell study indicated tremendous concern among officers and police management about the protection of each officer's rights in this process.[57] There was also a noticeably more sympathetic view of the value of a legalistic approach in the handling of allegations of police wrongdoing than one finds in police attitudes about how the judicial process (as one way of protecting the rights of the accused) handcuffs the police in their attempts to hold citizens accountable for wrongdoing. This was most apparent in a comment by an attorney interviewed as a part of this study. According to MM Bell, "the attorney interviewed noted that IIS interprets the preponderance of evidence standard to mean that the complainant must have more evidence than the police. So in cases where the evidence is based on the word of the officer versus the word of the complainant, the tie goes to the officer."[58] My point is not that officers ought to be treated with less concern for their rights, but that the department mobilizes different (and competing) stories about individual rights when the individual under scrutiny is a citizen rather than a police officer.

III. The Scandal and Beyond in the South Precinct

As was discussed earlier in this chapter, the corruption scandal was a catalyst for reform within the department. The police officer most responsible for exposing the payoff system was Tony Gustin. In order to protect himself after this disclosure he asked to be demoted from assistant chief to captain, a civil service rank, and was assigned to command the South Precinct. Following his departure, another department maverick, Romero Yumul, assumed control of the South Precinct, continuing many of Gustin's innovations and enlisting the services of another department outcast, Sergeant Chuck Pillon. This series of reassignments of outspoken members of the department to the South Precinct was described by Ezra Stotland as typical of any bureaucracy.[59] A bureaucracy, having civil service employees, requires a dumping ground. In this case, dumping proved to be a seeding process for innovation.

Bureaucratic Outcasts and Innovative Policing

According to Chambliss, Officer Tony Gustin was the honest cop courageous enough to swim against the tide in the department. Gustin became a major in charge of one of four divisions created by the department after the IACP study. Once promoted, he "began immediately to transfer anyone he knew to be collecting payoffs" and promoted those officers he felt would enforce gambling laws. "They had orders to begin slowly and in the safest areas; predictably they began harassing and arresting gamblers and whorehouse operators in the black ghetto."[60] Not surprisingly, pressure mounted to remove Gustin. Chambliss argued that he protected himself by allying himself with a reporter and an investigator from the U.S. Attorney General's Office. What the investigating attorney needed was evidence that would stand up in court. Tony Gustin provided it.

Gustin organized a surprise raid of the Lifeline Bingo Club, seizing its records. The chief criticized the raid as sloppy police work. "Gustin's life was threatened. He had risked his career. He had violated one of the sacred norms of police work: at all costs protect your brothers in blue."[61] Gustin's action forced the chief to resign and his replacement to demote Gustin to captain. This twist of fate worked to the advantage of the southeast when Captain Gustin was made commander of the South Precinct. In the South Precinct, Gustin's courage and imagination went to work on fighting crime outside the SPD. As commander, Gustin was now in charge of the department's bureaucratic dumping ground. He was a misfit in the department, and he would find the South Precinct a fertile ground for Seattle's first experiments with team policing.[62] Gustin met and shared his knowledge with interested members of the community. When his approach was noticed downtown, the chief removed him from command and reassigned him to Records. But the ideas and experiments, however short-lived, planted seeds in the community that would later blossom into Seattle's community policing program.[63] According to Fleissner, Fedan, and Stotland, Gustin

> was a strong advocate of team policing, which was a form of policing that was being attempted in several cities throughout the country. He established a form of team policing in the South Precinct, which included an emphasis on greater cooperation with local

> community groups. He encouraged the watch commander, sergeants and officers to attend community meetings and in other ways to take the initiative in working with residents in the area. He organized a successful seminar on door locks for the local business people. Some of the officers worked with an informal group of mothers to try to have speed bumps put in by the city's engineering department. And, quite significantly, he discussed the concepts of team policing with some local civic leaders. . . . However, the team policing program was terminated by the police chief before it was fully developed. In any case, team policing ideas which focused on the close ties between police officers and the community were introduced both conceptually and materially into the Southeast Seattle community.[64]

When Romero Yumul became commander of the South Precinct, he was also one of the SPD's more educated and community-oriented precinct captains. According to Stotland, Yumul was an idea man. He, like Gustin, "aggressively went about trying to stimulate the community to take more action."[65] Yumul continued the tradition of innovation in the southeast, working with the community to establish a graffiti hot line and a very successful program to target youth offenders before they become career criminals.[66] The man he put in charge of that program was Officer John Hayes. Detective Hayes is now the police coordinator for the much praised Seattle Team for Youth program.[67]

Perhaps the most important (and certainly the most sensational) Yumul innovation involved his creation of Seattle's first Anti-Crime Team under the command of Sergeant Chuck Pillon. ACT I was staffed by one sergeant and two officers with the assistance of a detective. According to the sergeant in charge, ACT I focused on confiscating or destroying drugs and breaking up their distribution networks. ACT I did not break down crack house doors or accumulate arrests. They harassed and confronted dealers to increase their cost of doing business. Stotland confirmed that Pillon, trained under the tutelage of Gustin, was not interested in arrests. "His job was to clean up an area of the community, get rid of the druggers and the burglars. Make it next to impossible for them to operate in a given area. In other words, this was a community policing philosophy, a rejection of normal law enforcement."[68] Pillon claimed that since ACT I operated with the "esteem and rapport" of the community none of his officers had ever been accused of excessive force or false arrest.[69] Pillon described the success of ACT I this way:

> It was a proactive formal extension of what I and very few patrol Sergeants had always done, confronting and defeating organized criminal activity. . . . The Anti-Crime Team concept, as a component in a truly effective scheme of team policing, is the absolute bedrock of the effort, because people that see cops in a reactive way don't have the respect for them they get for me, when they know that I and my troops were out there. We got the guy in the blue Mercedes with the California plates that was delivering dope to four houses on their block. They saw that car go down the road on a hook, and there was Sergeant Pillon, thumbs in his beltloops and triumphant. Those people could relate to us in block watch meetings and when they saw us in the coffee shop around the corner or whatever.[70]

According to Pillon, the chief had resisted establishing ACT I. Pillon publicly accused the chief of having a tolerance policy that accounted for the rise of street crime in the 1980s. What he meant by this was that the department did not devote resources to the kind of policing that works against street crime.[71] Instead of putting officers on the street, in touch with communities, assigned to beats long enough to know them and develop some sense of ownership in them, the chief followed national trends toward professional bureaucratic policing, that is, policing in which a significant amount of the police budget and personnel are absorbed into administrative tasks. The *South District Journal* quoted another patrol officer as saying:

> Police administrators have made those of us in patrol feel like there's something wrong with us because we feel the need to do more out there than is expected. Pillon is living proof of what we can expect if we go out and try to get involved. I'll do what's demanded of me and you can bet that the rest of my time will be spent drinking coffee.[72]

Instead of endless special units, Pillon argued that effective crime control required beat integrity, an idea he claimed Fitzsimons opposed.

When the chief, under community pressure, created ACT II, this new Anti-Crime Team became another special unit rather than an innovation within patrol. According to Pillon, it "became a gestapo-like element in that they . . . went out and stuck those doors, killed people. They damn near killed each other. They trampled children, they created alarm, and they fed the egos of the dope dealers, who realized that once again the gang was there."[73] ACT II became bureaucratized like the rest of the department. It did not gather information itself but acted as a mindless hit squad, a last link in a long bureaucratic chain.

It was not until Pillon was charged with improper paperwork that the chief was able to remove him, and after Yumul spoke out in Pillon's defense Yumul was transferred to Juvenile. The community was outraged at the transfer of Yumul and the eventual firing of Pillon.[74] The story here was of innovative policing that emerged out of the imaginations of those the department treated as outsiders. The chief was clearly under pressure from his own officers, from communities, and from elected officials to respond. ACT II was an initial and tragic response, reflecting his faith in professional stories about policing insulated from political influence. In addition to the Anti-Crime Teams, another important policing innovation began in the South Precinct: the Community Police Teams (CPTs). While ACT II was largely consistent with existing police practices and special unit orientation, the Community Police Teams, like ACT I, were potentially different.

Community Police Teams

> The mission of the Community-Police Team is to closely interact with the community to resolve neighborhood problems and concerns through the use of traditional and non-traditional police tactics and the coordinated application of resources beyond those available within the criminal justice system.[75]

In 1994, each of Seattle's four precincts had one Community Police Team. CPTs did not respond to 911 calls. They worked nine to five, Monday through Friday. Each CPT had six patrol officers commanded by one sergeant and, along with the ACT II teams, answered directly to the operations lieutenant. According to Sergeant Conn, the South Precinct CPT had five officers from the SPD budget and two from a Seattle Housing Authority Grant, including two black females, one black male, one hispanic male, and four white males. Sergeant

Manning told me that the East Precinct CPT was composed of two females, one Latino, one black, and two white officers.[76] CPTs were created in January of 1990 as a consequence of the successful South Seattle partnership arrangement. The early reception inside the department was cold. A CPT assignment "was something nobody wanted." But when the precinct commander approached Conn he decided to give it a try. "What he did was, he walked in and, I'm not kidding, he handed me a stack of literature about four feet high and a yellow note pad, and he said, 'design a CPT team. Here's what everyone else does, you figure out what we should do.' He gave me a month to sit down in a room and read that stuff and write, and that's exactly what I did."[77]

Projects and Cases. In South Seattle, CPTs operated as special units, receiving an additional 40 hours of special training under the command of the operations lieutenant.[78] As special units, Rainier Valley activist Kay Godefroy believed CPTs were vulnerable to a bureaucratic takeover that would seek to utilize them as fill-ins for other units. The special unit status and small size of CPTs weakened the SPD's claim that the department had shifted to a community-oriented mode of policing. The special status created some tension between patrol and CPTs. But being a special unit also created opportunities for experiments with new styles of policing. The South Precinct CPT did this by dividing its work into cases and projects.

The project function was a clear combination of crime attack and community service policing.[79] Projects were medium term, law-enforcement-oriented, task forces. On these task forces, CPTs often coordinated the activities of several units, including ACT II, the vice unit, the gang unit, patrol, detectives, and other city agencies such as the Department of Construction and Land Use, the Health Department, and the Liquor Licensing Board. In addition to coordination, the CPTs were primarily responsible for keeping "the lid on any potential neighborhood disturbance that might occur from an adverse reaction to a heavy police presence." The CPT was acting as an operationally based (rather than *strictly* public-relations-based) "community relations unit at a time of high enforcement."[80]

In 1991, the South Precinct CPT closed all six of its projects. Other than the citizen survey (project 6), each project had been a multiunit task force concentrating police efforts on specific areas of the precinct with particularly high amounts of criminal activity. In 1991, the South Precinct CPT devoted more than 20 percent of its time to the six projects, 28 percent to case work, and 27 percent to making neighborhood contacts.[81] In the course of its 1991 efforts in the southeast, the CPT received zero IIS complaints. A look at these projects will provide a picture of what CPTs did and a snapshot of the emerging meaning of community policing in Southeast Seattle.

Project 1 combined ACT, patrol, vice, and CPT in concentrated enforcement to reduce the problem of open prostitution in the South Park area. Tactics included 48 arrests, more than 50 towed vehicles, 15 notices of blight violations, and citizen efforts to clean up graffiti. In October, the Municipal Court designated South Park a SOAP (Stay Out of Areas of Prostitution) area, and both CPT and patrol immediately increased enforcement. CPT coordinated with the *West Seattle Herald* and the *Seattle Times* to inform citizens of the purpose of a SOAP and deter potential customers.[82]

The 1991 CPT annual report concluded that project 1 was an example of the department successfully responding to community concerns. "In 1990 there was a continuous outcry from the South Park Community about the open prostitution they were experiencing in their community. Sporadic efforts by Street Vice were insufficient to abate the problem. . . . The Precinct Command staff determined that this would be an ideal location for a SOAP zone and directed a task force operation to provide some immediate relief for the community residents and compile some statistics to justify a SOAP. . . . The community was extremely pleased with the results of the Task Force and it helped to invigorate them. They responded by cleaning several neighborhood site blights, including clearing the brush from a vacant lot behind one of the problem taverns."[83]

Project 2 combined patrol, ACT and CPT to make 60 arrests, tow more than 60 vehicles, serve 15 notices of blight violations, conduct more than 400 field interviews, and write more than 300 citations in an effort to reduce drug and gang activity in the Delridge Corridor and High Point areas.[84] Sergeant Conn told me that the "main purpose was to re-establish control of the streets, and give them back to law-abiding citizens. The kind of police presence it would require to maintain that control, I'm not sure the citizens of the United States of America would want that. Or be able to pay for it. So next to that, what you do is a temporary measure, incarcerate large numbers, and push the problem away and hope that when it comes back, it's at least scaled down to the point where people aren't terrorized and lose their streets. When it slowly but surely gets back to the point where it's that problem again, you need to do the same thing."[85]

Project 3 combined patrol, the Special Patrol Unit, Traffic, and CPT to make 16 arrests and issue 225 tickets to clean up Seward Park, which was a location for gang parties. Conn indicated that cleaning up this park subjected the department to some heat from the city council for harassing minority youth, "but surprisingly enough, as soon as that heat came, we got an overwhelming amount of support from the residents along the Seward Park and Lake Washington corridor who had been living with that nightmare for months before we came along. As fast as we got the heat, the support came and no more problem, everything was okay."[86]

Projects 4 and 5 both combined patrol, ACT, and CPT to make arrests, tow vehicles, and concentrate enforcement against gang and drug problems in Rainier Valley. Sergeant Conn argued that these task forces were an effective approach to problems that patrol or other individual units, such as vice, could not manage alone and that once the department "provided the muscle" it became the responsibility of residents to reclaim their parks, challenge undesirable elements, call the police, and be prepared to testify in court when the community can no longer manage the situation. "That's how the system has to work. If it doesn't work that way, you can throw all the cops in the world at it, and we can't do it."[87]

Project 4 was one of the CPTs' proactive efforts, planned in anticipation of criminal activity rather than in response to it. "The Rainier Corridor has a history of sporadic problems with Gang and Drug Activity and receives a heavy concentration of proactive patrol efforts as well as ACT and CPT attention. The Command Staff at the South Precinct determined that with summer coming and work load increases that come with summer a proactive effort to control the problem with the Rainier Corridor should coincide with school getting out. A Task Force effort was ordered beginning June 20th and was to run three weeks through July 7th. It would be staffed by Patrol, ACT and CPT and would involve maximum enforcement along the Rainier and Martin Luther King Way Corridors targeting that activity that is normally associated with gang and drug problems. . . . By the conclusion of the task force officers participating indicated it had been very successful and they were having a difficult time locating any criminal activity on the street. They had made 795 contacts and 223 arrests. This effort again generated no IIS complaints and the citizens were very pleased with the results. Statistical data was distributed to community groups and block watches."[88]

Project 5 was one of the CPTs' order maintenance efforts, an attempt to coordinate the activities of the police and city service providers. Citizens' complaints about lighting, abandoned cars, and blight in the public housing projects convinced the department to make a concentrated effort in these areas. "Beginning on August 19th, 1991 the South Precinct CPT went into Rainier Vista and Holly park and began removing junk and abandoned cars. We worked closely with the SHA [Seattle Housing Authority] on site blight and garbage removal. We advised residents of what would be occurring over the next few weeks and solicited their cooperation. Beginning on September 3rd, 1991, CPT, ACT, and Patrol conducted an enforcement emphasis to deter and eliminate drug and gang activity within Rainier Vista and Holly Park. During the two week period CPT towed 57 abandoned and junked vehicles out of those Garden Communities" and made 110 arrests.[89]

In addition to projects, CPTs did casework. Cases were short-term CPT work in response to citizen complaints about disorder problems. Through coordination with City Light, Engineering, the County Health Department, and the Department of Construction and Land Use, the South Precinct CPT addressed street lighting, street repair, rodent infestations, and garbage problems. Leaving "citizens in a mild state of shock," Conn argued, "the effect of the citizens having this type of access to city government was a gradual revitalization of their faith in the city system." Cases in 1991 also included 275 school visits, 26 precinct tours for schoolchildren, 599 business contacts, attendance at 331 community meetings (which generated another 450 cases), and 2,510 neighborhood contacts. In all, in 1991 the South Precinct CPT spent 2,546 hours on casework.[90]

The annual report provided selected sample cases. The cases focused on responses to citizen complaints and often entailed working with the Health Department or other city departments to cite residents for rodent problems and blight and, when necessary, to arrest residents or abate the property for noncompliance with these orders. CPT Officer Enriquez indicated that the department was successful in coordinating its activities with Health Department staff to secure warrants for early police intervention. Because the Health Department or DCLU (as in the

Charlie McDaniel's case) can gain access to a property without a warrant, it was often useful for officers to coordinate with their counterparts in these departments, who often observe contraband during an inspection and could provide this information to justify a warrant.

Responsive Patrol Officers. Officers seeking assignment to a CPT were expected to have three years of field experience (or other education or experience that might be the equivalent) and possess a set of skills not usually identified with police officers (such as sensitivity, interpersonal skills, a willingness to participate in specialized training courses, a demonstrated ability to maintain self-control in situations of high stress, and an above-average ability to write and speak effectively).[91] Sergeants Manning and Conn both indicated that these new skills created some tension between CPT and patrol and that initially they had some difficulty filling positions. But by 1992 there was a long waiting list for CPT positions.

Along with new skills, CPT officers were released from 911 responsibility. They focused on problem solving and regularly interacting with citizens in nonenforcement situations. Seattle's CPTs did not do foot patrol, did not work out of neighborhood ministations, and were not beat cops permanently assigned to patrol one area. However, CPTs mixed and matched these tactics to meet the needs identified by their interaction with communities and other units. Thus, while CPTs did not exclusively do many of the things that were popular symbols of community policing, they potentially did them all. Officer Wilson spent about half of her shift walking various beats. Officer Enriquez spent a lot of his time either speaking to apartment managers or collecting job-related information from a city agency to hand out at a community meeting. Being released from 911 did not create much free time for the CPTs. They knew almost everyone they passed by name. People recognized them and waved or came over to chat. The officers worked hard, and even made one arrest, but they seemed to become less tired as the shift wore on. This was in sharp contrast to one regular patrol officer I observed, who spent most of an entire day filling out traffic reports and seemed exhausted throughout.

CPTs were often asked to play the good cop in a good cop–bad cop scenario. Officer Enriquez did that when I heard him warn a resident in violation of a SODA (Stay Out of Drug Areas) that if she did not listen to him the next officers she spoke to would be breaking the door down and taking her away. Sergeant Conn described how CPTs knock on the doors of suspected dealers and patiently point out to them that Patrol will "beat your door down, guns all over, be really terrifying, little kids could get hurt. . . ." He continued, telling me, "You walk out, you give ACT the high sign. Next day they bust the door down, do their warrant, then you go back in a couple of days . . . it works."[92] This role became institutionalized in task forces, where the CPTs engaged in public relations at times of high enforcement to preempt adverse reactions in the neighborhoods.[93] In this sense, it is clear what a potentially valuable role a CPT can play for the chief in calming community criticism.

IV. Conclusion

It is clear from this review of the history of policing reform in Seattle that prevailing stories about policing are both consistent with long-term trends and, potentially, resources to support countertrends. Skid Road, the east-west pathway Henry Yesler once ran logs down to be milled, marked the boundary between Seattle's respectable elements and the Lava Bed, the brothels and gambling establishments that are concentrated just south of what is now Yesler Way. Prosperity brought population and with it vice and crime. The politics surrounding the policing of vice was central to the reformers' message in 1884, to policing in the Roaring Twenties and the 1940s, to the payoff and corruption scandal that engulfed the SPD in 1967, to the conflicts between Mayor Uhlman and Chief Toothman that led to the chief's resignation in 1973, and to understanding the tenure of recently retired Police Chief Patrick Fitzsimons.

Policing in Seattle has always involved its citizens, from "order committees" performing unauthorized health inspections in the homes of unwelcome Chinese laborers, to Neighbors Against Drugs, Operation Results, and the SSCPC. Policing has also consistently sought to coordinate a variety of resources, from multiagency assaults on Charlie McDaniel to CPTs coordinating Health, Fire, City Light, and DCLU inspectors to abate crack houses. And the police department has, since the turn of the century, steadily become more specialized and centralized, shedding social services in favor of a narrower law enforcement mission. All of these trends can still be seen playing themselves out in the struggle to define community policing.

Chapter 7

Reciprocity in Police-Community Partnerships

Community policing is just a word. It has different meanings to different people.

—President of a Seattle District Community Council

I. Introduction

State-centered stories about community policing can be traced through police failures in managing urban unrest in the 1960s, leading to a series of presidential commissions, each suggesting that poor police-community relations contributed to ineffective policing. The federally funded policing research that followed the 1968 Omnibus Crime Control and Safe Streets Act, taken together, challenged several basic assumptions of the twentieth-century professional policing model. Random preventative patrol, rapid response, and political insulation sought at the expense of beat integrity were found to be less efficient and less effective than had been presumed by law enforcement experts.

As a consequence, departments began to redesign the way that they respond to calls for service, tinker with police management, and consider reorienting patrol to improve police-community relations. Political pressure, research, and experimentation intersected with demands from citizens for government agencies to become more responsive to community concerns. The hodgepodge of reform ideas came to find an uneasy unity within a moving target: community policing, an intersection of two sets of overlapping, sometimes coherent, competing stories about policing and community.

The stories about community policing told by Fleissner, Fedan, and Stotland; Skolnick and Bayley; and the Seattle police chief have four things in common.[1] Because these also highlight the discursive overlap of competing stories, I use them to organize this section, which examines the emergence of a prevailing story about community policing in Southeast Seattle: (1) community-based crime prevention, (2) decentralization, (3) reorientation of patrol, and (4) accountability.

II. Community-Based Crime Prevention: The SSCPC

This section shows that in the most participatory component of community policing, the SSCPC, membership was restricted, outreach was weak, and their capacity and willingness to criticize the police department was constrained. But despite these limitations council activities, especially as they were manifested in early targeting practices and legal mobilization, can be seen to have both reaffirmed and challenged existing power relations. The most significant failure was that, while council activities both reaffirmed and challenged, the combined effect was more to empower the SPD than to encourage the reciprocity needed to revitalize community life. This is because the form of association established responded more vigorously to concerns about targeting street crime to protect commercial property than to equally salient concerns about reciprocity, that is, horizontal social capital (representativeness of the SSCPC) and vertical social capital (police misconduct and information sharing). These aspects of the partnership are examined under three headings: "Community Activities," "Legal Mobilization," and "Patrol Activities."

Community Activities. "The South Seattle CPC was designed as a council of organizations and community representatives, not as an open membership organization. Membership was by invitation only, and the regular meetings were not widely publicized."[2] Of the 17 original SSCPC members, three were black and two were Asian. About two months after the police-community partnership was institutionalized, following a meeting of black community leaders on racism and the police, a black member and an Asian member left the council.[3] This left the council, in an area of Seattle that was 60 percent minority, with a minority representation of only 18 percent. Not surprisingly, other community activists and even police officers expressed reservations about a perceived white business bias on the SSCPC.[4]

This concern was also apparent when, in 1994, the mayor formed a blue ribbon panel in response to a city Human Rights Commission finding of great hostility between the SPD and minority communities in the wake of conflict surrounding renewal of the Drug Traffic Loitering Ordinance (discussed below). This task force issued a report calling on the city to create a civilian review board. A central controversy in the work of the task force revolved around the composition of the city's Crime Prevention Councils, including the SSCPC. The task force report charged that these councils were dominated by business interests and thus were unwilling to push the department to address community concerns about police accountability.[5]

No recognized leader of any African American community in Southeast Seattle joined the SSCPC. When I asked one of the city's two most prominent black ministers about this, I was told that

> the African American community is reluctant to talk about increasing policing because we have police on every street corner as it is. The issues for us are about economic justice. Crime is an outgrowth of intolerable situations limiting people's access to the American dream. The businesses that are being closed through civil abatements initiated by the police and these councils should be closed. But the question is why is it that in African American communities it is only criminals that can afford to start businesses in the community? The issue is not drugs. There is not enough venture capital for legitimate businesses, because of bank lending policies, and the police punish those who seek underground capital. Trying to police in such a situation of serious neglect, when the government seems unconcerned, trying to solve crime in this context, is absurd. The Crime Prevention Councils serve more to justify police actions and act more as agents of the city than agents of the community.[6]

While a low priority, there were some early attempts at outreach. In 1988, 500 flyers were produced and distributed to warn Southeast Seattle businesses about counterfeiting, and another flyer was produced and distributed to explain the new abatement and nuisance laws and how to legally evict tenants suspected of dealing drugs out of their apartments.[7] The first quarterly review of the SSCPC showed that members met with 23 community groups and sent written overviews of the SSCPC to all the major groups in the community.[8] Founding member Robert Nordby organized a meeting of apartment owners in

March 1988. Jean Veldwyk met with the pastor of the Rainier Temple.[9] Also in March, Claude Forward organized a meeting with leaders in the black community, which lasted more than two hours, but did not lead to any additional minority representation on the council.[10] Outreach to the Southeast Seattle Community Organization was so successful that SESCO donated $300 from its benefit breakfast to the SSCPC in April 1988.[11]

Some time in the middle of 1989 outreach efforts were separated from crime control activities.[12] Outreach activities from then on have been handled by the SPD Community Crime Prevention Division as block watch questions or removed from the council entirely and handled by the Neighborhood Crime and Justice Center on a citywide basis.[13] While membership outreach received little attention, the council continued to sponsor graffiti paint-outs and it set up a hot line in the first quarter of 1988 for reporting crime-related information. The hot line gathered anonymous complaints and passed these on to the appropriate police units (see table 6).

The hot line enjoyed initial success, but concerns remained on the part of the SSCPC that not enough people in the community knew about it.[14] This may or may not have been a consequence of outreach difficulties, but calls to the hot line declined. The hot line and paint-outs were both forms of outreach and community-based crime prevention. The relative salience of these indicates the ambiguous and changing social position of the SSCPC. Direct, activity-based outreach, like graffiti paint-outs, characterized the group before it received official recognition. Anonymous information-gathering outreach for units of the police department, like the hot line, characterized the group's movement away from its roots in the community following official recognition.

TABLE 6. Number of Hot Line Calls through May of Each Year, 1989–93

Year	Calls
1989	303
1990	372
1991	212
1992	73
1993	72

Source: SSCPC meeting minutes, June 2, 1993.

While the charge that council membership was skewed toward white business interests was certainly not without merit and outreach activities were weak, the representative nature of the SSCPC was further compromised when the members of Neighbors Against Drugs and Operation Results did not feel welcome on the council. Fleissner, Fedan, and Stotland believe that this was probably because Neighbors Against Drugs remained critical of the chief. From this, they concluded that "with respect to the issue of the definition of the community, *the decision by the police to negotiate with the group associated with the Rainier Chamber of Commerce initially defined the community.* Others in the community were left out and protested vigorously and publicly, and created problems for the police department as well as the SSCPC."[15]

Frank LaChance told me that he attended a few SSCPC meetings, but when he insisted that the council could not be effective without a more representative membership he was shunned and assigned a very short-term position as chair of the Abandoned Vehicles Committee.[16] LaChance continued to work with patrol officers and community groups seeking his advice on street crime, but the cautious and very limited cooperation that characterized citizen efforts before the formation of the SSCPC was weakened by the recognition of the SSCPC as (1) the voice of the community and (2) the standard for SPD responsiveness to community concerns.

This exclusion set the stage for what Fleissner, Fedan, and Stotland called "chronic difficulties" in developing ties to the Rainier Beach area, the center of support for Neighbors Against Drugs. While Operation Results did cooperate with the chamber group on specific projects before 1988, interaction following the establishment of the SSCPC declined. Minutes indicate that Daykin attended occasional SSCPC meetings, usually trying to sell the council the services of Operation Results. But he, along with Neighbors Against Drugs, failed to find a role as a part of the community after the establishment of a police-community partnership. With the creation of the SSCPC, the concerns of citizens from Neighbors Against Drugs, Operation Results, and two new crime control groups (Mothers against Police Harassment [MAPH] and the Association of Community Organizations for Reform [ACORN]) were marginalized.[17]

MAPH, a nonprofit group organized in 1990, received a cool reception from the SSCPC.[18] Their mission is to "educate and coordinate parents and community organizations interested in addressing excessive police force. . . . One of MAPH's main goals is to hold the police in our community accountable to the *Law Enforcement Code of Ethics.* We urge everyone to know the code and help us demand that police officers live up to it."[19] In addition to publishing a newsletter, MAPH operated a hot line for reporting police harassment.

Godefroy described the invitation from the East Precinct Crime Prevention Council (CPC) to MAPH as the "best example of inclusion. The other groups [including the SSCPC] don't quite hit that standard. There wasn't a lot of new recruitment going on, some of the same people were showing up for meetings. They didn't have public meetings, sort of inbreeding and dying."[20] When I asked Harriet Walden about the participation of her group in East Precinct CPC meetings, she told me that the East Precinct had invited MAPH but added that most of the people there "don't see any problems with the police . . . and most of these councils were set up by the police anyway. They are an arm or tool of the police department."[21]

Godefroy insisted that the SSCPC was not created by the police, and the record is clear that the SSCPC initially grew out of a citizens' initiative. But other Crime Prevention Councils in the city were externally initiated by either the department or the Neighborhood Crime and Justice Center. Godefroy was aware that this issue was not simply a normative one but impacts directly on the potential for success of community policing in Seattle. When asked whether the perception that the police only cooperate with white business groups would eventually work itself out, she said: "No, it won't work itself out unless there are a lot of people working on it, particularly in the minority community. There is a great mistrust in the department. There is mistrust in government in general."[22]

Legal Mobilization: Citizen Efforts Expand the Powers of the Police. The second aspect of the partnership was the way that the police and citizens mobilized the law. Two of these programs began before the partnership and the other two were the result of police and citizen efforts to support new legislation. In this case, mobilizing the law meant both making it easier for the police to effectively enforce existing laws and actively seeking the creation of new legal tools for state-centered crime control. For this reason, the successes described here have contributed more to empowering the SPD than to encouraging specified capacities within communities.

The Criminal Trespass Program was developed before the partnership agreement was established. Precinct Commander Yumul and Kay Godefroy coordinated the effort to get businesses to provide the police with prior approval to arrest trespassers and a promise to press charges.[23] The trespass program also required the police to warn potential violators. The warnings were given by the officer on the scene or by the use of signs made available by the SSCPC advising that loitering was prohibited in the designated area. Department supervisors encouraged officers to observe individuals carefully to avoid obstructing the rights of people with legitimate business on the property.[24] This program increased police paperwork, but it also allowed the police to patrol private property in the same proactive manner that they patrol public property. In the Criminal Trespass Program, the partnership did not generate new laws but coordinated business and police department resources to improve the effectiveness of police enforcement of existing legislation.

The SSCPC expanded the scope of the Criminal Trespass Program. In order to combat loitering, which the department saw as a precondition for drug trafficking and other criminal activities, the council persuaded local business owners and managers to cooperate. By the end of the first year, more than 100 businesses had signed on and 1,044 citations had been issued. Eighty percent of the agreements in South Seattle were negotiated by SSCPC members.[25] According to Fleissner, Fedan, and Stotland, police supervisors considered the program an important tool for proactive policing. At the same time, however, there was some concern on the council and among property owners that this program contributed to higher vacancy rates, as wary managers became more reluctant to rent to potential drug dealers. Ironically, rising vacancy rates created economic pressure on managers to rent apartments without screening tenants. This pressure, combined with the way the civil abatement law was enforced, led one SSCPC founding member (the chief architect of the Civil Abatement Law) to leave the council. He charged that the partnership had been co-opted by the very agency it was meant to reform and was now blaming landlords for the criminal behavior of their tenants.[26]

The Civil Abatement Program was also developed before the partnership agreement was concluded. An owner notification program was started at the department's initiative as a way to notify property owners that their property was at risk of being abated. It later became an example of how the partnership could mobilize the law in the 1988

Civil Abatement Law. This law made it easier for landlords to evict tenants. Under it, a landlord was only required to give three days' notice to evict for nuisance when there was evidence of drug-related activities on the premises. Unlike normal evictions, the tenant could not delay eviction by posting a bond when the notice was for a drug-related nuisance abatement. According to a detailed flyer produced and distributed by the SSCPC:

> The 1988 Washington State Legislature recognized the need for landlords to evict quickly and efficiently those persons who engage in drug-related activities at rented premises. The new law provides: (1) a tenant has a responsibility not to engage in drug-related activities at rental premises . . . and (2) law enforcement has a responsibility to make reasonable efforts to identify and notify a landlord when illegal drugs are seized at rental properties.[27]

The flyer cited the 1988 changes in the Civil Abatement Law and the Nuisance Law as the legal basis for this type of eviction and notification process.[28] It was changes in both of these laws (together called the Drug Trafficking Civil Abatement Program) that made the abatement process such a potent weapon. The Civil Abatement Law was modified to require police to notify landlords, and the nuisance statute was modified to include drug trafficking as an abatable nuisance, placing the burden of proof on the landlord to show (1) no knowledge of the nuisance or (2) reasonable efforts to abate the nuisance and (3) a commitment to the court to "immediately abate any such nuisance that may exist at the building or unit within a building and prevent it from being a nuisance within one year thereafter; [then] the court shall, if satisfied of the owner's good faith, order the building or unit within the building delivered to the owner, and no order of abatement shall be entered."[29] Prior to these formal proceedings, both police officers and SSCPC members would informally notify landlords. Fleissner, Fedan, and Stotland report that almost 90 percent of owners were responsive to these informal notifications, taking action to clear up the nuisance.[30]

From January 1987 to March 1990, more than 700 property owners were encouraged to improve security measures, participate in the Criminal Trespass Program, hire a resident manager, evict a tenant, or close a building.[31] According to Fleissner, Fedan, and Stotland, the SSCPC was instrumental in assisting police efforts to deal with reluctant managers. When the police were unable to locate property owners, council members working in local real estate and title insurance businesses made their computer search services available. "They informally arranged to find new buyers or managers for some property. The Police, especially the Precinct Captain, became conduits for information about owners and managers, and in some instances put informal pressure on some managers to cooperate in this effort."[32]

According to the SSCPC's *1988 Year-End Report*, there were four abatements in the fourth quarter of 1988. Nineteen other premises were cleaned up in response to a formal threat to abate and numerous others through informal notifications by the SSCPC and SPD.[33] The abatement focus was also coordinated with the council's focus on nonrenewal of liquor licenses for businesses that failed to maintain a drug-free establishment and became nuisances to adjoining property owners and residents. These efforts affected several businesses in the southeast from 1988 to 1992: Jam's Broiler (closed), La Esquina (abated), the Hob Nob Tavern, Genessee Stop Tavern (closed), Columbia Cafe, Neighborhood Gathering Place (closed) Collins Gold Exchange, Rose Street Tavern, and Emerald City Market.[34]

As Fleissner, Fedan, and Stotland observed, the real estate connections of the SSCPC members, which accounted for part of its outreach difficulties, became a tangible resource for the partnership. In addition to providing access to computer networks and expertise about the real estate situation in the southeast, council members were able to use these connections to address part of the drug problem as an educational issue. Flyers like the one cited earlier and annual training sessions for owners and managers were part of the council's efforts to educate property owners.[35] "This issue was especially important since the drug dealers began to operate more from apartments and other residences as the police succeeded in driving them from the street by enhanced enforcement, especially through the use of the Criminal Trespass Program."[36]

The Criminal Trespass and Civil Abatement Programs originated in the southeast, but they contributed to citywide pressure for greater attention to crime control. In 1989, Seattle voters approved a $7 million Public Safety Action Program known as Proposition 1. This legislation, funded by a 12 percent increase in the city's B&O tax, provided funds for 125 new positions in the SPD, additional criminal attorneys for the City Law Department, expansion of the Municipal Courts, and youth violence prevention programs. The program components were based on the Buracker study of the SPD discussed in chapter 6.[37] In a letter to city council president Sam Smith, the mayor outlined the funding priorities of Proposition 1 (see table 7).

The mayor argued that Proposition 1 would increase police efficiency and accountability. Efficiency increases would result from reduced overtime, reduced paperwork by sworn officers (92 of the new positions were for sworn officers, 33 were for civilians), increased clearance rates due to expansion of attorney and court facilities, and improved information management. Accountability gains would result from the creation of Precinct Advisory Councils in each precinct, a citywide Police Advisory Council of representatives from the precinct councils, expanding community-based crime prevention, sensitivity training for officers, and a commitment to citizen participation in developing a department strategic plan for public safety.[38]

More than three million dollars for community policing was quite an investment in innovation. Looking more closely at the proposition's numbers, however, it becomes clear that the lion's share of this money had little or nothing to do with community policing. Of the 72 positions this money funded, 12 officers formed two Community Police Teams, one in the South and one in the East Precinct. Of the other 60 officers, 50

TABLE 7. Budgetary Allocations from Proposition 1 (in dollars)

Police	5,615,000
Management	1,030,000
Intelligence	740,000
Training	665,000
Community policing	3,180,000
Courts	660,000
Municipal Court backlog reduction	460,000
Municipal Court processing improvements	80,000
Criminal prosecutions enhancement	120,000
Youth Intervention	725,000
Antigang	225,000
Job training	175,000
Community-based programs	150,000
Police Guild recreation	175,000

Source: Mayor Royer to council president Smith, 1989.

were assigned to regular patrols and the others filled various supervisory positions at the precinct level. Despite being labeled community policing, the goal was to reduce response times, as recommended by the Buracker study. Of the $3.2 million, $95,000 was for the Neighborhood Crime and Justice Center (for staffing Crime Prevention Councils) and the SSCPC. Funding for the Precinct Advisory Councils was allocated to expand the SSCPC model to the rest of the city. The difference between these advisory councils and the existing SSCPC, as stated in exhibit 1 of the mayor's proposal to the city council, was that the "precinct commanders have input into board member selection, agenda setting, and group participation. [These are] critical to ensure that the precinct advisory councils are broad-based in membership and are not controlled by any one interest group." In addition to this alternate council system, funding from Proposition 1 created the Budget and Strategic Planning Unit of the SPD. The planning office was expected to "consider citizen concerns in the planning and budget processes."[39]

Proposition 1 was only the biggest crime control program of this period. There were others, and the SSCPC was involved in these as well. In 1988, the SSCPC requested that the city council consider a Drug Traffic Loitering Ordinance (DTL).[40] Like a later city ordinance sponsored by city attorney Mark Sidran to manage homeless panhandlers, the DTL ordinance grew out of concerns in the business community about how disorderly behavior (panhandling or loitering with the intent to sell drugs) hurt business by scaring customers away from shops. In 1990, the DTL allowed the police to regard the following behaviors as cause for arrest:

1. Being a known dealer
2. Repeated beckoning to passersby or passing motor vehicles
3. Circling an area in a motor vehicle and repeatedly beckoning
4. Being subject to a court order to stay out of drug-dealing areas (SODA)
5. Being recently evicted for drug activity[41]

According to Miller, the city attorney and the mayor's representative defended the proposed ordinance as responsive to community concerns. Speaking for the DTL were representatives from the business community and several Crime Prevention Councils, including the

SSCPC. Speaking against the ordinance was ACT-UP, the NAACP, the Public Defenders Office, the Seattle Commission for Lesbian and Gays, the Northwest AIDS Foundation, and the Hispanic Immigration Project. The ordinance passed with a vote of seven to two along with an ordinance requiring that the Seattle Human Rights Commission monitor complaints about police misconduct associated with the implementation of the law.[42]

Patrol Activities: The Double Edge of Reciprocal Targeting. A third aspect of the partnership was the ways in which patrol activities changed as a result of the cooperation. In chapters 5 and 6, I discussed the emergence of the Anti-Crime Teams (ACT I and II) and Community Police Teams. I will not repeat that discussion here. In addition to these, patrol officers were asked to target hot spots identified by the SSCPC, to follow up when citizens provided narcotics information, and to try to coordinate the delivery of public safety with the delivery of other city services. Part of the targeting included order maintenance concerns, such as converting 13 pay phones to call out only status and towing abandoned vehicles, but a majority of the officer hours devoted to targeting were spent on more professional forms of law enforcement.

While the SSCPC was involved in several types of activities, targeting became its focal point once the partnership was established. In a December 1987 meeting, which preceded the first formal meeting of the SSCPC, the chamber group and the police department had already agreed on the first seven targets (see table 8). In this program, the department decided, in cooperation with the council, to target hot spots or particular problems (such as abandoned cars and crack houses). Once a target was determined, the police were required to check targets at least twice per shift and carefully document their daily activities relating to the targets. At the monthly council meetings, the precinct captain reported on target activity. According to Fleissner, Fedan, and Stotland, however, "officers were not asked to do anything basically different from what they normally would do if they were patrolling aggressively. They were not asked to do walking beats or contact the law-abiding citizenry, as was done in some forms of community-oriented policing."[43] SSCPC members pressured the captain to target particular hot spots and persuade owners to clean up their properties. However, "these targets were, for the most part, those that the police had fairly well determined were major hot spots in Southeast Seattle [and] the SSCPC agreed with this selection of targets."[44]

In the interviews conducted by Fleissner, Fedan and Stotland, they found that police officers were suspicious of the business bias of the SSCPC. A Police-Community Relations Task Force formed by Mayor Rice in 1993 expressed similar concerns in its report.[45] The fact that many members of this group of citizen overseers owned both residential and commercial property close to these 1988 targets added to the concern that they were not representative of all residents in the Rainier Valley. The fact that their properties surrounded three of the initial seven targets, and that all of the targets were found along the commercial corridor and not in the neighborhoods or projects, also added to the impression that council activities were biased in favor of crime control that served the interests of a particular segment of the Southeast Seattle community (see fig. 9).

While ownership skewed target selections, the process of targeting itself also changed over time. Fleissner, Fedan, and Stotland report that initially the group met with the police weekly, vigorously discussing activity on established targets and potential additional ones.[46] This is confirmed by meeting minutes, which show detailed accounts given by the precinct captain followed by *equally detailed observations by the citizen overseer.* By the time I was observing SSCPC meetings, the target reports were very formal, involved little or no discussion, and other than passing on suggestions for additional targets community members were no longer involved in the decision-making process. In fact, by 1993 there was no longer any effort to assign individual citizen overseers to specific projects.[47]

TABLE 8. Initial Targets Established by the Partnership

Target	Suggested By	Council Overseer
Rainier and Genessee	Council	Claude Forward
Rainier and Martin Luther King	Cpt. Marquart	Linda Alhadeff
Rainier and Henderson	Cpt. Marquart	Gladys Jordan and Robert Nordby
4319 South Webster	Cpt. Marquart	Ron Ellison
39th and Pearl	Council	Buzz Anderson and Jean Veldwyk
Rainier and Graham	Council	Doug Merrill and Lou DeFranco
Abandoned Cars	Council	Frank LaChance

Source: SSCPC meeting minutes, various meetings; Seattle Police Department 1988c; Fleissner, Fedan, and Stotland, 1991.

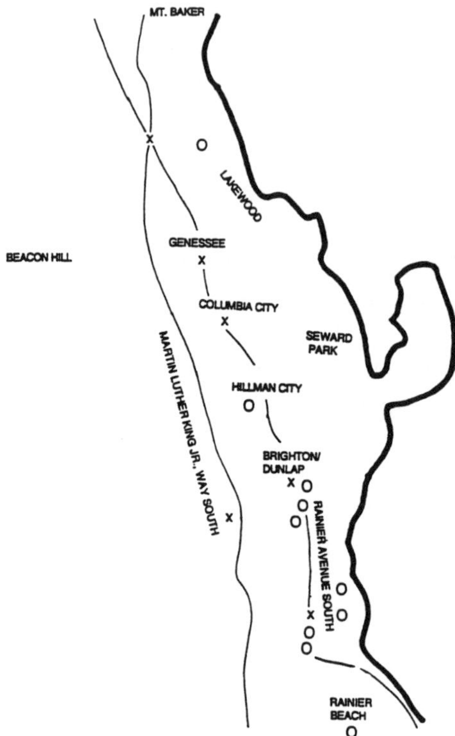

Fig. 9. Location of initial targets and property owned by core SSCPC members, 1989–95 (x = target, O = property)

In addition to the targets identified by the SSCPC, the department assigned a two-officer patrol car to the Garden Communities in the southeast, calling it the Garden Car Program.[48] This emerged from the work of a July 1991 task force established to address concerns of citizens in the Garden Communities about rising crime. As noted earlier, Fleissner, Fedan, and Stotland attributed this increase in criminal activity to the more aggressive enforcement efforts targeted for the southeast's commercial routes by the SSCPC. According to the 1991 CPT report, patrol officers, Seattle Housing Authority officials, and residents had repeatedly recommended a concentrated effort in this area, but these public housing projects were not targeted by the SSCPC.[49]

This task force was an excellent example of prevailing state-centered stories contributing to democratizing more than to disciplinary forces. This task force shows what was new (administratively encouraged attention to order maintenance and interagency coordination) and not new (a short-term task force approach with a heavy emphasis on professional law enforcement tools). According to the CPT report, overtime was to be minimized, the lieutenant in charge of ACT and CPT would command the task force, and "enforcement will be to the maximum levels legally possible. All pertinent laws will be enforced including traffic laws. The use of FIRs [and] Criminal Trespass Admonishments will increase our ability to dislocate and cease much of the criminal activity that is diminishing the quality of life of our citizens."[50]

This operation was divided into three stages. In stage one, the CPT walked through the area, placing warning stickers on suspected abandoned vehicles and inspecting for garbage accumulation or other site blight. The CPT made contact with the on-site managers and other city agencies. ACT sought warrants to be served in stage two. Stage two began one month after stage one. From 3:30 A.M. on September 3 until the same time on September 16, the task force provided 24-hour maximum enforcement. Watch commanders were instructed to assign a two-officer car exclusively for each of the two projects in this period to concentrate on arresting violators of the Criminal Trespass Program. ACT focused its efforts on this area for the same period. CPT spent half of its hours assisting with enforcement, and all officers were encouraged to patrol the area on foot. At the end of stage two, CPT repeated their stage one walk-through and two patrol cars remained assigned to the two areas for the remainder of 1991.

In stage three, the CPT had planned on organizing a cleanup day involving youths ages six to 12, but "liability waivers, transportation, and parental supervision" proved logistically difficult and the event never occurred, though the report noted that there was enthusiastic support in the community for a cleanup day. The other half of the CPT's time was spent on administration, since its role in the task force included gathering and reporting task force information from all involved units. The task force towed 57 cars, made 83 arrests, issued 38 criminal trespass warnings, conducted 34 FIRs, and wrote 225 tickets.[51] This task force focused on a low-income area of the southeast not targeted by the SSCPC. It shows the department responding to a wider range of concerns than those covered by the partnership, though with a distinct emphasis on professional law enforcement.

TABLE 9. Breakdown of 332 NARs Collected in Fourth Quarter, 1988

Eviction	48
ACT	47
Unfounded/other jurisdiction	13
Arrest	11
Pending	213

Source: Seattle Police Department 1988c.

Finally, patrol activities expanded the use of Narcotics Activity Reports (NARs). NARs were developed by the SPD in response to crack usage several years before the partnership agreement was signed. Using this reporting system, citizens passed narcotics-related information to the police through any officer at the precinct office, by mail or by phone. Each report was forwarded to the Narcotics Division, which conducted a computer analysis of crime trends to determine hot spots. The division decided which reports to pursue. Whether or not official action was taken, an officer was assigned to contact the complainant and provide the feedback necessary to encourage continued reporting and information sharing. At the council meetings, the captain reported on the status of NARs (see table 9).

III. Decentralization: SPD Organizational Change Following the Partnership

The logic of community policing would lead one to expect this section to focus on reforms that reduced the power of the chief, shrunk the police hierarchy, and redistributed command and control to precinct commanders and patrol sergeants. But there was no effort to shift authority to precinct commanders, patrol sergeants, or the community. Ministations, foot patrol, beat integrity, smaller precincts, or reductions in the number of prestigious citywide special units located downtown were not part of the story. Thus, this section is short and focuses on one issue related to decentralization, which may account for the absence of reforms to alter the command and control hierarchy of the SPD: department fears of micromanagement by the community.

On November 25, 1987, an article in the *Seattle Times* explained that the city council had sent a letter to the chief of police requesting that he testify before the council to justify his budget requests with "specific plans for combating crime in Southeast Seattle."[52] The chief was able to use the pending formation of the partnership, an initiative he opposed, as evidence of his commitment to fighting crime in the southeast. To the chief, community policing was more a new philosophy than a particular approach to patrol or organization.

SPD senior administrator Dan Fleissner argued that this philosophy was more a new management strategy for improving service delivery than a department reorganization.[53] Further, the limited decentralization that had occurred was not in response to community concerns but in response to agency needs.[54] For the department, responding to citizens meant improving the delivery of existing services by cooperating with other city agencies, inviting customers to provide marketing information to the SPD, and escaping from the "prison of 911."[55]

But customer concerns about department management and personnel decisions (like extending beat tenure) received a cool reception in the department. The department expressed its opposition to SSCPC interference in stories about confidentiality and micromanagement. Meeting minutes report that both Captain Marquart and Jean Veldwyk were concerned enough about confidentiality to warn the council about legal liability and schedule special meetings of the Executive Committee to avoid overaccess by the community to SPD information.[56] Concern about the confidentiality of crime-related information shows that the department was still focused on its monopoly control of data.

Concern about micromanagement focused on personnel questions and dated back to the founding of the SSCPC.[57] In 1988, the SSCPC strongly protested the transfer of two narcotics detectives as a violation of the partnership agreement and an example of poor communication within the department. Discussions with police officers indicated that the department was wary of micromanagement for two reasons. Officers expressed concerns about the undue influence of a business group like the SSCPC. They believed that policing was best left to professional law enforcement experts and that the council did not represent all the communities the police interacted with each day. The department's response to this issue of multiple constituencies, however, reflected a second concern: autonomy. The department chose to cooperate with one of several community groups because the chamber group was more willing to limit discussions to crime concerns and table concerns about department management or personnel policy.

In response to a strong letter from Jean Veldwyk, Captain Joiner

(Narcotics Section commander) responded with a long letter expressing frustration with her comments. He explained that, even though the two narcotics detectives assigned to the SSCPC pilot project had been reassigned to work with a federal task force, this did not violate the partnership agreement because (1) that task force would be targeting the southeast and (2) the two detectives would be replaced with two other detectives, giving the southeast two extra detectives during this period. He concluded: "I do not apologize for the amount of attention and commitment of resources the South Precinct has received and is receiving from the Narcotics Section. Forty percent of the Section's proactive detectives are concentrating on that area, and at least fifty percent of all the warrants obtained by the Section's City Wide Street Team have also been in the South Precinct."[58]

The captain's response was detailed, articulate, and forceful. But it was an after-the-fact explanation, giving no indication of a willingness to cooperatively determine proper personnel allocation. It also showed the precinct commander to be more of an information conduit than a decision-making authority. Fleissner, Fedan, and Stotland listed five micromanagement incidents. Three of these involved requests by members of the council for a response to a crime-related situation. According to Fleissner, Fedan, and Stotland, some in the department perceived these as evidence of undue influence and interference. The two other incidents that raised the issue of micromanagement were the suspension of ACT I and the replacement of the South Precinct commander by the chief soon after the announcement of the partnership agreement. Community concerns in these cases were treated as beyond the scope of the partnership. One consequence of the group's public support for ACT I (and their desire to preserve their relationship with the department) was that one of the original core members, the editor of the *South District Journal*, withdrew from the council. The chief did not meet with the community to discuss alternatives. He fired Sergeant Pillon the same year that the *South District Journal* named him officer of the year.

In the second incident, the council and the southeast's minority community protested the transfer of Captain Romero Yumul. "Although some members of the group expressed misgivings at losing the precinct commander who had helped them, the group backed down from a confrontation on this matter."[59] Captain Yumul, "a casualty of the turmoil," was reassigned to Juvenile.[60] The chief gave no quarter to the idea that community concerns included personnel policy. His explanation was simple: department policy required rotation every two years to avoid the corruption that can result from close relations between police officers and the communities they serve.[61] According to one officer, who wrote a letter to the editor in support of ACT I, the suspension of ACT I and the transfer of Commander Yumul sent a clear message to patrol officers that proactive policing would not be rewarded in the SPD.[62] It also sent a clear message to citizens: the role of the community was to provide information and support for police crime-fighting activities and not to meddle in police administration. As a result, Fleissner, Fedan, and Stotland indicated that an unstated compromise was reached. The police agreed to accept citizen input on targeting and patrol priorities. In exchange, the SSCPC refrained from providing unwanted input on personnel matters.

The April 1994 minutes reported that the SPD planned to transfer South Precinct commander Harv Ferguson to the Internal Investigations Section after only 18 months in the southeast. Captain Ferguson was replaced by the commander of the Coordinated Criminal Investigation Section (gang unit), Captain John Mason, a southeast resident. What is interesting about this decision is that, in contrast to the SPD decision to transfer Captain Yumul out of the precinct in 1988, there was no reaction from the SSCPC, even though the popular Captain Ferguson was being transferred before his two-year tenure had elapsed. This indicated both the taming of the council and the success of the SPD in defining personnel questions as beyond the scope of the partnership. It also indicated that, even in a precinct with a strong community voice, decentralization toward greater precinct autonomy, extended beat tenure, or decentralization to the community of a role in how the agency itself should operate was not part of prevailing stories about community policing.

IV. Reorientation of Patrol: CPT and ACT

The one potentially significant organizational change within the Seattle Police Department was the creation of Community Police Teams. Because this unit was not tied to 911 and focused on problem solving, this small organizational change expanded stories about policing in Seattle. A focus on CPT, however, can obscure the fact that, while not a neat match to the logic of community policing, the second Anti-Crime

Team (ACT II) was another addition to the department's specialized street units. And ACT II was not a new style of policing. Thus, in reorientation of patrol the SPD failed to send a clear message of openness to change.

ACT I emerged directly from the informal citizen-police partnership in the southeast prior to the SSCPC, but it was discontinued by the chief in 1987. Citizens in the southeast were so outraged by the chief's action that he formed a revised ACT II. But ACT II did not involve innovative order maintenance like ACT I did. Its primary tool was arrest, not the disruption of illegal business.[63] The department still evaluated patrol according to professional criteria such as response times, overtime hours, and arrests, so it is not surprising that downtown's revision of ACT would create a unit that could be measured according to this criteria. Thus, while ACT was new it did not represent a very significant commitment on the part of the department to change the way it patrolled in the southeast. While CPTs were more innovative, they were small and did not change what more than 97 percent of the officers did every day. And even what CPTs did was not always very different from the professional practices of using patrol officers to saturate high-crime areas for the short-term displacement of criminal activity.[64]

Both CPT sergeants I interviewed described the CPT as a support unit for other patrol units in task forces. Manning of the East Precinct CPT focused on the educational role of CPTs. "The philosophy of community policing is getting to know the area where you work, people getting to know you, knowing that you are touchable. . . . The primary function [of CPTs] is to get the community involved in their neighborhoods, to get the people together to talk, empowering them to understand what they can and can't do and how much control they have in their neighborhoods."[65] Conn of the South Precinct CPT focused more on how CPTs coordinated department resources, especially when task forces were attacking long-festering community problems like those addressed in the Garden Car Program. In addition to identifying long-term problems and coordinating resources, Sergeant Conn stated that the "particular function [of CPTs] in these task forces quite frequently was to go to the residents and neighbors and let them know there was a task force, ask them to support it, tell them why we were doing it, put down rumors that there were mass arrests. *Basically to act as a commu-*

nity relations unit at a time of high enforcement. Even though we do some enforcement, CPT's job mostly was to keep the lid on any potential neighborhood disturbance that might occur from an adverse reaction to a heavy police presence."[66]

CPTs assisted patrol through backups, cleaning up hot spots, and getting other city agencies to coordinate with policing efforts by cleaning up site blight or other problems. Linking with other government agencies was not just for CPT, though being released from 911 allowed them the time to devote to such coordination. Pressure from citizens to respond to their concerns and from management to increase the efficiency of service delivery intersected in CPT efforts to coordinate enforcement actions with health inspections, zoning enforcement, and efforts by the SHA to evict problem tenants.[67]

ACT and CPT, targeting and NARs, all indicate some reorientation of patrol in response to demands from citizens. However, very few of these broke with professional law enforcement practice and none evaluated officers on a set of performance criteria that rewards behavior other than professional law enforcement. This indicates that the department treated the reorientation of the patrol component of community policing like a continuation of police-community relations units, that is, as a marginalized special unit that had little direct impact on what the large majority of patrol officers actually did.

V. Accountability: SPD Responses to Citizen Complaints

The final component of stories about community policing in the southeast was accountability. A significant amount of concern was expressed by Seattle communities about this issue in this period, though little of it came from the SSCPC. The establishment of a police-community partnership, a police auditor, CPTs, and the hiring of a new police chief known for his work on community policing all indicated that Seattle was moving in the direction of a new style of policing. However, department resistance to organizational changes, reorienting patrol, and improved accountability also indicated that the SPD was more willing to focus its efforts on increasing its resources and controlling crime-related information and less willing to respond to concerns about centralization, professional patrol practices, and police misconduct. As table 10 shows, in the first year of the partnership citizen complaints about police misconduct in the southeast increased, while they decreased in each of the other three precincts.

The Police Auditor. While my discussion of the SSCPC and organizational changes indicates that the SPD was less responsive to some community concerns than to others, it was in the area of complaint processing that the department's limited responsiveness was most clear. The police chief controls accountability procedures in Seattle through the Internal Investigations Section (IIS). Along with the micromanagement controversy and the exclusion of Neighbors Against Drugs, Operation Results, MAPH, and ACORN, the department's control of complaint information removed certain kinds of community concerns from the police-community partnership.[68] In this way, public concerns from outside the SPD about the SPD itself were effectively deflected. The city council and the mayor's office provided a partial response, however, by creating the police auditor position.

At a Public Safety Committee hearing, a parade of irate citizens, concerned about police harassment associated with the enforcement of the Drug Traffic Loitering Ordinance, were told by the city attorney that the data on this invaluable police tool, contrary to their experience, did not indicate that it had been used to harass minorities. Community concerns about federal control of Weed and Seed left the mayor's office publicly disputing the position taken by the Department of Justice, directing citizens to the city's grant proposal for reassurance that the city would be in control.[69] According to the Police Guild, public concerns about police misconduct, described by the city's Human Rights Commission as responsible for "a deep distrust," were without merit.[70] Under pressure, the city finally did accept these concerns as meritorious enough to begin gathering its own information. This led to the creation of the position of police auditor.

TABLE 10. Changes in Number of Complaints of Police Misconduct, 1987 to 1988

Complaints	IIS	Line Referrals	Contact Log	Total
South	7/18	6/3	19/14	32/35
North	4/14	2/4	28/12	34/30
West	11/19	6/1	34/15	51/35
East	7/13	8/3	25/13	40/29

Source: Seattle Police Department 1988c.

The auditor, former judge Terrence Carroll, was confirmed by the city council in a nine to zero vote on March 16, 1992. While the *Seattle Times* later reported that the auditor position was largely perceived as a move by Mayor Norm Rice and city council member Jane Noland to "head off calls for a full-scale review board," the decision to appoint Terrence Carroll received widespread support.[71] According to the mayor's assistant for public safety, the creation of the position was a thoughtful response to serious community concerns about police misconduct.

> There was clearly some calls for a look at the disciplinary process, and there were a number of ideas floating around that people wanted and ways in which they felt it ought to be changed. In trying to be responsive to that, we felt it would be much more prudent to have a deliberate objective view of what was actually going on in assessment, of the kinds of things that were involved in the process, to make an informed decision about how best to improve an area that there's been a lot of controversy and a lot of concern about. So rather than emotionally react to any number of proposals, many of which had some merit, many of which we didn't know if they had any merit [we decided to take] a very analytical look at the entire issue and to try to make informed decisions about the entire process . . . because what was important was that you had a good product, a good basis for decisions being made versus a reaction to some problems that people saw.[72]

The police auditor's report was issued in April 1993, and, while it did not recommend additional changes to the complaint handling process, it was critical of both SPD resistance to oversight in general and SPD reaction in particular cases of alleged misconduct.

Studies Preceding the Creation of the Police Auditor Position. While the auditor's report may provide a catalyst for the mayor and city council to pressure the SPD for further reforms, it is important to remember that three major studies since 1989 recommending reforms in this area have been largely ignored by the department.

The MM Bell study of the police complaint-handling process, commissioned by the city and completed in 1989, reported the following findings:[73]

1. Concerns about the process were not new.
2. Many indicated no knowledge of how the process worked.
3. Many indicated a preference for an external process.
4. There was insufficient effort to publicize its procedures.
5. Misconduct complaints had increased over the last 10 years.
6. Allegations of excessive force in 1988 were up 150 percent compared to 1984.
7. IIS officers had no special experience or training.
8. The time required to investigate complaints had increased to four to six months.

The results of the MM Bell study focused on two recommendations: publicize complaint procedures and the disposition of cases and redefine the purpose of the complaint-handling process. This means reconceptualizing the process as "one aspect of quality assurance . . . another way of assessing citizen satisfaction."[74] Julya Hampton of the ACLU agreed, saying: "One way of learning about community concerns is through the complaint process. In other words, when complaints are filed with the police department about actions of a particular officer or officers, that is one way for them to learn about the views of the community. [The current practice is] not a very good process, I think, for learning."[75] Action on the MM Bell recommendations was slow, so slow that the city council felt it was necessary to initiate another investigation of SPD complaint-processing procedures.

Seattle City Council Resolution 28198, adopted June 15, 1990, directed the Seattle Human Rights Commission to "monitor and investigate citizen complaints of police harassment" in response to strong public opposition to the Drug Traffic Loitering Ordinance. The Seattle Human Rights Commission (SHRC) issued its report almost exactly one year after the MM Bell study. The commission found "a deep and disturbing lack of trust of the police," particularly regarding the department's perceived unwillingness to investigate and punish officer misconduct. "In the view of the Commission, this attitude results from a general lack of public accountability which is inherent in the existing philosophy and procedures which the Department follows when investigating citizen complaints of police harassment. . . . The problem is also exacerbated by the fact that the Department is investigating itself and is very resistant to any changes in this process."[76] The report continued to argue that the passage of the Drug Traffic Loitering Ordinance had increased distrust of the police and catalyzed the organization of MAPH and Queer Nation's Q Patrols to "combat police harassment and the failure of the Department to provide adequate protection."[77]

The Human Rights Commission recommended that the SPD improve the accessibility and accountability of IIS by giving citizens the information they need to file complaints, providing the information they need about the investigation of complaints filed, removing the offices of the IIS from the Public Safety Building, and adding two civilian participants to IIS investigations. These recommendations can also be found in the MM Bell study. According to the SHRC, the secrecy of the process was a source of cynicism and a shield for officers who chose to retaliate against complainants. "The fear of retribution combined with inaccessibility and cynicism regarding the integrity of the system, discourages the filing of complaints. Moreover, there is a strong community perception that the Seattle Police Department cannot monitor itself. A number of those interviewed requested the implementation of a civilian review board."[78] Like MM Bell, the SHRC did not recommend an external review at this time, but it did express exasperation at the resistance within the SPD to its investigation.[79] The commission also recommended sensitivity training, minority and female recruitment and promotion, shifting hiring decisions from the SPD to the Public Safety Civil Service Department, and convening a public hearing so the mayor and city council could hear from the community directly.[80]

A problem became apparent when the recommendations in the MM Bell study were found in the SHRC report and then appeared again in the ACLU report issued on July 10, 1992, almost two years after the MM Bell study was released.[81] The ACLU report again focused on opening up the process, providing citizens with information about the investigation of complaints, an explanation of the 75 percent of complaints that were not investigated, and data concerning the disposition of complaints that were investigated. Repeating other recommendations from the MM Bell study, the ACLU suggested that the SPD develop an early-warning system to weed out officers with conduct problems. Such a system would include analyzing the majority of complaints, which are currently stored outside the system in the contact log. Also following MM Bell, the ACLU recommended extending the length of time a complaint is kept in an officer's file from 3.5 to 7 years and including contact log entries in these files. Since the MM Bell study had found that over a three-year period only 1.4 percent of officers accounted for 18 percent of excessive force allegations and in the same period 18 officers were the subject of more than 10 investigated complaints, it was clear that an early-warning system could target that small portion of the SPD to protect the reputation of the rest of the officers and improve public safety and confidence.[82] Finally, the ACLU repeated the recommendation made by MM Bell and the SHRC for citizen patricipation on the Complaint Advisory Board.

VI. The Rise and Fall of the SSCPC

The SSCPC passed through at least three stages following its inception in 1988. In the founder's phase (1988–91), the council was headed by Jean Veldwyk and the relationship between the council members and the SPD was one of a precarious balance, with more reciprocity than in later phases. The council focused on targeting, monitoring police performance on targets very closely, personnel, and resource allocation questions. While secondary, the council also devoted attention to legislation, license renewals, and graffiti cleanups. As early as the end of the 1988, council minutes reported that no one had volunteered to run for president, targeting reports were getting shorter, and the detailed quarterly and year-end reports on crime in the southeast had been discontinued.[83]

Godefroy left the SSCPC to head up the NCJC in 1990, which precipitated a split on the council over the advisability of setting up a citywide agency and losing local control.[84] By 1992, the SSCPC had entered a second phase under the leadership of Dr. Joseph Smith, a vice principal of Rainier Beach High School. His leadership was reflected in the council's growing attention to guns in schools.[85] While other issues remained, this new issue and the removal of NCJC staff support from the southeast to downtown office space defined this period. In this period, the SPD presence on the council became compartmentalized into crime prevention, CPT, and target reports. Citizen overseer reports on target activity disappeared.

In the third phase (1993–94), under council president Grover Haynes, few of the founders attended meetings and the initiative of Dr. Smith was passed on in the form of an Education Committee, headed by Kerry Trobec, which focused on grant writing.[86] Perhaps the most telling evidence of change in the character of the council by stage three was found in two incidents: a brief exchange between Haynes and

Veldwyk and Lou DeFranco's doubts about council vigor and police responsiveness. In the first instance, meeting minutes record that Veldwyk called Haynes to request council (and presumably SPD) attention to a specific crime problem in the southeast. Haynes "requested that she send a letter (put her concerns in writing). To date he has not received correspondence from her."[87]

In September 1992, founding member Lou DeFranco expressed dissatisfaction with the role of the SSCPC and the removal of staff to downtown offices. While on vacation, his home was burglarized, and in a separate incident his son-in-law's car was prowled near the Arches Apartments. According to meeting minutes, "Lou also indicated that he was not too happy with the service he received at the South Precinct when he went there to report the incident. Additionally, Lou expressed his concern regarding the SSCPC's role in Southeast Seattle. He finds the current staffing arrangement unacceptable. He feels strongly that the SSCPC must maintain an office in the area as it did in the past—at least two days per week."[88] The minutes added that the Executive Committee encouraged Lou to attend the October 7 meeting to further discuss these issues.

The October 7 minutes do include a hot line report that summarized Lou's situation, yet no further action was discussed.[89] In this period, DeFranco's complaints appeared regularly in the meeting minutes. He was unhappy when the Social Security Agency closed its office in the southeast because it contributed to the perception of the area as dangerous. He was also upset that the SSCPC only heard about SPD personnel changes after the fact, and after discussing the issue the council took no action.[90] On December 2, 1992, the SPD Crime Prevention Division reported to the council that the burglars responsible for the DeFranco burglary had been arrested. While DeFranco's crime-

TABLE 11. Change in Total Part I Offenses, 1988 (by precinct)

Precinct	Change
South	−7.1
North	+2.3
East	−1.5
West	+4.0
City	−0.5

Source: Seattle Police Department 1988c.

fighting concern was addressed, his concerns about council and police agency were not.

This examination of partnership activities indicates that the community-based crime prevention component of community policing in Southeast Seattle atrophied with the establishment of a formal partnership with the SPD. In chapter 6, I argued that historically the SPD has devoted most of its reform resources to managerial tinkering rather than innovative street operations. This examination shows that this pattern has continued in the SPD's stories about community policing in the southeast. Thus, the most significant impact on the crime rate in the southeast came from citizen action leading up to and during the first year of the SSCPC. A reversal of crime rates in the southeast was achieved without foot patrols, beat integrity, ministations, decentralization, or enhanced accountability. For this and other reasons examined here, I conclude that it was stories about more decentered policing that accounted for the early successes of community policing in Southeast Seattle and the social capital that provided the foundation for those successes was now less manifest in the operations of the SSCPC and in the communities' relationship to the SPD (see table 11).

Chapter 8

Getting Back to Mayberry

In this final chapter, I summarize and examine the findings of this study. First, I organize this material around an image—Getting Back to Mayberry—that captures the intersection of community activism and policing reform, state-centered and more decentered stories, and the dialectical relationship between democratic and disciplinary mechanisms of social control in this case. Getting Back to Mayberry is an image that immediately conjures up positive feelings among those who would implicitly expect to be part of the peaceful and prosperous middle-class community Mayberry refers to, just as it lacks that immediate appeal for those who do not hear their stories or see their faces in the concrete social relations referred to in both the traditional and now nostalgic presentations of that image.

Second, I provide an illustrative list of democratic and disciplinary characteristics manifest in this study of community policing. Then I proceed to examine these as competing and overlapping stories, both moderating and normalizing, both enabling critical public scrutiny and enhancing disciplinary surveillance, that both constrain reciprocity in important ways and also enable moments of more reciprocal interaction and effective political action. Finally, I conclude with a discussion of the political utility associated with the particular mixture of democratic and disciplinary mechanisms of social control in this case.

> Whatever happened to Mayberry, that small, fictitious town with the friendly sheriff and deputy who spent more time chatting over pie and coffee at the local drugstore than chasing after criminals? The best guess is Mayberry grew up. Development brought more people and the police force grew. There wasn't time for an afternoon snack and a rambling talk with a drugstore owner. Mayberry's probably a lot like Redmond now. And Redmond, with its 51 officers, is trying to get back to Mayberry.[1]

As a nostalgic image, Getting Back to Mayberry encourages folks to imagine better days by comparing the present unfavorably to an idealized past, but as such the image is both constructed to strengthen state agency and continuously reconstructed by the memories, dreams, and fears of citizens. It becomes a medium for transmitting an uncritical traditional vision of community life that also subverts normalization as it encourages imagination; it encourages folks to see physical, social, and political disorders as linked; even as it normalizes the fears, problems, and solutions of particular segments of the community. The image of getting back to something asserts that which must be achieved; just as it also manifests a critical perspective on liberal politics with what Walzer calls the power of a "communitarian correction."[2]

Like the white, middle-class town brought to mind in nostalgic images about Getting Back to Mayberry, policing that invests in the social capital of communities can, as in this case, support more democratic forms of social control. In the Seattle case (1988–94), democratic impulses were present at several points in the police-community partnership.

First, focusing on the concrete social relations supported by competing stories about community and policing showed that long-term investments in social capital by community members accounted for initial successes. Success at both crime prevention and integrating crime prevention efforts into ongoing struggles over community revitalization was a consequence of citizen coordination of formal and less formal resources, and the moderation of competing concerns forged in their cooperative problem solving activities. The selection of the Rainier Valley Chamber of Commerce group as the official voice of these diverse Southeast Seattle communities was a consequence of the vertical and horizontal social capital that the members of this group were able to mobilize. This meant mobilizing private resources, their status as long-standing neighborhood business leaders, and their personal and professional relationships with other citizens and city leaders to pressure the police department to accept a police-community partnership.

Second, the partnership failed to target their policing efforts on poor and minority neighborhoods or to conduct outreach to ensure that partnership activities continued the pattern of building upon and contributing to the social capital of Southeast Seattle communities that characterized citizen efforts prior to the partnership. Instead they insisted on policing efforts that would clean up areas surrounding their own personal and commercial properties, allowing the rapid atrophy of community groups that had been active players in the southeast community crime prevention story before the partnership formed. This failure mobilized democratic impulses from within the police department. Police officers, suspicious of a white business bias in the partnership, noted conscious efforts to not follow through on commitments to patrol partnership targets more aggressively. Police officers, supervisors, and administrators mobilized a professional discourse to resist the biases of the partnership by providing resources for other southeastern communities in the Garden Car Program and rebuffing potentially vigilante citizen attitudes with rights-based stories limiting the breadth of the net in the Criminal Trespass Program and discouraging the development of citizen mobile watches.

Third, the stories examined here include a candid recognition of the limits of state power that highlights the relational basis of social control and the contingent nature of law enforcement in society. This was seen in stories about disorder that did not remain limited to stories about physical and social disorder but expanded to include stories about political and economic disorder in community demands for zoning control, efforts to recall the mayor, pressure for a new chief who would support community policing, and calls for more citizen participation in the review of complaints of police misconduct. Further, pushing beyond policing that privileges those chosen few citizens partnering with the police, stories about the importance of aggressively dealing with disorder also meant, in this case, that powerful pressure on property owners to clean up their properties was mobilized in the Criminal Trespass Program, civil abatement, and partnership educational initiatives. Here, like the increasing visibility of state power manifest in the minor reorientations of patrol constitutive of community policing, this use of the spectacle is turned on both state agents and that segment of the community partnering with the police. The apparent inability of the police to fill in the microphysics of power—because they are not less but more visible, not more but less omnipresent, and both more and less the subject of critical public scrutiny—links state agency to the lowest levels of power in a way that highlights an inescapably contingent characteristic of any attempt to tap the resources that inhere within indeterminate relational networks.[3]

While Getting Back to Mayberry, then, does provide an image of community and policing that contains identifiably democratic characteristics, the image is neither immediately nor unambiguously appealing to everyone. The brief moment of high reciprocity characteristic of the creation and first year of the police-community partnership examined here was a consequence of the capacity of citizens to mobilize the diverse nonstate resources noted, supported by a network of police-citizen relationships that (for a short time) both reduced crime and strengthened communities by investing in social capital. But eventually the partnership atrophied as a consequence of several relational factors, which reveal a more disciplinary side of Getting Back to Mayberry.

First, the composition of the SSCPC remained a biased segment of Southeast Seattle communities when the members decided to exchange a less critical membership for a more cooperative police department. Second, when the founding leadership of the partnership moved on, their replacements were not able to command the same respect from the department or support from the community because they lacked the status as long-standing civic leaders, the experiences shared with other citizens' groups and police officers that led to the establishment of the partnership, and the social capital that would inhere within these. Third, the power of the Seattle Police Department contributed to both of these shifts in the relational character of the partnership when the department mobilized a professional discourse to rename reciprocity as micromanagement, to resist the biases of the partnership by providing resources for other communities to support a professional approach to law enforcement, and to encourage a one-way information exchange focused exclusively on the police crime-fighting mission and not on police agency or council representativeness.

Getting Back to Mayberry captures in a single image the complex and intoxicating allure of community policing; an aspiration of all people to be free from fear and live with dignity in safe and prosperous associations with others. The same image also encodes a vision of community based on partnerships that exclude the least advantaged, empower state agents, and are limited to targeting those disorders most feared by more powerful communities and most amenable to intervention by professional law enforcement agencies. When more resources from the community were needed by the police department, stories about active communities taking responsibility for crime prevention spurred citizen partners to lobby the city council or contribute volunteer labor. When these same partners challenged the police administration's failure to extend beat tenure, stories warning against community micromanagement, citizen mobile watches, and a loss of information control constrained citizens, encouraging passive communities dependent on professional law enforcement agencies.

Different stories about community or policing were mobilized at different times, and the image of Getting Back to Mayberry captures these multiple meanings. Like privacy or individualism, which also carry competing and sometimes contradictory meanings that can be mobilized differently at different times, the net effect of this conceptual richness and ambiguity in this case was to privilege stories that reinforced existing power relations.[4] Nostalgic stories about communities with police officers everyone knows by name mobilize different visions of community and policing at different times "to create or impose order within the community, to define and deflect change, and to articulate a philosophy of individualism and equality that could also be reconciled with their tenacious defense of the status quo."[5]

I. A Dialectic of Democratic and Disciplinary Stories

Prevailing stories tended to privilege state-centered professional law enforcement, but where these stories necessarily intersected with more decentered stories about community and policing they introduced discursive resources for resistance to prevailing stories. This necessary intersection, it turns out, has both a discursive and an empirical component. The logic of prevailing stories depends on the discursive link between police practice and revitalizing communities with specified capacities for its persuasiveness in larger communities, where what Scheingold calls "symbolic policing" thrives on images and stories with powerful political utility.[6] Not surprisingly, however, this symbolic form of regulation cannot easily be decoupled from its more instrumental construction in the narrower communities where police officers interact with more and less law-abiding citizens on a daily basis.

Scheingold argues persuasively that this entanglement of symbolic and instrumental regulation tends toward the local moderation of more hysterical symbolic stories about crime and punishment. This is the empirical component of the necessary linkage between state-centered and more decentered stories: police officers ultimately must interact with citizens face to face, and we know that most officers, even at the height of the now mutating professional model, depend on their local knowledge, community connections, and ability to alternately act as an agent of the state or member of the community to manage disorder and fight crime.

The local reconstruction of stories about community and policing that takes place between and among patrol officers and citizens can, however, moderate or normalize. In this case, that local reconstruction tended to support state-centered law enforcement, integrating more decentered stories to the extent that these strengthened state agency and privileging more disciplinary mechanisms of social control when the partnership was less than reciprocal. When the partnership was more reciprocal, in its initial period, both the decentered and state-centered stories tended to support the moderation of competing concerns in concrete activities that did not privilege a state interest in information and resource control but included subjecting state agents to critical public scrutiny. When the partnership atrophied, this reciprocity was lost and the capacities that supported moderation were linked more directly to state-centered stories about normalization, as a particular form of moderation, and to surveillance, as a particular form of information sharing, both forms that privileged the state interest in order, docility, and dependence.

This interweaving of democratic and disciplinary impulses has both short- and long-term consequences. More reciprocal forms of association mean both potentially more democratic forms of social control in the present and more resources to support future efforts to resist prevailing stories if current problem solving efforts reduce crime in a way that also strengthens communities. In this case, the police department was able to use the partnership to secure large increases in federal funding for community policing and to broaden its mandate and legal tools. Each of these increased police power in relation to other city agencies and strengthened the power of professional stories about policing and community. At the same time, these created the potential for additional constraints on police power through expanded networks of cooperation with the Department of Construction and Land Use, Health Department, Housing Authority, Department of Housing and Human Services, City Domestic Violence Coordinator, and Harborview Injury Prevention and Research Center. While state-centered stories about community and policing remained the core of prevailing stories, the arrival of a new police chief with a commitment to a vision of community policing closer to that articulated by community groups provided a new resource for the community. The controversial selection of an outsider by the mayor (and the creation of a police auditor position) also indicated the resilience of political narratives highlighting reciprocity and community revitalization in the struggle to define community policing.

Community Police Teams, the early targeting practices of the SSCPC, the new police chief, and the creation of the new police auditor position each represented tiny but potentially significant democratizing changes in policing. Each of these were small arenas where the interactions between citizens and police were more open and reciprocal. CPTs were structured to recognize and adapt to the fact that policing remains embedded within social networks as surely as it is an activity of a centralized city bureaucracy. They were more a part of the communities they served, less insulated than regular patrol. They were released from 911 and expected to be conduits for effective two-way communication between citizens and the department. And CPTs grounded this increased reciprocity in concrete neighborhood policing activities. In communities, they contributed to more reciprocal relations, but this also meant that their ability to act was more constrained by citizens, just as their capacity to play the good cop to patrol's bad cop *loosened* constraints on the department as a whole.

A "possibility of power" was manifest in these small changes in the discourses and practices of policing.[7] While the organization and philosophy of policing had not changed all that much, what changed was the way people talked about policing. In the period from the middle 1980s until the formation of the SSCPC, steady media attention was focused on community policing. Numerous reports about community policing in other cities appeared in the two citywide newspapers. There were reports about citizen activities in the southeast and other parts of the city to combat crime and about the appeal of community policing in Federal Way, Kent, Redmond, Bellevue, and other cities in the Seattle metropolitan area. In December 1987, the *Seattle Times* reported that Captain Marquart, the new commander of the South Precinct, was working with community groups on what then city council member Norm Rice called "a prototype for neighborhoods."[8]

In March 1988, a Neal Pierce editorial praised Lee Brown's success with community policing in Houston saying: "It's hard to imagine a more dramatic reversal of traditional authoritarianism. In the semi-military world of policing, Brown is introducing innovative principles borrowed from Japan and US industry. Among them: participatory management, bottom-up decision making, and emphasis on the individual's creative powers."[9] Articles in June and July praised the efforts in Southeast Seattle. In May 1989, *Pacific Magazine* did a cover story on the SSCPC. In April 1989, there was a long editorial by the chief of the University of Washington Police Department. In October, a long op-ed piece by the former Bellevue police chief praised this revolution in American policing. And the *South District Journal,* whose editor was a founding member of the SSCPC, was even more attentive to what Professor Ezra Stotland of the University of Washington called a "quiet revolution."[10]

The sustained media attention may weaken the case that this was a quiet revolution, but it does indicate that journalists, local activists, elected officials, and most of the police chiefs in the area were clearly telling different stories about community and policing. These articles were filled with promises about how the organization and philosophy of policing would dramatically change with the adoption of community policing. It would empower street cops and other law enforcement professionals to reduce fear through problem solving partnerships and revitalized communities. Community policing would return city neighborhoods to the days when foot patrol officers knew residents by name because they walked the same beat every day. These more decentered stories about Getting Back to Mayberry reinforced state agency *and* provided discursive resources for resistance to prevailing stories by giving voice to democratic aspirations. While community policing was both democratizing and disciplinary, the paths toward freedom and servitude intersected in this case around efforts to legitimize state agency rather than invest in local social capital.[11]

The Power to Say What Policing Is: The Militarization of Mayberry. Prevailing stories about community and policing advanced by advocates were efforts to construct history to support state-centered stories about social control. Prevailing stories about policing drew discursive resources from references to empowering communities with specific capacities, while at the same time they narrowed the possibility that policing in those communities most victimized by crime and disorder would invest in the social capital of residents living there. Stories about community revitalization were central to the political appeal and coherence of prevailing stories about policing reform, but the logic of these stories was left to wither as prevailing stories narrowed their meaning to problem solving and reducing fear, both police-led activities that tapped community partnerships only insofar as they were a resource for the police department, reversing the power flow from empowering communities to empowering the police.

Police interest in community policing reflects more what Garland calls a combination of adaptation and denial, an evolutionary adjustment of the professional policing model to better fit it to changing social circumstances, than a quiet revolution.[12] This tension between professional stories and stories about the failure of the professional model frames police internal struggles over policing reform, increasing the tendency of police leaders to try to sell community policing as just another tool—that is, as an improvement on the professional model. This ends up being reflected in patrol practices that are called community policing despite their focus on the techniques of professional law enforcement. Public stories about a quiet revolution justify this redredging of tired city trenches, as administrative energies are not focused on leadership or innovation but are sapped in an endless shifting of bureaucratic boxes characteristic of the professional model's emphasis on command and control. And, while organizational charts change above them, patrol officers are increasingly drawn into partnerships with state and federal law enforcement agencies that extend the professional approach to policing with lucrative federal financial support for special units and task forces mobilizing powerful stories and military hardware.[13]

Kraska argues that much of this focus on hyperprofessionalization reflects the impact of national and international legitimation efforts on city politics.[14] He argues persuasively that the war on drugs amounts to a gradual nationalization of local law enforcement—what he calls the "militarization of Mayberry."[15] Local policing, he notes, is increasingly expanding its use of SWAT teams that are no longer just limited special units but engage in standard and routine police work as part of an increase in high risk no-knock entries related to the war on drugs.[16] This militarization of Mayberry is a descent of symbolic policing to the local level, transforming a moderating force in the politics of law and order, by emphasizing its links to larger efforts to normalize deference to state agency and legitimize state power.

Like the Seattle Police Department's Gang Unit (which is heavily and conspicuously armed, dressed entirely in black, with a cobra insignia not unlike the symbol a gang might use), the Narcotics Unit, and the second Anti-Crime Team, this colonization of routine patrol by specialized, paramilitary units is justified with stories about fighting violent crime through professionalization in multiunit task forces expanding the use of military tactics in local policing. Joseph McNamara, former police chief of San Jose and Kansas City and now at Stanford's Hoover Institute, concluded that the message here is that community policing is an illusion. "Despite the conventional wisdom that community policing is sweeping the nation, exactly the opposite is happening."[17] But stories about community policing are sweeping the nation as a part of a larger discourse legitimizing state-centered mechanisms of social control by rearranging the power to punish.[18]

Rather than expressing a collective responsibility to participate in democratic politics, then, community policing encourages active deference to state authority and passive acquiescence to state agency. To justify shifting the grounds for legitimation from politics to law, the professional discourse constructed stories about policing as an apolitical and scientific profession appropriate for insulation from critical public scrutiny. These early professionals could be identified by their new radio-equipped patrol cars, link to 911, brainy individual detectives taking fingerprints in their pursuit of cagey career criminals—and by their visible power as agents of a citywide middle-class community rather than members of any particular working-class neighborhood community. To justify shifting the grounds for legitimation from law to order, community policing constructs stories about policing as professional fear reduction through problem solving partnerships. As the shift to law has confined the scope of democratic politics, so has a focus on (dis)order and fear confined the scope of law. These latter-day professionals can be identified by their military weapons, enhanced information systems, release from the burden of 911, multiunit partnerships privileging professional participation—and by their visible power as agents of a symbolic national community with outposts in militarized Mayberries.

Legitimation here is further separated from democratically achieved consent and is linked to fears that justify state agency and expand the professional insulation of police experts. Prevailing stories expanded less accountable forms of state power into communities by increasing the capacity of the SPD to shield itself from critical public scrutiny. This shielding occurred in two stages. First, in defining the community as the chamber group the SPD excluded more critical voices from membership in the community of community policing. This decision, along with a commercial property bias in SSCPC targeting, cut the partnership off from developing reciprocal relationships with a significant portion of those southeast communities most victimized by crime and *normalized cooperation with the SPD as a precondition for living in a safe community.* Second, with the decline of reciprocity in targeting, the SPD treated the partnership like an impersonal budget line to be tapped rather than a relational network to be nurtured. This cut the partnership off from even the modest vertical social capital it had enjoyed in its initial period, reducing the SSCPC to a pool of volunteer labor watching Southeast Seattle for the police. This confirmed suspicions that the council was more an agent of the city than the voice of the community and *normalized uncritical cooperation with the SPD as a precondition for living in a safe community.*

Department power was manifest in its control of information. In the Narcotics Activity Reports Program, for instance, the department was willing to accept additional paperwork and provide prompt feedback to citizens who filed crime-fighting complaints. In one year, the department was able to review and follow up on 1,219 complaints. Contrasting this with department resistance to providing complainants with follow-up information on complaints of police misconduct indicates a willingness to be more open with the public regarding some types of confidential information and not others. Rick Anderson of the *Seattle Times* made a similar observation: "You can learn all you want about the private citizens of Seattle when they attack each other on the streets or behind closed doors. But you are not allowed to know what happens when a public officer and a citizen crack one or the other's head. This is secret."[19]

Like Progressive Era reforms, prevailing stories about policing here are inescapably political; and the political utility of these reforms serves to extend state control over a widening range of centralized and decentered social control resources. Prevailing stories constructed history to make more decentered stories about policing either less visible or only visible to the extent that they legitimated (an expanding) state agency. Seeing this privileging of stories about state-centered law enforcement helps us to understand how the atrophy of community actually contributed to this particular construction of (community) policing.

The Power to Say Who the Community Is: Fortress Mayberry. While the composition of the South Seattle Crime Prevention Council (SSCPC) was skewed toward white business interests, the representative nature of the SSCPC was further compromised by the absence of participation from Neighbors Against Drugs, Operation Results, Mother's Against Police Harassment, ACORN, or any recognized leader from the minority communities in Southeast Seattle. Fleissner, Fedan, and Stotland concluded that "with respect to the issue of the definition of the community, *the decision by the police to negotiate with the group associated with the Rainier Chamber of Commerce initially defined the community.* Others in the community were left out and protested vigorously and publicly, and created problems for the police department as well as the SSCPC."[20] This decision constructed Mayberry as a fortress community, a place that survives through its dependence on the state cavalry, and (by excluding neighbors) eschewing the reciprocal basis of social capital, making future dependence on state social control resources more likely.

Since the SSCPC was the only component of this partnership that incorporated active citizen participation in decision making, the composition and activities of the council were critical factors in evaluating the democratizing and disciplinary elements of community policing. Minority and nonbusiness representation was weak, and council activities were, as a consequence, skewed in favor of concerns about one police mission (street crime in commercial areas) and against concerns about agency itself (SSCPC representativeness, beat integrity, or police misconduct). By moderating critical stories and normalizing stories more consistent with existing professional police practice, the partnership made the public scrutiny of state agents more difficult. The establishment of the SSCPC granted the SPD the power to define the community. This power contributed to the focus on displacement strategies and response times—rather than beat tenure, accountability, information sharing or a recognition of the competing stories about policing and community struggling for ascendance in the southeast.

The atrophying of the SSCPC was apparent with its declining role in targeting, its failure to cooperate with new community groups, and the decline in its tenuous cooperation with older community-based crime prevention groups in the Rainier Valley. After the department recognized the chamber group, it appears that this altered its position in the community. On the one hand, its composition added to the suspicion in African American communities that crime prevention councils are agents of the police department. And this suspicion reduced the possibility of generating horizontal social capital in relations with other groups in the southeast. At the same time, SPD power and the council's limited vision of police responsiveness reduced the possibility of sustaining a reciprocal relationship between the council and the SPD, lending credence over time to the impression that the council was not an agent of the community but was dependent on the police department.

The eventual colonization of the police-community partnership by the police did not end the dialectical relationship between democratic and disciplinary mechanisms of social control. The members of the excluded community groups remained active in the southeast, continuing to voice their criticisms of the police administration, resisting department stories about community and policing in the creation of the police auditor position, supporting the selection of a new police chief committed to a vision of community policing markedly dissimilar from the outgoing chief, and even trying (with little success) to market their crime prevention services based on their achievements in Southeast Seattle. Similarly, the members of the SSCPC used both the success and the atrophy of the partnership to catalyze their own stories about community and policing in the above efforts along with efforts to combat homelessness, provide public education, organize crime prevention councils citywide, and pressure the new chief for a serious commitment to community-based storefronts or miniprecincts.

The members of each of these groups continued to struggle to define community and policing as pieces in a larger struggle to revitalize Southeast Seattle. But, while the efforts of these citizens and the police officers they worked with mobilized both disciplinary and democratic mechanisms of social control, the constraints on reciprocity embedded within the relational networks constitutive of their partnership contributed to the dominance of disciplinary mechanisms and the restriction of more democratic mechanisms to those that reinforced state agency.

II. Constraints on Reciprocity in Police-Community Partnerships

Constraints on reciprocity were found in the prevailing stories about community and policing, in the insulation of police agencies, and, at the macrolevel, in the structuring of our political economy. Investment decisions had a direct impact on social order and the capacity of citizens to build social capital. The inability of workers with families who live in crime-threatened neighborhoods to control investment decisions was reflected in the decreased capacity of their communities to protect themselves from either the crime or the police action that divided and weakened their communities. But, to the degree that stories about community and policing linked social control to community revitalization through more reciprocal vertical and horizontal relationships, prevailing stories also provided resources to challenge larger political and economic power relations.

One the most interesting combinations of democratic and disciplinary stories in community policing surrounds the relationship between policing, community, and property. Tomlins noted that stories about professional policing "elevated the maintenance of order above mere politics, which simultaneously labeled economic activity a private realm and segregated it from purposeful public direction." In this story, Tomlins argued, social order was constituted principally by protecting property rights from democratic politics.[21] The bias in the composition of the SSCPC was manifest in the fact that the partnerships' targets surrounded their residential and commercial properties in the valley, first ignoring neighborhood violence and later displacing criminal activity into neighborhoods already more victimized by crime. Their stories, in part, imparted a higher moral position to commercial property than to public housing, providing a mechanism for the privileging of a story about community policing that devoted more community and police resources to the policing of commercial property than to enabling safe communities in those areas most victimized by crime and violence. But it was not only the composition and targeting practices of the SSCPC that reflected the impact of property on policing and community.

The Criminal Trespass Program empowered the police to intervene as proactively on private commercial properties as they do on public properties. Tenant screening and monitoring related to the Drug Trafficking Civil Abatement Program and Narcotics Activity Reports provided decentered surveillance and an enlarged police information system to enhance the police/state capacity to proactively police *inside* of these private commercial facilities. This capacity was strengthened by grant-encouraged coordination between the SPD and other city agencies such as the Department of Construction and Land Use, the

Seattle Housing Authority, and the Health Department. These agencies provided information and access to police officers, making otherwise unattainable warrants achievable. And this coordinated state-centered integration of decentered policing continued a trend in law enforcement established by the coordinated harassment of Chinese residents by Citizen Order Committees performing public health inspections under the supervision of the chief of police and of restaurant owner Charlie McDaniel for refusing to cooperate with the operators of a cardroom on his premises. Taken as a whole, these coordinated efforts amount to a preservationist impulse in community-based crime prevention that reinforces state agency.[22]

These stories reinforced the police/state as the preservationist public agent of a social order based on a hierarchy of property rights.[23] These stories also increased the state's capacity to hold property owners more accountable for maintaining the space surrounding and within their properties. While the disciplinary characteristics of this accountability are clear, this can also serve as an insurgent resource since absentee (or simply nonresponsive) property owners are often an obstacle to community revitalization (as shown in the effective use of SSCPC real estate connections to identify and pressure property owners, city-owned blighted property in the Southeast Seattle coming under attack, and civil abatements successfully initiated by citizens seeking to hold these public and private property owners accountable).

While a focus on property continued trends in policing, these are embedded within different Mayberries today. Stories about community policing combine community-based initiatives with more centralized, resource-rich, professionally insulated, state-centered, crime-attack strategies without strong ward-based networks of information exchange and accountability, further reinforcing state agency through structurally imbalanced partnerships. Professional policing, it turns out, is only insulated from certain political influences; it is much more exposed to the vertical influence of state and federal law enforcement professionals providing funding and policy research. This imbalance contributed to favoring the certainty of rule through bureaucratic expertise over the indeterminacy of community activism in Community Action Programs, Model Cities, and community policing.[24] As the citizens opposed to Weed and Seed had feared, one consequence of this particular policing reform has been a more powerfully coordinated but less reciprocal and accountable police presence in their communities.

While decentered stories focused on a broader vision of self-governance, it is no longer 1848. Communities are weaker, more fragmented, and, in the case of community policing, plugged into an immensely more powerful picket-fence federalist system. State-centered stories about coordination and problem solving partnerships redirected this self-governance energy to support more effective state action. Policing, once the subject of political control and legitimation, then subjected to juridical oversight, is now also managed to strengthen the administrative capacities of the state. Legitimation shifted from politics to law to order, and it is "impossible to reconcile law and order because when you try to do so it is only in the form of integration of law into the state's order."[25] As the shift to law confined the scope of democratic politics, so does the focus on order confine the scope of law to constructing systems of social control that more efficiently reinforce the power and agency of the police.

Fear and Other Constraints on Reciprocity. People fear crime. People also fear homelessness, cancer, unemployment, poverty, and the inability to pay for their medical care. Most of us fear police officers. People are afraid when they are unable to protect themselves and their families; when they are vulnerable to the vicissitudes of modern urban life beyond their control; when they are subjected to the humiliations and degradations of arbitrary authority and unaccountable power.

While people have many fears, we are exposed to fear-filled stories about crime, especially violent crime, much more often than to stories about other fears. Scheingold argues that this distortion contributes to a myth of crime and punishment that privileges a punitive approach to crime control.[26] Fear-filled, personalized, dramatic, fragmented, and normalizing crime stories fail to provide a basis for citizens to understand the power relations beneath particular stories about police or community.[27] These characteristics of our information system exaggerate the voices of those less likely to be victimized but most likely to support an expansion of crime control practices that reinforce state agency.

A focus on the fear of crime distorts public opinion and impoverishes public debate about crime control. Individual responses to this fear are of limited effectiveness and the capacity to engage in target hardening depends on the availability of disposable income to pay for additional locks, insurance coverage, taxi rides, and other miscellaneous expenses incurred in efforts to insulate oneself from interactions with others. Collective responses are also limited to the extent that community life has atrophied and additional state intervention may be associated with unacceptable costs in the form of increased taxes or police brutality. Further, a focus on the fear of crime rather than on the full range of fears and vulnerabilities may lead to a policy response that encourages citizens to remain passive consumers of social order. As Machiavelli observed, "men love as they themselves determine but fear as their ruler determines."[28] Policing that focuses on fear reduction, then, may be a response to perceptions encouraged by state agency itself.[29]

Policing narrowed to focus on the fear of disorder, while containing the democratic impulses discussed earlier, may lead the fearful to voluntarily seek to reduce their freedom through insulation. Instead of learning to cooperate with others, a focus on the fear of disorder is likely to encourage more isolation in more fragmented fortress communities. This may encourage citizens to seek recourse to violent (personal or state) confrontation long before less tragic responses have been exhausted. When there is no forthcoming solution from the police and absent any capacity of communities to act independently, violence may *become* the only thinkable path to the preservation of self, family, and community.[30]

Stories with Political Utility: Moderation and Normalization. Both community and police department stories moderated and normalized maverick police officers, vigilante community groups, and critics of the department. Pressure to moderate came from the tradition of police professionalism in the SPD and from citizens working with other citizens to forge a more integrated understanding of their collective concerns. Many of the more radical law and order activists—while failing to overcome racial and class biases in the composition of their groups—did moderate their perspectives over time, but the dynamics of the moderating process cut in several directions.

When the activities of Operation Results raised concerns in other segments of the community, the police department applied pressure by characterizing citizen mobile watches as attempting to pass themselves off as officers. When one sergeant, despite being named officer of the year by the community, ignored department procedures in his zeal for harassing crack dealers, the chief fired him. When some members of the SSCPC pushed for more aggressive enforcement of the Criminal Trespass Program, the precinct commander held his ground, reminding the group that some individuals have a legitimate right to be in these places. In response to the perceived business bias of the SSCPC, several patrol officers indicated that they were being less than proactive in their efforts to police SSCPC targets. In these cases, the police department's commitment to professional policing, impartial law enforcement, and individual rights merged with their concern about excessive community influence over police policy in the mobilization of moderating discourses.

The forces of moderation not only muted radical law and order demands, maverick police officers, and vigilante community groups; they also marginalized concerns about community control and police accountability. When the SSCPC tried to expand the scope of their partnership to cover concerns about police agency itself, the department strongly resisted community micromanagement of the police department. While the department mobilized micromanagement concerns to normalize the SSCPC, other groups that resisted moderation were marginalized by the department's suggestion that their input would be more appropriately channeled through the SSCPC. Criticism of the police was screened out when the police defined the community as the SSCPC and an uncritical attitude toward the SPD became a criteria for official recognition and normalization as a part of this community.

The department restrained citizen input by resisting decentralization, civilian oversight, beat integrity, and reciprocity. Further, while there were some minor changes in patrol activities, these new units were small and continued the professional model of a task force approach to law enforcement. The SSCPC's efforts to mobilize the law by supporting new legislation to empower the police department focused on expanding professional, state-centered forms of crime control: arrest, prosecution, and incarceration. Efforts by some in the community to collect anonymous tips on hot lines or photos from citizen mobile watches were easily integrated into existing police information systems, but efforts by others in the community to collect anonymous tips about police misconduct did not become a part of prevailing stories because these neither reinforced state agency nor normalized an uncritical deference to police expertise.

Insulating Partnerships: Critical Public Scrutiny and Surveillance. Twentieth-century professional policing attempted to insulate police officers from their embeddedness in communities. For the past 100 years, cities and states have hired more police with more sophisticated equipment, built more prisons, and watched crime rates continue to rise. Police reformers since the Progressive Era have argued that more firepower, better communications technology, more efficient centralized administration, and insulation from corrupting influences in the community would create a more professional police force and effectively fight crime. Current interest in community policing is, at least in part, a response to the failure of this model.

Today law enforcement officials claim that community policing is the new answer to crime and community decay. With Republicans threatening to shift community policing funding in the recent Omnibus Crime Bill into prison construction, there is pressure to demonstrate that community policing is not a break with professional law enforcement (it is not soft on crime) *and* that it is not just another fashionably ineffective bureaucratic program (it is a revolution in policing). My findings indicate that community policing is, indeed, a continuation of professional law enforcement, a modest break with these practices, and another fashionably ineffective bureaucratic program. In the Seattle case, community policing was a mixture of reform and stasis, and the particular form of this mixture empowered the police department more than it empowered communities.

Insulation reduced police corruption and professionalized some aspects of police work, but it also alienated the police from community support without reducing crime. As citizen groups in these communities today seek a more cooperative and responsive police department, this relationship offers them, like it offered nineteenth-century ward captains, the possibility of power. The South Seattle Crime Prevention Council was initially empowered by its partnership with the police department to select targets, monitor police action, and serve as a community-based fiscal agent. This was a power that distinguished them from other community groups, but it also reduced the incentive for the organization to see itself as part of the disorderly networks of reciprocal relations that constitute community life. The conferring of this power granted a privileged status to the intersection between the SSCPC's particular vision of community policing and that of the Seattle Police Department.

The possibility of power, therefore, had its costs. While cooperating with the police may have given a particular group the leverage in the community to define policing practices and community concerns, the cost was a slow concession of control over this leverage to the police department. The SSCPC sought authority to control crime but lacked the power and incentive to direct this authority toward a crime control strategy that could revitalize community life. Community policing in Seattle failed to contribute to revitalizing the social relations that constitute communities capable of informal social control because it favored bureaucratic relations of dependency and insulation over reciprocal and accountable relationships. The intersection of the concerns of a selected segment of the community with the bureaucratic needs of the police department created a story about community policing that favored reproducing, rather than challenging, existing power relations.

Seeing this as a political struggle highlights larger questions about the relationships between stories and practices in community policing and how these support techniques that constitute systems of social control. In community policing, there are two techniques of note: problem solving partnerships and fear reduction strategies. Both of these contributed more to normalizing deference to state agency than they did to providing resources for communities to subject unaccountable power to critical public scrutiny. To the degree that scrutiny was enhanced, it contributed to the capacity of the state to surveil public places more effectively and it expanded the capacity of the state to surveil private places.

> The marginalistic integration of individuals in the state's utility . . . is obtained in this new political rationality by a certain specific technique called then, and at this moment, the police. . . . [T]he main characteristic of our political rationality is the fact that this integration of the individuals in a community or in a totality results from a constant correlation between an increasing individualization and the reinforcement of this totality.[31]

Problem solving partnerships reinforce a totality of increasingly isolated and frightened individuals when they integrate decentered individuals and groups into state-centered policing efforts only insofar as they reinforce state agency, expanding responsibility but not resources for more decentered policing. Fear reduction strategies subtly shift police resource allocation from victims to frightened but less likely to be victimized middle-class white residents, normalizing Wilson's conception of middle-class values in place of moderating the competing demands of diverse urban communities. Since these are the same residents who are more likely to vote, the political utility of fear reduction strategies trumps its perverse effect on crime control policy.[32]

And these two techniques form the center of a web that injects disciplinary meanings into other, more decentered, policing techniques mobilized in community policing. These include *joint targeting* of criminal hot spots that favor allocating police resources to protect the property of business owners in an area; balkanizing *patrol reorientation* into special units and structuring these units to encourage a continued emphasis on professional law enforcement; *encouragement of community-run anonymous hot lines* for crime tips and discouragement of community-run hot lines to report police misconduct; *citizen patrols* that antagonize minority members of the same geographic community; *citizen lobbying* for legislation to provide the police with new legal tools and other resources; and *community organizing* that both excludes groups critical of the police department and precludes a continuation of the informal intergroup cooperation that characterized Southeast Seattle prior to the establishment of the partnership. In Seattle, each of these techniques could have supported more democratic forms of social control but did not. While not unambiguously, each contributed more to the expansion of disciplinary mechanisms by reinforcing state agency.

III. Broken Windows and Other Stories about Rearranging the Power to Punish

Community policing in Seattle has been both disciplinary and democratizing. It has been both but not in an undifferentiated way: It partly colonized community life and partly manifested the potential for more democratic forms of social control. The path toward freedom intersected with the path toward servitude. The outcome remained contingent on the forms of association that emerged as agents from two related and interpenetrating spheres—the state and society, the system and the life-world, the police and communities—struggled to control urban social space and the power to say what policing is and who communities are. This study has argued that the discursive struggles to define community and policing were central to understanding the democratic and disciplinary characteristics of community policing and the political utility of prevailing stories, beginning with Wilson and Kellings "Broken Windows" thesis.

"Broken Windows" is about sending a strong message to potential criminals that a particular community will not tolerate minor disorders. "Broken Windows" and the war on drugs are also stories for law-abiding communities that the message senders hope will reduce their fear and enlist them in state-centered social control efforts, including supporting police efforts to more aggressively police minor disorders. As we have seen in this study, however, these are not the only stories about community and policing constitutive of the struggles to define community policing. Tending to broken windows without also attending to the reciprocity constitutive of horizontal and vertical social capital contributes to police-community partnerships that primarily legitimate and insulate police agency, reducing the democratic and enhancing the disciplinary face of community policing. While the citizens opposed to Weed and Seed have no particular affection for the plethora of broken windows decorating their neighborhoods, they also expressed a fear of messages about subjecting their children to a disproportionately harsh and less accountable power to punish. Abner Louima, and others like him in New York, heard a message about a new style of policing, in which state agents partner with communities that do not include them. And there are other messages being sent in the ways we choose to control crime.

"We are sending a strong message . . . that the U.S. government takes very seriously the need to attack the production [of marijuana]."[33] This message from the U.S. attorney general supported increasing the power of military personnel to arrest, as was seen in the 1989 Department of Justice interpretation of *posse comitatus* revisions to mean that U.S. soldiers could legally arrest drug traffickers, which they did less than two months later, invading Panama and arresting Manuel Noriega not long after he had been praised by George Bush as a key ally in the war on drugs. This story also sent a message. One neighborhood activist in Seattle asked how to understand the message sent by leaders who are telling kids "just say no" while these same leaders were cooperating with a military leader later charged with drug trafficking.[34] The message to this citizen partner was that government leaders are not good role models; the message to our international partners in the war on drugs was that we practice what we preach, that the stories we tell do, in fact, structure our policing efforts.

Prevailing stories about community and policing intersect around legitimation and constitute an emerging social control discourse about managing citizen inputs by constructing who the community the police serve will be, whose fears will become most salient, and where control over problem solving resources will be located. Similar to the way that the militarization of local policing highlights legitimation efforts in a changing international political economy, community policing is a part of the changing political economy of cities, including what Katznelson calls a transformation of urban politics into a politics of dependency.[35] This process has turned cities into a terrain of social control that has less to do with substantive problem solving and more to do with controlling discontent—and this is reflected in the stories about problem solving and fear reduction, which are more about information system improvements to support a state-centered rearranging of the power to punish than about addressing the broad range of problems facing urban residents. This larger context highlights how local, national, and international messages about social control contribute to efforts to manage the consequences of making capitalism work by separating legitimation from consent and linking it to fear and dependency. Community policing is a local component of this emerging social control discourse. To the extent that the relationships constitutive of community policing fail to invest in the social capital of those communities most victimized by crime and disorder, this policing reform arouses the democratic aspirations associated with policing as a collective responsibility as it makes the realization of these less likely by disproportionately enhancing the power of the police to punish individuals and communities.

Appendix: Supplementary Materials

Southeast Seattle Area Profile

Demographics

A predominantly residential population of 42,400

Commercial development is concentrated along Martin Luther King Jr. Way and Rainier Avenue South

24.4 percent of the population is less than 16 years old, compared to 15 percent citywide

62 percent of the population is people of color, compared to 25 percent citywide

From 1980 to 1990, there was a 20 percent decrease in the white population and a 25 percent increase in people of color

Housing

58.6 percent of housing units are owner occupied, compared to 46.5 percent citywide

72.7 percent of housing units are single-family structures, compared to 53.1 percent citywide

Median rent was $354, compared to $425 citywide

92 percent of the land was zoned for residential use, compared to 75 percent citywide

From 1980 to 1990, the number of housing units increased 1.6 percent, compared to 8.3 percent citywide

Income and Employment

Per capita income was $13,255, compared to $18,308 citywide

24.2 percent of the population 18 and under lived in poverty, compared to 15.7 percent citywide

21 percent of jobs were in retail, compared to 14 percent citywide

Unemployment rate in 1990 was 7.7 percent, compared to 4.9 percent citywide

Two jobs per gross acre, compared to nine citywide

Source: 1990 Census, District profiles prepared by the City of Seattle Planning Department.

Total Number of Violent Crimes by Census Tract of Occurrence in Seattle, Five-Year Average, 1989–1993

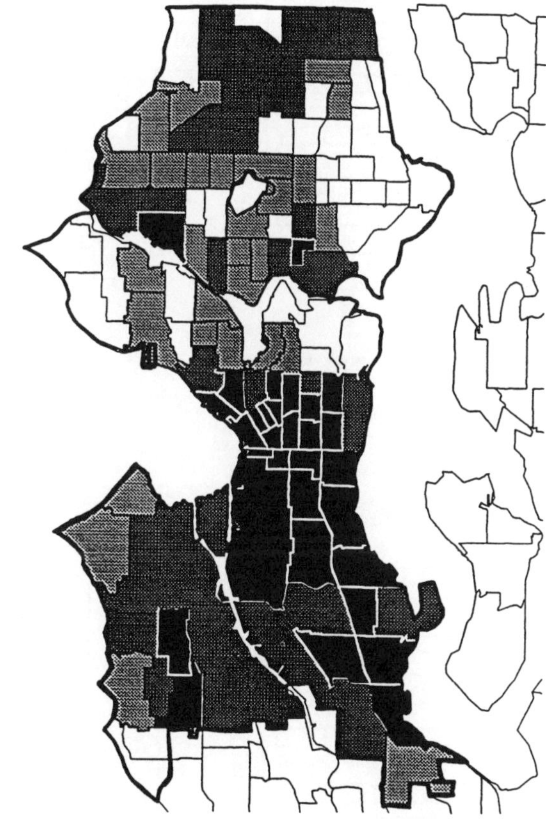

Source: Krieger, 1994, fig. 2.24.

Index Crime Rates, 10-Year Profile

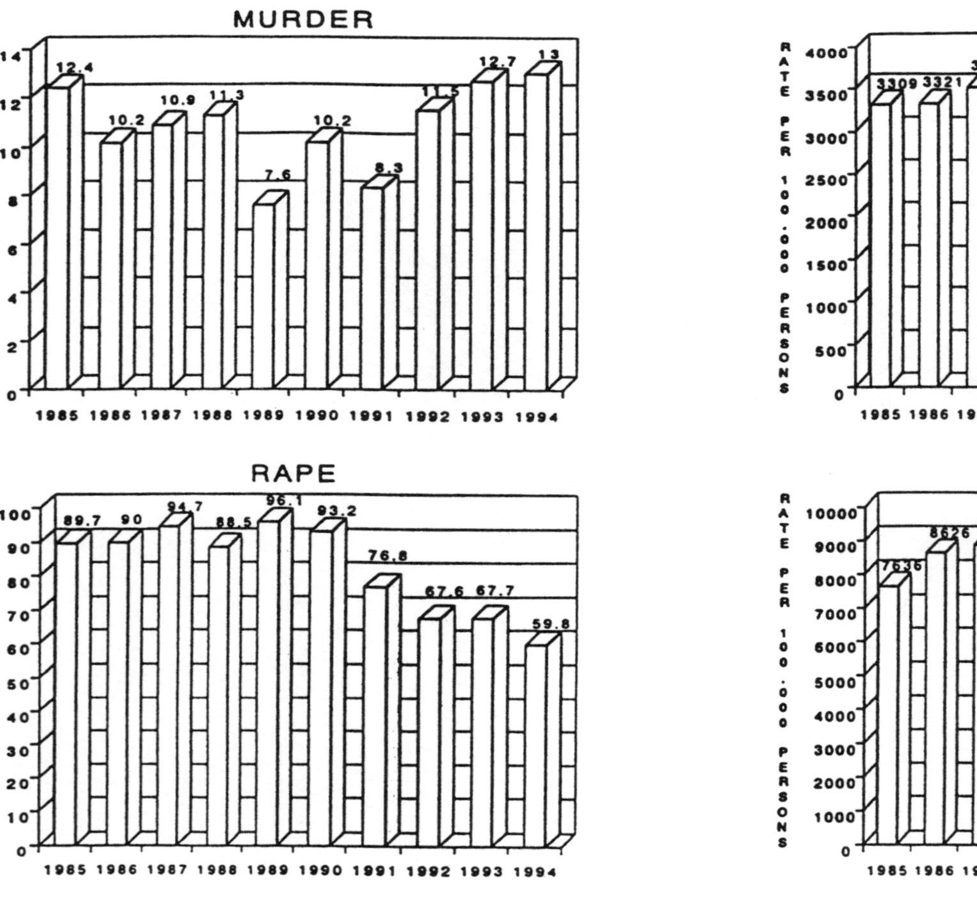

Source: Seattle Police Department 1994.

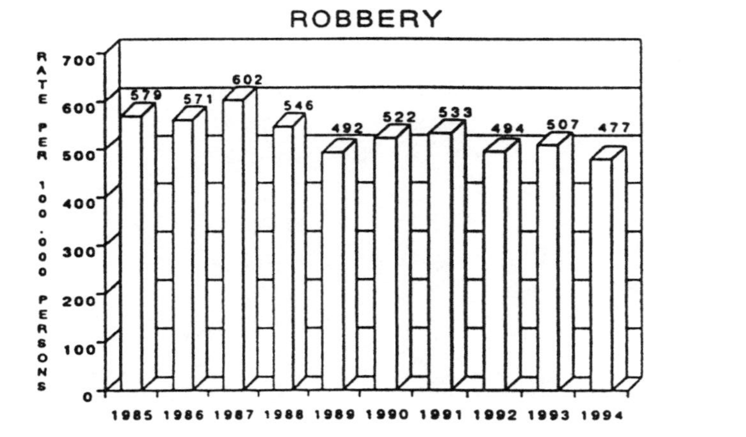

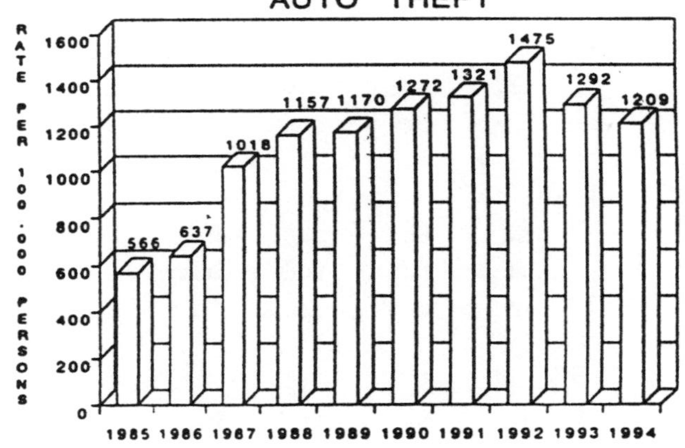

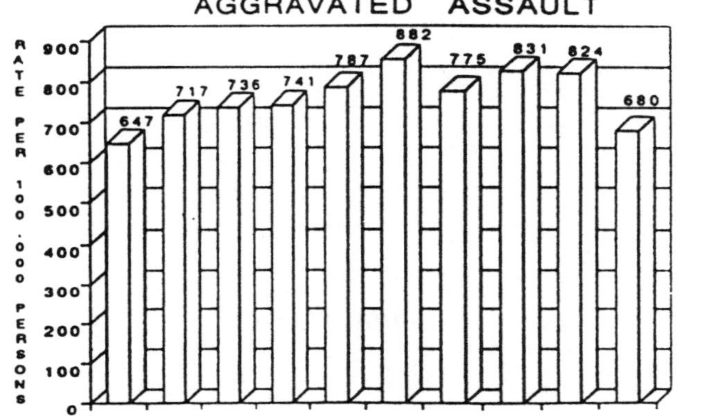

The 1994 Seattle population of 531,400 is based on April 1994 figures provided by the Washington State Office of Financial Management. The rate at which a particular crime occurs per 100,000 population is derived by multiplying the total number of occurrences of the particular crime during a given year by 100,000 and then dividing that product by the total population. The result is the crime rate per 100,000 persons. This measure provides a meaningful method of comparing crime statistics from year to year by adjusting for yearly fluctuations in population.

Ten-Year Profile: Violent Crimes

Year	1985	1986	1987	1988	1989	1990	1991	1992	1993	1994
Murder										
Total	61	50	54	56	38	53	43	60	67	69
# cleared	35	48	37	51	33	34	31	40	54	41
% cleared	57	96	69	91	87	64	72	67	81	59
Rape										
Total	441	443	465	439	478	481	398	353	357	318
# cleared	234	208	247	211	253	237	201	180	174	140
% cleared	53	47	53	48	53	49	50	51	49	44
Robbery										
Total	2,843	2,792	2,959	2,709	2,448	2,695	2,761	2,577	2,676	2,536
# cleared	765	737	927	781	790	690	636	763	624	634
% cleared	27	26	31	29	32	26	23	30	23	25
Aggravated Assault										
Total	3,178	3,505	3,618	3,675	3,914	4,551	4,017	4,337	4,349	3,615
# cleared	2,124	2,223	2,193	2,156	2,211	2,407	2,217	2,614	2,380	2,037
% cleared	67	63	61	59	57	53	55	60	55	56

Source: Seattle Police Department 1994.

Ten-Year Profile: Property Crimes

Year	1985	1986	1987	1988	1989	1990	1991	1992	1993	1994
Burglary										
Total	16,262	16,215	17,254	16,880	14,162	11,181	10,640	9,250	9,252	8,186
# cleared	1058	1181	1205	946	884	820	761	739	696	562
% cleared	7	7	7	6	6	7	7	8	8	7
Theft										
Total	37,534	41,625	43,586	43,196	39,540	39,522	40,502	41,125	39,216	36,758
# cleared	8,992	9,780	9,512	9,489	8,366	8,384	8,562	8,764	7,486	6,605
% cleared	24	24	22	22	21	21	21	21	19	18
Auto Theft										
Total	2,783	3,110	5,001	5,739	5,816	6,570	6,842	7,698	6,819	6,423
# cleared	419	483	641	688	725	854	833	872	756	687
% cleared	15	16	13	12	13	13	12	11	11	11

Source: Seattle Police Department 1994.

Rate of Reported Violence in Seattle 1985–1993

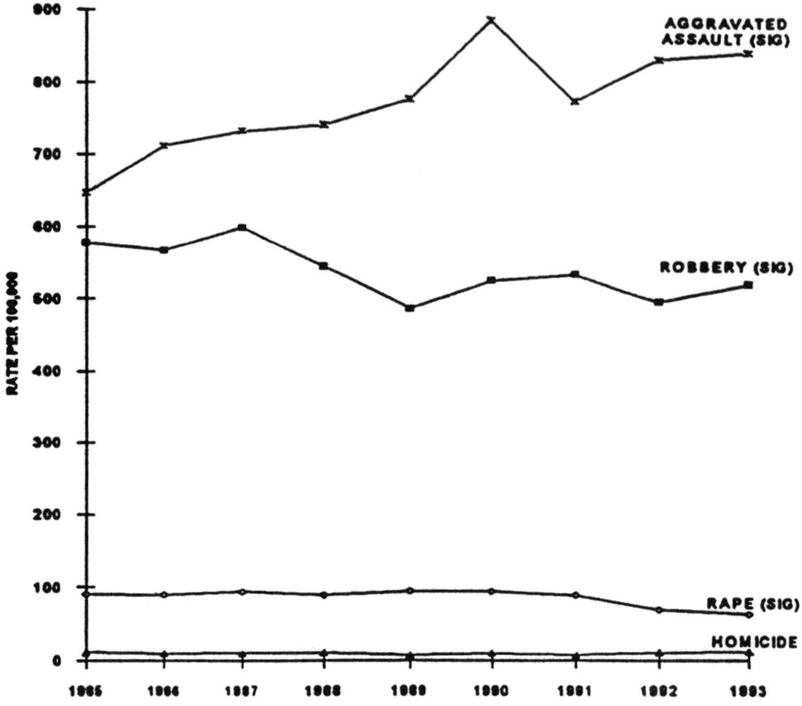

Source: Krieger 1994, fig. 2.8. (SIG indicates that the trend since 1985 is statistically significant.)

Total Sworn Employees vs. Total Calls for Service

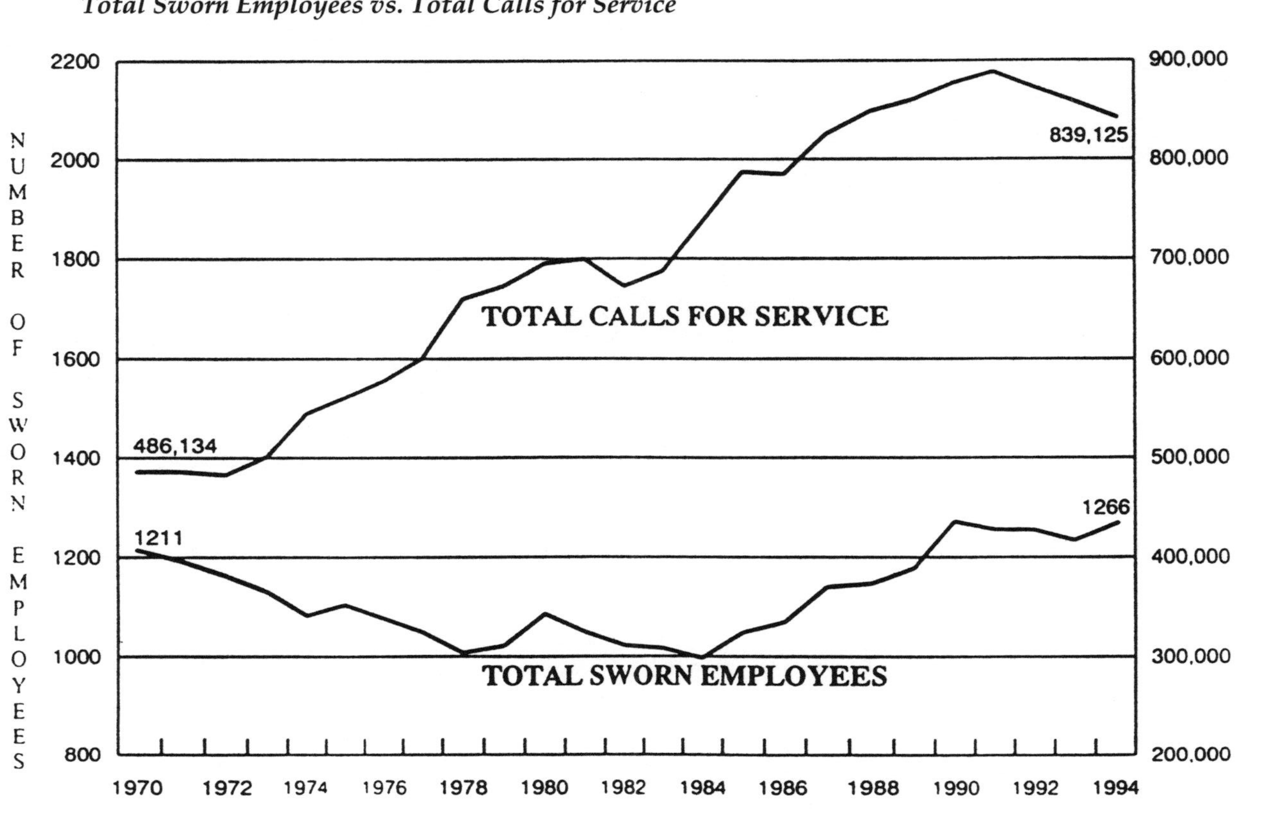

Source: Seattle Police Department 1994.

Notes

Chapter 1

1. In fact, the Seattle Police Department was awarded additional Weed and Seed funding for a second and then a third year. In addition to this money, by virtue of being a Weed and Seed site, Seattle was able to secure other grant funds, bringing the total Weed and Seed associated funding for Seattle in a three-year period to more than $4 million.

2. ACLU to Mayor Rice, 1992. More than four-fifths of the attendees were nonwhite, and most of these were African American.

3. The ballot initiative to return to a district council did not pass, and the recall drive did not get on the ballot. In response to citizen pressure for a district council, however, the city council itself has elected to make each member responsible for one or two neighborhood districts. There are 12 districts and nine council members.

4. *Seattle Times,* April 14, 1992 ("Weed and Seed: A Problem or a Solution," by Don Williamson).

5. A story from the *New York Times* reprinted in the *Providence Journal-Bulletin,* August 22, 1997 ("Critics: Brutality is Flip Side of New NY Police Policy").

6. *Washington Post,* weekly edition, July 21–28, 1990.

7. A story from the *Washington Post* reprinted in the *Providence Journal-Bulletin,* August 19, 1997 ("New York Police-Brutality Case Prompts Federal Civil-Rights Probe").

8. Foucault 1977: 80–87, contrasts the illegalities of property with the illegalities of rights; see also Reiman (1990), who contrasts the capacity of the system at every stage to favor mercy toward the already powerful and punishment for the power poor, and Kelling and Coles 1996. While the veracity of claims attributing this statement to the officer have subsequently been put in doubt, this does not change the fact that city and police leaders insisted there was no connection between community policing and police brutality. Even given the extent to which these leaders punished the officers involved, this remains a failure to construct a public discourse that connects police administration to police conduct or citizen fear of crime to fears of official misconduct.

9. See Tonry 1995 on foreseeable consequences as these reflect a similar failure of political leadership in the war on drugs.

10. *Seattle Police Department 1994 Annual Report.* 1994.

11. National Institute of Justice 1992.

12. Scott 1990.

13. Many thanks to the University of Michigan Press reviewer for our conversation regarding this point.

14. Ewick and Silbey 1995: 200–201.

15. Greenhouse, Yngvesson, and Engel (1994: 2) define discourse as "an interrelated set of cultural meanings—symbols, values, and conventionalized interpretations—that shape and make comprehensible the terms people use to converse in everyday life." My use of stories is close to the way these authors use the conversations between court officials and citizens; like these conversations, the stories I document here map out the mobilizations of conventionalized interpretations as well as countermobilizations contesting them. For this reason, I distinguish between competing stories about community and policing and examine how this discursive struggle contributes to the constitution of those interrelated sets of cultural meanings with political utility that we call discourses.

16. Lyons and McPherson 1998.

17. Wilson and Kelling 1982; Trojanowicz and Bucqueroux 1990; Kelling and Moore 1988; Reiders and Roberg 1990; Bayley 1988; Sherman 1997; Eck and Rosenbaum 1994; Bayley and Shearing 1996; Kelling and Coles 1996.

18. Cohen 1985.

19. In the 1997 Seattle Leadership Sessions, one officer candidly noted that "our windows were broken internally," arguing that before the problem solving era the department structure encouraged and rewarded unethical police behavior. Lyons and McPherson 1998.

20. Cohen 1985: 84–85.

21. Cohen 1985: 78.

22. Foucault 1977; Cohen 1985: 66. See also Handler 1990 on participatory exceptions.

23. Skogan 1988 contrasts preservationist and insurgent forms of community-based crime prevention organizations.

24. Kelling and Coles (1996: 3, 109, 222) discuss the politics of order maintenance as a discursive struggle to construct more persuasive stories when they disparage advocates for the homeless and recommend a strategy of renaming these individuals as disorderly. Kelling and Coles describe this discursive struggle in democratic terms when they note that "police and citizens negotiated a 'disorder threshold' for the neighborhood. They did not merely prohibit specific acts . . . but often defined the conditions and manner under which activities could be carried out" (17–18).

25. Skogan (1990) distinguished physical and social forms of disorder, though his focus was on disorders linked to the activities of the poor.

26. Foucault 1977: 177.

27. Foucault 1977: 189.

28. Foucault 1977: 200.

29. Foucault 1977: 213.

30. Foucault 1977: 214.

31. Foucault 1980: 220.

32. Giddens 1979: 93.

33. These four components of community policing were taken from the work of Skolnick and Bayley (1988).

Chapter 2

1. Wilson and Kelling 1982; Reiders and Roberg 1990; Trojanowicz and Bucqueroux 1990; Bayley 1988; Eck and Rosenbaum 1994; Goldstein 1990.

2. Crawford 1996: 250–54.

3. Lacey and Zedner 1995; Crawford 1996.

4. The earliest references to "community policing" as a single notion emerged within a subfield of police studies: police-community relations (Germann 1973). This subfield, like the creation of municipal police departments themselves, emerged in response to urban unrest and the discovery that existing mechanisms of social control were less equipped to manage this than was previously supposed (Walker 1977; Fogelson 1977; Kelling and Moore 1988).

5. Greene and Taylor 1988; Bayley 1988.

6. Lacey and Zedner 1995: 310.

7. Santos 1982.

8. Putnam 1993: 35–42.

9. On the republican visions of the founders, see Hanson 1985; on the possibility of cooperation, see Taylor 1982.

10. Mastrofski 1988; Manning 1988; Klockars 1988; Bayley 1988.

11. Exploiting gaps such as these can be a key component of political mobilization and can contribute to community building (see Scheingold 1974). It is also possible that, as Crawford (1996) argues, strong communities are criminogenic. My treatment of communities focuses on the reciprocal internal and external relationships that constitute forms of association with specified capacities. Seen this way, criminogenic communities are both inconsistent with the logic of community policing and with the possibility of more democratic forms of social control *in ways that can be identified and criticized.*

12. Crawford (1996: 254) argues that communitarians' failure to account for power imbalances allows them to celebrate community responsibility regardless of resource inequities, such that crime is constructed not as a political failure of government but as a moral failure of communities. Similarly, Lacey and Zedner (1995: 305) contend that community-based policing defuses problems of political legitimacy by reallocating responsibility for crime control to communities while simultaneously undermining "the very infrastructures that might be thought to make references to community meaningful."

13. Interview, 27.

14. Skogan 1990: 161.

15. Cohen 1979; Lacey and Zedner 1995.

16. Cohen 1979.

17. John Winthrop, citing Matt. 5:14, in "A Model of Christian Charity" (1988).

18. Hofstadter 1955.

19. Ericson, Haggerty, and Carrier 1993: 39; Holmes 1993.

20. Crawford 1996; Etzioni 1993; Dahrendorf 1985.

21. Etzioni 1993; Dahrendorf 1985; Wilson 1968; Kymlicka 1989.
22. Crawford 1996: 250–52.
23. Ericson, Haggerty, Carriere 1993: 39.
24. Okin 1989; Crawford 1996: 251.
25. While it is clearly unfair of me to imply that the communitarians themselves speak in such simplistic terms, it is not unrealistic to argue that their tendency to reduce liberalism to a communityless doctrine of extreme individualism and contrast this with our search for community contributes to such simplistic thinking. The reason I present it this way is to highlight the fact that the way they pose the question constructs a philosophical inquiry around a dilemma to which liberalism cannot, by definition, respond. They choose an aspect of the question that makes it appear to be a perennial question revisited: individual liberty or community? As Wittgenstein argues, however, perennial questions are more useful for keeping philosophers employed than for focusing our intellectual efforts on living. "The way to solve the problem you see in life is to live in a way that will make what is problematic disappear" (1937: 27).
26. Kymlicka 1989: 254.
27. Kymlicka 1989: 253.
28. Kymlicka 1989: 254.
29. Kymlicka 1989: 19.
30. Kymlicka 1989: 85.
31. Kymlicka 1989: 90.
32. Crawford 1996: 251. "He [Etzioni] chooses to ignore the contemporary (and historical) research literature on the horrors which lie behind domestic bliss. It is as if decades of feminist research on gender-based violence has been neatly and conveniently brushed under the 'family' carpet."
33. Kymlicka 1989: 90.
34. Taylor 1982: 53–59.
35. Tinder 1991: 100.
36. Ackelsberg 1992; Okin 1989.
37. Ackelsberg 1992.
38. Okin 1991.
39. The concept of being drawn into another's movie comes from *The Electric Kool-Aid Acid Test* (Wolfe 1969).
40. Lacey and Zedner 1995: 305.
41. On soccer hooliganism, see Crawford 1996. See *Eyes on the Prize: Fighting Back* for a visual introduction to the meaning of mobilized community groups in opposition to the implementation of *Brown v. Board of Education.* See *The 18th Brumaire of Louis Bonaparte,* (Marx 1852: 76) where Marx describes the use by Bonaparte of his community-based Society of December 10 as his own private mass army mobilized by state-initiated fears of disorder.
42. Skogan (1990: 124) argues that this conflation of state agency trumps democratic interaction, allowing police officers and chiefs to avoid confronting views that conflict with their own and further weakening the possibility of accountability. It also becomes less clear what accountability means, since these partnerships "dispel the idea that crime is the problem of government" (Lacey and Zedner 1995).

43. Walker 1983: 390–406; McCann 1986; Scheingold 1974.
44. Abel 1982; Harrington 1985.
45. Taylor 1982.
46. Polsky 1991: 120.
47. Polsky 1991.
48. See Donovan 1980 and Greenstone and Peterson 1973 (225–315) on Community Action Programs. Greenstone and Peterson conclude that the experience with Community Action Programs reveals the tensions inherent in reforms claiming to be both community based and efficient. The effort failed to generate the level of participation by the poor necessary for community control because, in the end, it and local political institutions favored the certainty of rule through bureaucratic expertise over the indeterminacy of community activism. Greenstone and Peterson argue that what critics missed was the importance of the power relations that underlie local politics. Specifically, they overlooked the disjuncture between forms of association that recognize citizenship based on bureaucratic classifications, such as income level, and other forms of citizenship and identity, such as race, which challenge existing power relations by positing the possibility of alternative forms of political association and community.
49. Polsky 1991: 130. Polsky argues that modern caring professions, "while professing support for government responsiveness and accountability, mounted a strong attack on participation, condemning it as incompatible with the maintenance of social order under modern conditions."
50. Sennett 1970.
51. It might be argued that this robs the concept of its historical specificity, losing the sociological thrust of Tocqueville. While it is true that the definition of community is most meaningful in a specific historical context, as Hanson argues about the definition of democracy, this does not preclude the identification of characteristics common to various particular stories about communities. For democracy, Hanson identifies as a core characteristic that the stories about democracy be democratically achieved. For communities to be capable of informal social controls, the core characteristic is reciprocity, which has traditionally been built on direct and multifaceted forms of local association.
52. Taylor 1982: 25–29; italics in the original.
53. Taylor 1982.
54. Social movements can generate this sense of community as a resource for mobilization for the limited periods when activism is high, interaction routine and direct, and relations between participants multifaceted (Goodwyn 1978). Existing communities can mobilize this resource to encourage members to defer immediate payoffs and value more highly future payoffs, such as those that were finally achieved in the Buffalo Creek Disaster (Stern 1976).
55. Fraser 1992.
56. See the discussion in Fleissner, Fedan, and Stotland 1991 about the stages a community must go through before it can cooperate with the police department. This is also consistent with Skogan's (1988) distinction between preservationist and insurgent crime prevention groups.
57. The substitution of private resources in the resolution of collective action

problems is discussed by Mancur Olson (1965) as the provision of selective benefits and is one example of how private resources can substitute for the weakness of communities. Since corporations and other large organizations can also threaten communities, there are no reasons, other than pith, parsimony, and presentation, for me to limit my attention to state agents.

58. Lacey and Zedner 1995; Taylor 1982; Hanson 1985; Lustig 1982.

59. Coleman 1988: S98.

60. Sale 1976; Putnam 1993.

61. Tonry (1995) suggests a Rawlsian formulation of this idea when he argues that police reformers have an obligation to ensure that new policy initiatives will be structured to minimize harm to the already least advantaged (and most criminally victimized) communities. Braithwaite's (1989) valuable work on reintegrative shaming is another case in which respecting the integrity of intercommunity and intracommunity relations supports policing reforms that enable communities with the sought-after informal social control capacities. Intracommunity reciprocity refers to the relationships among members of a single community; intercommunity reciprocity refers to relationships with members of other communities, including members of police departments. This cannot be construed as a replication of the pluralist error of treating state agents as just another group because the treatment of police departments as a community in this context makes explicit their responsibility to manifestly respect (in their stories and practices) intra/inter community reciprocity.

62. Sennett 1970; Sale 1976.

63. Evans and Boyte 1982: 56.

64. Crawford (1996) and others refer to this as semiautonomy.

65. Habermas 1989.

66. Katznelson 1981; Polsky 1991; Cohen 1979.

67. Boyte 1992: 211.

68. Sennett 1970.

69. Boyte (1992: 212) identifies the need to revitalize publics in three specific and interdependent ways: as deliberative bodies, as problem solvers, and as an insurgent force.

70. Spitzer 1982.

71. Hanson 1985; Lustig 1982; Cohen and Rogers 1986.

72. Katznelson 1981.

73. Katznelson 1981: 42–44; Tomlins 1994: 38; Lustig 1982: 47.

74. Katznelson 1981: 36.

75. Katznelson, citing Tilly 1981: 42.

76. Santos 1982: 261.

Chapter 3

1. Skolnick and Bayley 1988: 1–19. Skogan (1990: 91–92) also argues that community policing has no fixed set of program components but is only a general agreement on a set of guiding principles: problem orientation, two-way

communication with citizens, responsiveness to citizen demands, and helping neighbors help themselves.

2. Skolnick and Bayley 1988: 23–33.

3. Skolnick and Bayley 1988: 23–31.

4. Skolnick and Bayley 1988: 32.

5. Walker 1984; Manning 1988; Tomlins 1993.

6. Tomlins 1993: 5–7; Walker 1977, 1980.

7. Tomlins 1993: 19–20.

8. Muir 1977; Klockars 1985; Sadd and Grinc 1994.

9. Tomlins 1993: 6–7; italics in the original. For a related treatment of the history of policing, see Foucault 1988.

10. Appleby 1993: 36.

11. One consequence of the emergence of the modern industrial state has been the decline of communities. Without strong communities, stories today about police departments (re)turning to the community would seem to lack a meaningful empirical referent. Professional policing and its extension as community policing is insulated only from certain types of political influence. Political influence from within the professional law enforcement bureaucracy (most powerfully in the form of federal funding opportunities) has increased as political influence from citizens and neighborhood political leaders has decreased. Further, the seeming absence of an empirical referent, it turns out, is an empirical void that is filled with the particular segments of local communities most willing to uncritically cooperate with police departments.

12. I am not arguing that state-centered discourses are always disciplinary or that self-governing discourses are always more democratic. Tomlins's two categories are used here to identify competing discourses about policing and to highlight the power relations woven within the prevailing state-centered discourse about policing reform. While prevailing stories obscure more decentered stories about policing, both stories can support policing activities that are disciplinary or democratic. Demonstrating this claim is central to my work. There are, however, illustrations from America's communitarian tradition of policing (vigilantism, citizen councils, exclusionary zoning) that provide a prima facie case for understanding each discourse as a resource that can be mobilized in democratizing or disciplinary ways.

13. Greene and Mastrofski 1988; Rosenbaum 1994.

14. Wilson and Kelling 1982; Reiders and Roberg 1990; Wilson 1983.

15. Goldstein 1990: 21.

16. Manning 1977; Klockars 1985; Muir 1977.

17. Eck and Rosenbaum (1994) redefine these standard terms, for purposes I consider momentarily, as crime control, emergency aid, serving justice, and nonemergency services.

18. Eck and Rosenbaum 1994: 8.

19. These efforts often rely on professional law enforcement, where police saturate an area for a short time and then wait for citizens to reclaim their neighborhoods. One drawback of this approach is that in neighborhoods with

long and consistently unsatisfying experiences with government programs that enlist their participation and then dry up due to a lack of funding or a change of administration these efforts to reduce fear end up replacing fear with a combination of fear and anger that can generate officer hostility toward citizens who eschew partnerships and are perceived by officers to be apathetic. See Sadd and Grinc 1994: 44–47.

20. Eck and Rosenbaum 1994: 9.

21. Eck and Rosenbaum 1994: 10.

22. Eck and Rosenbaum 1994: 12–17.

23. Kelling and Moore 1988: 6.

24. Kelling and Moore 1988: 6.

25. Kelling and Moore 1988: 19–22. Order maintenance, in contrast to law enforcement, refers to those gray areas of policing such as disorderly conduct, neighborhood noise problems, or teenagers hanging out in a park. It is a gray area because it is often unclear what constitutes disorder or good policing. Statutory language is often vague, and police officers, especially when operating without community support, have limited tools for managing disorder. The professional model encourages officers to either dismiss these as social work and not law enforcement or to enforce the law, that is, arrest someone, which can often escalate an order maintenance situation. For a good discussion of this dilemma, see Wilson 1968.

26. Kelling 1985: 300.

27. Kelling 1985: 306; Kelling, Wasserman, and Williams 1988: 4.

28. Wilson and Kelling 1982: 43.

29. Wilson and Kelling 1982: 32. This cooperation takes the form of citizen councils, block watches, or other community-based organizations that provide the police with a pool of volunteer labor, access to locally specific information, and residents who can apply significant pressure on drug dealers—and on mayors, city councils, and state legislatures in support of police budget requests (Wilson and Kelling 1989: 51). This helps departments by reducing labor and information-gathering costs, pressuring local elected officials for additional funding, and making more federal funding available. Departments interested in experimenting with community policing have access to generous amounts of Department of Justice funding. The Seattle Police Department, in its initial Weed and Seed grant proposal, placed heavy emphasis on the department's community policing program. That grant eventually brought more than $4 million to the SPD. The South Seattle Crime Reduction Project, which preceded the Weed and Seed grants and was the catalyst for community policing in Seattle, was also funded by the DOJ.

30. Goldstein 1990: 26.

31. Goldstein 1990: 24–27. "[I]n such situations, [officers should] work with those specific segments of the community that are in a position to assist in reducing or eliminating the problem."

32. Walker 1977: 7; Trojanowicz and Bucqueroux 1990; Sherman 1986.

33. Fogelson 1977: 20–21.

34. Katznelson 1976; Trojanowicz and Bucqueroux 1990: 42, 44–46. According to Samuel Walker (1977: 5): "Businessmen, concerned about the safety of their property, took the initiative. During the 1854 election riots [in St. Louis] they mobilized a volunteer vigilante force to guard the city."

35. Fogelson 1977: 17–19; Walker 1977: 8–9.

36. Fogelson 1977: 19.

37. Fogelson 1977: 19.

38. Fogelson 1977: 32–38.

39. Fogelson 1977: 42.

40. According to Walker (1977: 94), reform stories focused initially on both crime prevention and law enforcement. In the 1930s, professional law enforcement came to dominate and stories about crime prevention withered.

41. Sherman 1986: 354–60. The single-complaint strategy refers to the system in which police patrol in automobiles, waiting for the radio dispatcher to direct them to a crime scene on the basis of a single phoned-in complaint. The assumption is that police can be visible in a larger area, thus deterring criminal behavior, and also, by increasing response times, they can more effectively fight crime.

42. Sherman 1986 (emphasis added); Skolnick and Fyfe 1993: 145. For other representative discussions of these studies see Goldstein 1990: 8–11; Walker 1984: 77; Trojanowicz 1990: 43; and Kelling and Moore 1988: 15–17.

43. Conversations with officers in the SPD indicates to me that long ago patrol officers recognized the ineffectiveness of random patrol and modified this patrol strategy by randomly patrolling hot spots in anticipation of criminal activity.

44. Kelling 1992.

45. Greene and Klockars 1991; Klockars 1985; Manning 1977.

46. Klockars 1985; Muir 1977; Manning, 1977; Handler 1990.

47. Klockars 1988: 250.

48. Klockars 1985: 317. Disorder statutes that have survived Supreme Court scrutiny are further from the ideal of clear and unambiguous prohibitions such as those against Part I crimes. This means that order maintenance activities are more open to criticism and more likely to politicize those areas of criminal law that have the lowest levels of social consensus, and for these reasons a more systematic attention to order maintenance activities will mean increasing officer discretion in precisely those areas furthest from the reach of current formal mechanisms of command and control. For an excellent discussion of these issues, see Wilson 1968.

49. Klockars 1985: 317.

50. Farrell 1988: 76.

51. Wycoff 1988: 115; see also Trojanowicz 1990: 7.

52. Muir 1977; Handler 1990.

53. Sadd and Grinc 1994: 50; Greene and Mastrofski 1988. Seattle is an exception.

54. On New York City, see Farrell 1988 and Weisburd and McElroy 1988; on

Houston, see Oettmeier and Brown 1988; on Baltimore, see Cordner 1988. On Portland, Minneapolis, St. Louis, Los Angeles, and Savannah, see Fleissner, Fedan, and Stotland 1991; see also Sadd and Grinc 1994.

55. Skolnick and Bayley 1988: 49; Skogan 1990.

56. Oettmeier and Brown 1988.

57. Mastrofski 1988: 66.

58. Manning 1988. Crank 1994.

59. Greene and Taylor 1988; Rosenbaum 1994.

60. Wycoff 1988. Rosenbaum 1994.

61. Klockars 1988; Manning 1988.

62. Wilson and Kelling 1982.

63. Mencke, White, and Carey 1982.

64. Block 1971: 91–100; Black 1991: 341. Sadd and Grinc (1994: 44–46) find that in eight cities experimenting with community policing citizens are afraid of both the unaccountable power of gangs and of police officers in their neighborhoods.

65. Manning 1984, as cited in Greene and Taylor 1988: 204.

66. Greene and Taylor 1988: 205.

67. Walker 1984.

68. Wilson 1968; Kelling and Moore 1988. In this context, using *traditional* as a neutral descriptive (meaning existing) is unacceptably confusing. In an otherwise superb piece, Sadd and Grinc (1994: 38) also replace *professional* with *traditional,* allowing them to attribute the professional arrest fetish to the police subculture rather than to the professional administration that spawned both the fetish and the subculture. They also criticize the lack of formal coordination in the eight cities they analyze rather than praising the more informal and personalized coordination that actually did emerge in these experiments and would be seen as a promising achievement were it not that this is inconsistent with the professional ideal of formal forms of coordination among state agents (41). Further, they find that citizens lack knowledge of this Department of Justice program, though it seems unlikely that any of us would have this kind of knowledge about most federal government initiatives that routinely impact our lives, thus leaving us with a question: other than to the bureaucrats filling in the reports no one will read, is it more significant to know what citizens know about one short-term program or to know what citizens think should be done to strengthen their communities and how current police practices might encourage or block these efforts?

69. Eck and Rosenbaum 1994: 5.

70. Eck and Rosenbaum 1994: 11.

71. Eck and Rosenbaum 1994: 14–15.

72. Prevailing constructions of problem solving also empower-state-centered discourses about policing. By defining partnerships as operational only, police exclude legitimate community concerns about the agency itself (such as about patterns of misconduct or corruption) and ignore potential long-term impacts on the problem-solving capacity of weaker communities from short-term, police-initiated, problem-solving efforts.

73. Skogan 1990: 108.
74. Tonry 1995.
75. Braithwaite 1989.

Chapter 4

1. Reiss 1986: 17–18.
2. Reiss 1986: 20.
3. Reiss 1986: 23.
4. Schuerman and Kobrin 1986: 93–94.
5. Schuerman and Kobrin 1986: 99; Sennett 1970.
6. Altshuler (1971) persuasively defends community control as consistent with the American ethos and African American empowerment. A local African American activist observed that community policing could be of tremendous assistance to the African American community, but community policing should mean enhanced community control and public accountability. Then it may improve public safety *in a way* that strengthens African American communities. (Interview, 29:6).
7. Sale 1976: 5.
8. *Seattle Times,* October 26, 1993.
9. *Seattle Weekly,* March 27, 1991 ("Valley Forging," by Eric Scigliano).
10. *Seattle Weekly,* March 27, 1991.
11. Sale 1976: 33–37.
12. Sale 1976: 80–85.
13. Sale 1976: 108.
14. Stone 1988.
15. The Bogue Plan was an ambitious set of recommendations presented by civil engineer Virgil Bogue to the city council, and through the council to the voters. The plan included a civic center, a public transportation system, and large increases in green space (including the suggestion that the city eventually acquire Mercer Island and turn it into a "people's playground, worthy of the city of millions which will someday surround Lake Washington" (Bogue's words). The Bogue Plan was defeated by a ratio of almost two to one. According to Sale, "Seattle was becoming various Seattle's, and, by and large, the Seattle of the wealthy just dropped away" (1976: 95–105).
16. Sale 1976: 107.
17. Sale 1976: 193.
18. Sale 1976: 233; *Seattle Weekly,* March 27, 1991.
19. *Seattle Post-Intelligencer,* February 18, 1974 ("Columbia City Caught in Web of Crime: Trouble is That People Are Living in Fear," by Linda Rockey).
20. Sale 1976: 249.
21. *Seattle Weekly,* March 27, 1991.
22. "Southeast Seattle Revitalization Plan" 1991.
23. "Southeast Seattle Background Report" 1989: 7.
24. Fleissner, Fedan, and Stotland 1991: 48.
25. "Southeast Seattle Background Report" 1989: 15.

26. Interview, 37:1.

27. "Southeast Seattle Background Report" 1989: 18–20.

28. A 1988 study by a University of Chicago sociologist found that Seattle remains one of America's most segregated cities (*Seattle Times,* November 23, 1988 ["Seattle Gets Poor Marks in Survey of Segregation" by Alex Tizon]). City voters rejected an open housing ordinance by a ratio of two to one (Sale 1976: 218).

29. Sale 1976: 216.

30. *Seattle Post-Intelligencer,* October 25, 1991 ("Dispute Over Store Settled: Mayor Orders an End to City's Campaign to Revoke Liquor License," by Steven Goldsmith); *Seattle Post-Intelligencer,* July 17, 1983 ("Asians Bring New Look to the Rainier Valley," by Don Tewkesbury); *Seattle Times,* December 8, 1979 ("The Rainier Valley: A River of Memories," by Don Duncan); *Seattle Times,* October 23, 1977 ("Judkins-Rejected Area Not Rejected Anymore," by Salley Gene Mahoney).

31. Sale 1976: 218.

32. "Southeast Seattle Background Report" 1989.

33. "Southeast Seattle Revitalization Plan" 1991: 6. Due to the inclusion of different census tracts, this number used in the "Revitalization Plan" is slightly different from the numbers in table 2.

34. *Seattle Weekly,* November 7, 1990 ("Drug War on First Avenue," by Eric Scigliano).

35. Sale 1976: 181.

36. Sale 1976: 182–83.

37. Sale 1976: 188–92.

38. Sale 1976: 232.

39. *Seattle Weekly,* March 27, 1991.

40. *Seattle Times,* November 12, 1990 ("Columbia City Isn't Safe, Blind Student Says," by Diane Brooks).

41. *Seattle Times,* March 14, 1991 ("South End Gets Fewer Loans," by Dick Lilly).

42. *Seattle Times,* October 24, 1991 ("How Bank-Loan Rules Can Affect Minorities," by Michele Matassa Flores).

43. "Southeast Seattle Background Report" 1989: 12.

44. "Southeast Seattle Action Plan" 1991: 12.

45. "Southeast Seattle Action Plan" 1991: 14. The report states that there are 60 to 65 human service agencies in Rainier Valley, with proposals to add a new parole office, substance abuse center, alcohol treatment program, and special needs housing. In my interview with Tom Lattimore of SEED, he told me that this concentration was due in large part to the failure of the Housing Authority to market these certificates as aggressively in other parts of the city. This seems unlikely, since residents can choose where to live. It seems more likely that the concentration reflects the state of the private rental market there, which, this section argues, is largely a legacy of choices made in the decades following World War II.

46. See *Seattle Weekly,* March 27, 1991, and October 6, 1992, on the freeway.

See *Seattle Times,* November 26, 1993, on the call for district level elections; and *Seattle Times,* February 22, 1992, on minority opposition to redistricting.

47. "Southeast Seattle Revitalization Plan" 1991: 46.

48. "Southeast Seattle Action Plan" 1989: 13. According to the Rainier Chamber of Commerce, there is a real debate in the valley on this question. Some, like one of the founders of the SSCPC, Lou DeFranco, oppose all social services in Rainier Valley. The chamber's position, however, is that it is better to have a probation office to monitor felons than not to monitor them. The chamber focuses on the lack of positive public facilities, like a cultural center, and private facilities like a theater.

49. *Seattle Post-Intelligencer,* July 17, 1983; *Seattle Times,* October 23, 1977.

50. *Seattle Times,* December 8, 1979.

51. *Seattle Times,* November 12, 1990 ("Columbia City Isn't Safe, Blind Student Says," by Diane Brooks).

52. *Seattle Weekly,* March 27, 1991.

53. *Seattle Times,* September 9, 1991 ("New School Another Sign of Bloom Back in Judkins," by Steven Goldsmith).

54. *Seattle Times,* October 6, 1992 ("State, Tenants in Dispute Over Rent," by Constantine Angelos).

55. Fleissner, Fedan, and Stotland 1991: 48.

56. The Fleissner, Fedan, and Stotland report (1991) views this as an outgrowth of a 1984 subcommittee of Mayor Royer's Economic Renewal Task Force of the Rainier Valley, but the state Secretary of State's Office lists the Crime Prevention League as having been incorporated as a nonprofit in 1981.

57. Interview, 19; Interview, 34; *Seattle Times,* August 22, 1992 ("City, Nightclub Owner Spar," by Kate Shatzkin).

58. Fleissner, Fedan, and Stotland 1991: 51–52.

59. *Seattle Weekly,* March 27, 1991.

60. Hearde made this comment at the Ultimate Convention—the final meeting of SESCO—but it was quoted in the *Seattle Times* on June 24, 1978 ("Neighborhood Says Leave Us Alone," by Wendy Walker) and in the *Seattle Sun* on June 28, 1978 ("Feds Look into Urban Districts").

61. This is based on my observations of the SESCO Ultimate Convention on September 27, 1991.

62. In 1990, 41 percent of minority children from the valley were bussed north, while just 17 percent of white children from the north were bussed into the valley. The effect was to keep underenrolled northeast schools open and dangerously reduce enrollment in southeast schools, which hurt communities built around the multifaceted interactions that come with a thriving neighborhood school. See *Seattle Weekly,* March 27, 1991.

63. SEED information packet.

64. Interview, 17:2.

65. Interview, 17:3. Lattimore also commented that the South Precinct commander expressed strong support for the project upon learning that it would include the Southend's first Starbucks coffee shop.

66. SEED information packet.

67. "Southeast Seattle Action Plan" 1991: 34.

68. *Seattle Weekly,* March 27, 1991.

69. *Seattle Times,* May 3, 1991 ("Mayor's Call for Action Cheers Rainier Valley," by Dick Lilly).

70. In a speech to the City Club, the mayor asserted that he intended to address both the "reasons for and results of" crime by "throwing out the either/or way of thinking" and adding police, penalties, social services, and citizen activism because "creating a safer and stronger community is going to require that we do all these things." *Seattle Times,* June 18, 1993 ("Improved Public Safety Requires a Multi-Level Approach, Says Mayor," by Helen Jung).

71. *Seattle Times,* October 1, 1993 ("Public Safety Top Issue in Rice, Stern Debate," by Dick Lilly); *Seattle Times,* May 9, 1993 ("This Year's List of Winners"). Initiative 593 required that third-time violent offenders be sentenced to life without parole.

72. *Seattle Times,* October 27, 1991 ("Rice Unveils Loan Program to Boost Two Communities," by Ronald Fitten).

73. *Seattle Times,* July 9, 1993 ("Rice's 'Village' Plan Promises a Boom in Southeast Seattle," by Sally Macdonald).

74. *Seattle Times,* March 19, 1993 ("SEED Money for City's Southeast Section," by Constantine Angelos).

75. *Seattle Times,* October 12, 1992 ("Mayor, Banker Issue Challenge," by Dick Lilly).

76. *Seattle Times,* March 14, 1991 ("Male Teens: Gun Deaths Exceed All Natural Causes," by Paul Taylor); *Seattle Times,* May 3, 1991 ("Mayor's Call for Action Cheers Rainier Valley," by Dick Lilly); *Seattle Times,* May 26, 1992 ("Bank to Offer Economic Uplift," by Dick Lilly).

77. *Seattle Times,* May 3, 1991.

78. The program distributes $1.5 million per year (with $275,000 reserved for projects of less than $5,000). In 1992, eight southeast groups received a total of $255,000 for projects ranging from $10,000 to design a new performance hall, to $22,000 for SEED, to $63,000 for Powerful Schools, an innovative local effort in the valley to pool the resources from four adjoining schools to make their facilities available for after-school and evening activities. Community members organizing Powerful Schools hope to improve public education and make it possible for their neighborhood schools to become cornerstones of a stronger community. See *Seattle Times,* May 13, 1993 ("Small Grants for Big Help," by Sally Macdonald).

Chapter 5

1. Skogan 1988.

2. Skogan 1988. Sherman (1986: 374) also highlights the relationship between community groups and state agency, arguing that state attempts to organize community are hard to sustain because they tend to lack the participation of key neighborhood leaders and citizen efforts fail because they lack government support.

3. Scheingold 1991: 62–66.

4. Skogan 1990.

5. "You can't sit around and wait for 20 years for the neighborhood to change back. It's gotta be now" (Interview, 34:3). Jon Daykin has an master's degree in sociology from the University of Mississippi and has done graduate work in criminology at the University of Washington and George Williams College (from an Operation Results information sheet).

6. Interview, 34.

7. Interview, 34:1; Davis et al. 1991: 46; *Beacon Hill News,* July 3, 1991 ("Crime-Fighting Group Gets Results," by Peter Clarke).

8. The hot line sometimes averaged as many as 40 calls per week (Davis et al. 1991: 48). One member of Operation Results called their operation "an extra set of eyes for the police" (*Beacon Hill News,* July 3, 1991). This information was also used to assist Operation Results when it lobbied the city council or state legislature for passage of tougher crime control legislation such as the Drug Traffic Loitering Ordinance (Davis et al. 1991: 48–49).

9. Interview, 34:1.

10. Craig Detmer to Jon Daykin, February 5, 1990.

11. *Beacon Hill News,* November 23, 1989 ("We Are Not Vigilantes," by John Colwell).

12. Interview, 34:2. Daykin identified Candace Carrol as the administrator, Arthur Wilson as a man with street sense, and himself as the problem solver.

13. Interview, 34:1. Some other community leaders suspect that Operation Results was more Jon Daykin the maverick than a community group. In nearly every conversation I had about this group, including those with Daykin, the word *vigilante* was mentioned without any prompting from me.

14. Interview, 34:1.

15. Davis et al. 1991: 41.

16. *Seattle Post-Intelligencer,* May 1, 1992.

17. Davis et al. 1991: 43.

18. Interview, 34:3. The general thrust of this observation was confirmed by the Neighborhood Crime and Justice Center.

19. *Beacon Hill News,* November 23, 1989. Praise from Veldwyk appears in this same article. Praise from Norm Chamberlain appears in the *Seattle Post-Intelligencer,* May 1, 1992 ("Some Take a Dim View of Point of Light Winner," by Steven Goldsmith). For a brief time, Jon Daykin was the Hillman City Neighborhood Association's representative on the SSCPC.

20. *Seattle Post-Intelligencer,* April 17, 1992 ("Crime Busters," by Steven Goldsmith).

21. Margaret Pageler to Operation Results, April 17, 1992.

22. *Seattle Post-Intelligencer,* May 1, 1992.

23. Derived from personal correspondence from Daykin to Shubert, April 21,1992, and from Daykin's attorney to Shubert April 22, 1992. Daykin was eventually allowed to receive the award from President Bush as originally planned, on May 1, 1992, despite a letter and fax campaign against him from other members of the Rainier Valley community.

24. *Seattle Post-Intelligencer,* April 17, 1992. The president of the Columbia City Neighborhood Association called Daykin a "wacko." Kay Godefroy and area merchants echoed this sentiment when Godefroy said: "He markets himself very well. I think he's envisioning making a living at this" (*Seattle Post-Intelligencer,* May 1, 1992).

25. Interview, 34. Daykin's split with this group led to the incorporation of Operation Results as a nonprofit organization in December 1989.

26. Interview, 34:2–5.

27. *Seattle Times,* January 13, 1994. The reverse sting netted 14 arrests of drug buyers, most of whom were from outside the Rainier Valley corridor and white.

28. Chambliss 1978.

29. *Seattle Times,* June 26, 1992 ("Holly Park Puts Spotlight on Crime," by Peyton Whitely).

30. Davis et al. 1991: 74.

31. A search of the *Seattle Times* in the period 1987–88 found 19 articles about Neighbors Against Drugs.

32. In *Rules for Radicals* (1971), Alinsky recommends personalizing the struggle in this way in a chapter entitled "Tactics."

33. The biggest rallies were held on December 1, 1988, at the Seattle Municipal Building and on November 21, 1987, at Van Asselt Playground, which is across the street from the South Precinct Station. There are no reliable estimates of the size of these rallies, but Frank LaChance remembers that most of the Neighbors Against Drugs rallies at this time attracted more than 100 local citizens. In addition to these rallies, the group used several marches on crack houses in various neighborhoods as forums to attack the chief. The largest of these were held on May 22 and June 12, 1988. The rallies or marches listed here are only those that I can confirm from newspaper searches. Interested parties claim that there were several more. LaChance recalls marching on a different crack house each weekend for perhaps two months, but there are no public records for these.

34. Interview, 19:1–2.

35. *Seattle Times,* January 12, 1988.

36. Interview, 19:3–5; Interview, 8:5; *Seattle Times,* December 2, 1988 ("Neighborhood Groups Call for More Action on Drugs and Gangs," by Joe Haberstroh).

37. Interview, 19:4–5.

38. *Seattle Times,* February 19, 1988 (Police Chief Says Raids Will Continue but Activists and Family of Slain Man Want Answers," by Dave Birkland).

39. *Seattle Times,* February 19, 1988.

40. *Seattle Times,* February 19, 1988.

41. In one crack house, LaChance reports that the owner was getting $750 a month when even $350 would have been high (Interview, 19:1).

42. Interview, 19:2. See also *Seattle Times,* December 9, 1988 ("The Fear of Gangs," by Marsha King), for a statement of the group's commitment to bringing people together.

43. The most distant group appeared in Yakima, Washington (*Seattle Times,*

May 19, 1988 ("Yakima: Eye of the Needle," by Mark Matassa). Within Seattle, but in the Northend, some citizens in Ballard similarly chose to adopt the Neighbors Against Drugs model. They held a large public meeting to criticize the police chief on January 11, 1988, and invited Frank LaChance to speak. See *Seattle Times*, January 12, 1988 ("Frustration Erupts at Anti-drug Meeting," by Anne Christensen). LaChance noted a group in the Garfield neighborhood (Interview, 6). The *Seattle Times* reported that the Central Area also formed a Neighbors Against Drugs group.

44. Interview, 19:1.

45. LaChance chaired the Abandoned Vehicle Committee.

46. Interview, 19:3. An SSCPC founder agreed (Interview, 11:2).

47. Interview, 19:3.

48. Interview, 19:5.

49. Chief Fitzsimons did this in a response to Neighbors Against Drugs criticism. Similarly, in a speech to the City Club, the chief cited a rise in search warrants from 81 in 1985 to 447 in 1987, a rise in felony arrests from 807 to 3,101, and an increase in calls for service of 400,000 since 1971, while the number of officers had been reduced (*Seattle Times*, January 15, 1988 ["Police Chief Takes Offensive, Demands Help in Drug Battle," by Richard Seven]).

50. Interview, 19:5. LaChance sites a recent blackout in downtown Seattle as evidence that it is not just too few officers. It is too few officers on the street. (During the blackout, officers were pulled from desk jobs and put back on the street, and expected crime problems did not materialize.)

51. *Pacific Magazine*, May 7, 1989.

52. *Pacific Magazine*, May 7, 1989.

53. It later changed its name to the Seattle Neighborhood Group.

54. Interview, 27:1.

55. Fleissner, Fedan, and Stotland 1991.

56. *Seattle Times*, July 17, 1974 ("Court Watch: Volunteers on Lookout for Lenient Sentencing," by Ross Anderson).

57. *Seattle Times*, April 24, 1975 ("Hanson Asks Study of Judge's Practices," by Larry Brown).

58. *Seattle Post-Intelligencer*, June 10, 1976 ("Group Rates Judges on Basis of Sentencing," by Stan Nast); *Seattle Times*, June 9, 1976 ("Eight of 29 Judges Rated Unacceptable"). For similar treatment of this group, see Fleissner, Fedan, and Stotland 1991 and Scheingold 1991. While the prosecutor, Christopher Bailey, supported this citizens' group (he was pushing for sentencing reforms to constrain judicial discretion), the Washington State Bar Association was opposed, and several judges spoke out against the group as a dangerous threat to democracy and the rule of law (*Seattle Times*, July 27, 1974).

59. Interview, 15:1.

60. *Seattle Times*, April 29, 1982 ("South Seattle is Safe," letter to the editor by Buzz Anderson).

61. Interview, 32:18; Interview, 29:1; Fleissner, Fedan, and Stotland 1991; Interview, 27.

62. *Pacific Magazine*, May 7, 1989.

63. *Pacific Magazine,* May 7, 1989.

64. Fleissner, Fedan, and Stotland 1991: 54–55. The Criminal Trespass Program involved citizens persuading business and property owners to sign an agreement with the SPD to (1) allow officers to enter their premises without first seeking the owner's permission and (2) promise to cooperate with the police in the prosecution. The program also involved citizens posting signs and included efforts to transfer some pay phones to call-out only.

65. Interview, 27:6. Larry Montgomery, vice president of SEED and president of the Rainier Valley District Council, agreed with this assessment of the chief. Montgomery argued that, since "Fitzsimons is from New York, he's seen [police corruption], so he's kind of cautious in that regard. He still doesn't like his officers doing drug buys and drug busts and stuff. He's still kind of leery about that" (Interview, 31). It may be this belief in professional law enforcement that led council member Jane Noland to say: "I don't think Fitzsimons is open to anything. I think he's a brilliant politician who has outlasted his usefulness here. And I've been very open about saying that. I mean I think he's a real big part of the problem" (Interview, 26).

66. Fleissner, Fedan, and Stotland 1991: 63–64.

67. Interview, 27:21.

68. SSCPC minutes. Since the SSCPC is the central focus of this study, the composition question will be taken up in greater detail in chapter 7.

69. *Pacific Magazine*, May 7, 1989.

70. Interview, 32:4.

71. Fleissner, Fedan, and Stotland 1991: 160–63.

72. Skogan 1988: 39.

73. Abel 1982: 9–10.

74. Scheingold 1991: 62–66.

Chapter 6

1. Seattle Police Department 1982: 18–32.

2. Morgan 1960: 73.

3. Morgan 1960.

4. Morgan 1960: 81.

5. Morgan 1960: 82.

6. Morgan 1960: 88.

7. Morgan 1960: 91.

8. Seattle Police Department 1982: 20.

9. Chief Rogers said at the time: "I can hardly overstate its assistance . . . equivalent to an increase of 35% in the number of patrolmen" (Seattle Police Relief Association 1900: 15).

10. Seattle Police Department 1982: 31.

11. Skogan (1990: 88–89) argues that police departments turn away from order maintenance and toward law enforcement when organizational reforms structure departments in such a way that order maintenance becomes inefficient, unprofessional, and inconsistent with bureaucratic needs.

12. Seattle Police Relief Association 1900: 17.
13. Seattle Police Relief Association 1900: 13.
14. Seattle Police Relief Association 1900: 13.
15. Seattle Police Department 1923.
16. Seattle Police Department 1923.
17. Seattle Police Department 1923; italics added.
18. Seattle Police Department 1923. For a public health approach to drugs and violence currently responding to this imbalance in the Seattle area, see Krieger 1994.
19. Seattle Police Department 1923.
20. For the details of how the payoff system worked, see Chambliss 1978.
21. Chambliss 1978: 33–49.
22. Chambliss 1978.
23. Chambliss 1978: 91.
24. Chambliss 1978: 72.
25. Chambliss 1978: 130.
26. Chambliss 1978: 117–25. See also Scheingold (1991: 91–92), who argues that the scandal opened a window for reform, but, since the officers closed ranks, it also made the success of any reforms unlikely. The officers who exposed the corruption were not seen by other officers as good cops but as opportunists.
27. Scheingold 1991: 89.
28. Scheingold 1991: 93.
29. Scheingold 1991: 94.
30. Scheingold 1991: 106.
31. Scheingold 1991: 83.
32. Scheingold 1991: 107.
33. Seattle Police Department Annual Report, various years.
34. Scheingold 1991: 114–15.
35. This meant that the three top law enforcement officials in the city (mayor, chief, and prosecutor) shared the common name of Norm, raising the specter that community policing is a transition from the rule of law to the rule of norms. Perhaps.
36. Seattle Police Department 1980: 18–19.
37. Seattle Police Department 1980: 2.
38. Seattle Police Department 1980: 2.
39. Seattle Police Department 1980: 9.
40. Seattle Police Department 1980: 10.
41. Seattle Police Department 1980: 11.
42. Seattle Police Department 1980: 61.
43. Seattle Police Department 1980: 105. According the Buracker report (Seattle Police Department 1989b), this experiment began in 1981 and proved to be a success. The Decentralized Detective Squads significantly out performed their counterparts downtown (142).
44. Seattle Police Department 1980: 96.
45. Seattle Police Department 1989b: i.

46. Seattle Police Department 1989b: v–xiii.

47. The city's request for a proposal specifically identified neighborhood policing, problem oriented policing, and fear reduction.

48. Seattle Police Department 1989b: 178.

49. Seattle Police Department 1989b: 180.

50. Seattle Police Department 1989b: 180.

51. Seattle Police Department 1989a: 3.

52. Seattle Police Department 1989a: 39, 67.

53. Seattle Police Department 1989a: 3–5.

54. Seattle Police Department 1989a: 59.

55. Seattle Police Department 1989a: 5.

56. Seattle Police Department 1989a: 6; italics added.

57. Seattle Police Department 1989a: 13.

58. Seattle Police Department 1989a: 84.

59. Interview, 7:1. Ezra Stotland was the co–principal investigator in the 1991 landmark study of community policing in Seattle. He was also an esteemed member of the University of Washington faculty, who kindly spent many hours discussing community policing with me.

60. Chambliss 1988: 131.

61. Chambliss 1988: 131–37.

62. There is very little information available on the South Precinct's experiment with team policing other than that it started under Gustin. It was a precursor of community policing, funded by the Law Enforcement Assistance Administratio (LEAA) (see Scheingold 1991). Team policing means assigning a "team of patrolmen and supervisors to a small area, say, one precinct or a few beats, and to leave them there . . . to meet the demands of the area" (Wilson 1983: 68).

63. Interview, 7:1; Fleissner, Fedan, and Stotland 1991: 50.

64. Fleissner, Fedan, and Stotland 1991: 50.

65. Interview, 7:2.

66. *South District Journal,* January 24, 1987 ("Project Targets the Young and the Lawless," by Terry McGuire).

67. Seattle Team for Youth is a coordinated effort by the Seattle schools, public and private agencies, and the SPD to assist at-risk youth through early intervention and coordinated case management. See *Seattle Times,* June 22, 1992 ("Trust is Key in Reaching Out," by Constantine Angelos).

68. Interview, 7:2.

69. Interview, 8:2.

70. Interview, 8:3.

71. Interview, 7:3; Interview, 8:3; *South District Journal,* February 25, 1987 ("Anti-crime Team Appears to be Dead," by Denis Law).

72. *South District Journal,* February 25, 1987.

73. Interview, 8:4.

74. Interview, 8:2. Pillon said that it was "a signal to all on patrol that you better not ask any hard questions, and you sure as hell better not ask them publicly." Community outrage was reported in the *South District Journal,* February

25, 1987 ("Anti-crime Team Appears to Be Dead," by Denis Law); March 11, 1987 ("Police Anti-drug Effort Questioned"); March 18, 1987 ("Fans Say Goodbye to a Fighter [Pillon]," by Terry McGuire); and March 25, 1987 ("Petition Drive Seeks Sgt. Pillon Return," by Terry McGuire). The *Seattle Times* only covered the police administration's charges against Pillon (on March 2 and March 3), who was portrayed as a renegade cop.

75. Seattle Police Department 1991. This was a large three-ring binder that South Precinct CPT Sergeant Bill Conn distributed to the numerous law enforcement and city officials who visit Seattle each year. It was not paginated continuously.

76. Interview, 22:29; Interview, 23:22. Sergeant Conn's numbers do not add up because at the time of our interview his team was in the process of being strengthened. Additional officers were to be funded through the recently passed Proposition 1 and Weed and Seed, Sergeant Conn was the South Precinct CPT Sergeant; Sergeant Manning headed up the East Precinct CPT.

77. Interview, 22:11.

78. CPT officers receive special training in sensitivity, utilization of community resources, public speaking, writing, problem-solving techniques, crisis intervention, and other areas designed to improve police-community relations (Seattle Police Department 1991).

79. Wilson 1983.

80. Interview, 22:5.

81. Calculated from Seattle Police Department 1991.

82. A SOAP designation by the court makes simply being in the area a crime (for a previously convicted offender). A SODA (Stay Out of Drug Areas) designation does the same for convicted drug dealers.

83. Seattle Police Department 1991.

84. Field interviews are a form of aggressive order maintenance in which police officers without sufficient information to make an arrest stop and interrogate known dealers, sometimes confiscating drugs or other contraband to disrupt their operations.

85. Interview, 22:8.

86. Interview, 22:8.

87. Interview, 22:10.

88. Seattle Police Department 1991.

89. Seattle Police Department 1991.

90. Seattle Police Department 1991.

91. Seattle Police Department 1991.

92. Interview, 22:18.

93. Interview, 22.

Chapter 7

1. Fleissner, Fedan, and Stotland 1991: 28; Skolnick and Bayley 1988. In Chief Fitzsimons's letter of support for the city's 1991 application for a federal Weed and Seed grant, he included the South Seattle Crime Prevention Council,

CPTs, the Buraker Management study, the MM Bell Complaint Process study, and a new philosophical orientation as components of the department's "community-oriented quality service" approach to policing.

2. Fleissner, Fedan, and Stotland 1991: 69. The advantage of this form of association is that it made cooperation with the police easier because confidentiality and criticism of the police would be less of a problem. Restricting membership in this way, according to Fleissner, Fedan, and Stotland, was an essential precondition for SPD cooperation. While there is little indication that the chamber group was itself interested in a larger, more diverse membership, the department did provide positive incentives to the SSCPC for minimizing criticism of the department, which may have intersected with the group's own interest in limited outreach.

3. Fleissner, Fedan, and Stotland 1991: 87–89.

4. Fleissner, Fedan, and Stotland 1991: 99; Interview, 31; Interview, 33; Interview, 9; Interview, 29.

5. Mayor's Task Force Report 1993. The task force was a 13-member council. Five members were appointed by the mayor, five by the city council, one from the Seattle Human Rights Commission, one from the Seattle Police Management Association, and one from the Seattle Police Officers Guild. This report focused on the need for community control and police accountability, citing the composition of the CPCs as an obstacle to these (7–9).

6. Interview, 33.

7. Seattle Police Department 1988c: 8.

8. Seattle Police Department 1988b.

9. SSCPC meeting minutes, April 6, 1988.

10. The meeting was attended by Chief Fitzsimons and city council member Jane Noland (SSCPC meeting minutes, March 16, 1988).

11. SSCPC meeting minutes, April 20, 1988. Other funding for SSCPC came from the Medina Foundation ($5,100), the International District Rotary ($1,995), the Neighborhood Business Council ($18,720), the NIJ ($4,500), and U.S. West ($2,000) for 1989 (SSCPC meeting minutes, December 7, 1988). An undisclosed amount of emergency funding from the City Council for staffing at the NCJC was reported in the minutes of October 5, 1988. Fleissner, Fedan, and Stotland (1991) reported that initial funding for the SSCPC came from several sources: private donations, fundraisers, a city block grant, and contributions from local businesses.

12. SSCPC meeting minutes, August 2, 1989; January 10, 1990; February 7, 1990.

13. SSCPC meeting minutes, August 24, 1989.

14. Fleissner, Fedan, and Stotland 1991: 84. According to the minutes of the meeting of October 3, 1993, the SSCPC president reported that he had attended a community meeting concerning a proposed halfway house for the southeast and discovered that the hot line number was not widely known, even among these more active residents of the Rainier Valley.

15. Fleissner, Fedan, and Stotland 1991: 67; emphasis added.

16. Interview, 19.

17. ACORN, organized in 1992, focused its efforts on redlining and crime control, issuing a list of demands to the mayor, chief and city council on October 14, 1993. After the group gave the mayor its Turkey of the Year Award (*Seattle Times,* November 16, 1993 ["Thanksgiving Menu: Turkey and Rice."]), the mayor met with the 15-member group and persuaded it to look into working with the SSCPC. That was the last we heard from ACORN.

18. This work does not treat MAPH as one of the significant citizen crime control groups in the Rainier Valley for three reasons. First, MAPH operated out of the Central District, which is just north of the valley. Second, MAPH did not organize until 1990 and thus did not play a role in the creation of the police-community partnership that is the focus of this work. Third, as this section argues, MAPH was marginalized by both the SPD and citizen crime control groups in the southeast. It is included here because its activities spread into the southeast and because the concerns it raised were not addressed in the partnership, nor in any other part of Seattle's community policing initiative in this period.

19. *MAPH Newsletter,* July 1992.

20. Interview, 27:13.

21. Interview, 9:5.

22. Interview, 27:14.

23. *Pacific Magazine,* May 7, 1989.

24. Fleissner, Fedan, and Stotland 1991: 77.

25. Fleissner, Fedan, and Stotland 1991: 78–79.

26. Interview, 35.

27. SSCPC flyer, "Expedited Evictions for Drug-Related Activities."

28. RCW 59.18.130(6) and RCW 59.12.030(5).

29. New Section 11 (2) contained in 1988 amendments to the Nuisance Law, passed by the Washington State Legislature on March 9, 1988, by a vote of 94 to zero in the House and 49 to zero in the Senate. Certificate of Enactment for Substitute House Bill No. 692.

30. Fleissner, Fedan, and Stotland 1991: 78.

31. Fleissner, Fedan, and Stotland 1991: 79.

32. Fleissner, Fedan, and Stotland 1991: 81.

33. Seattle Police Department 1988c: 10.

34. SSCPC meeting minutes, December 7, 1988; October 4, 1989; February 7, 1990; April 1, 1992; May 6, 1992; January 10, 1990.

35. SSCPC training sessions provided owners and managers with information on how to legally screen potential tenants for previous drug activity, check credit histories, and use the Drug Trafficking Civil Abatement Program, the Criminal Trespass Program, and Housing Code violations to maintain drug-free apartment buildings.

36. Fleissner, Fedan, and Stotland 1991: 79–80.

37. Mayor Royer. press release, August 23, 1989.

38. Mayor Royer's "Questions and Answers" memo, which was enclosed with his transmittal letter to the city council.

39. Exhibit 1 of the mayor's letter to council president Sam Smith.

40. SSCPC meeting minutes, October 7, 1992. For the discussion of the Drug Traffic Loitering Ordinance that follows, I am indebted to the work of Lisa Miller at the University of Washington. The information is from an unpublished 1994 manuscript, entitled "Competing Visions of Drug Policy and Crime Control: An Exploration of the Seattle Drug Traffic Loitering Ordinance." While the DTL was certainly the most important legislation after Proposition 1, there was also SSCPC support for the state's "Three Strikes and You're Out" initiative and for City Attorney Mark Sidran's Anti-homelessness Law, which criminalized sitting on sidewalks in an effort to clear them of panhandlers from Seattle's growing homeless community. My focus is on Proposition 1 and the DTL because it is in these cases that the SSCPC role was most direct.

41. Miller 1994: 7.

42. Miller 1994: 9. Despite a highly unfavorable report from the Human Rights Commission, discussed in chapter 6, the DTL ordinance was renewed by the city council in 1992 along with another ordinance creating a Police-Community Relations Task Force.

43. Fleissner, Fedan, and Stotland 1991: 72.

44. Seattle Police Department 1988c: 14, and SSCPC meeting minutes of February 17, 1988 show that four of seven initial targets were proposed by the council, suggesting more council initiative than Fleissner, Fedan, and Stotland observed a year later.

45. Mayor's Task Force Report 1993.

46. Fleissner, Fedan, and Stotland 1991: 73.

47. At the January 20, 1988, meeting of the SSCPC, Captain Marquart presented the council with a 15-page report logging target activity for the previous week. He also provided copies of several memos regarding blight removal and police accountability on target areas. By 1993, there were no such reports, though at the November 3, 1993, meeting Janice Corbin of Crime Prevention passed out a 31-page photocopy of the section from the mayor's proposed 1994 budget that covered the SPD.

48. Fleissner, Fedan, and Stotland 1991: 86. There are two large public housing projects in the southeast area covered by the SSCPC. Neither of these, euphemistically referred to as Garden Communities, appeared on the SSCPC list of targets.

49. Seattle Police Department 1991.

50. Seattle Police Department 1991. FIR is a field interrogation report, which is filed with the department any time an officer stops a suspect for questioning but does not proceed to arrest. It is designed to gather information and make it difficult to conduct illegitimate business operations, and it is considered a classic example of aggressive order maintenance. Of all the FIRs conducted, more than three-fourths were for suspected narcotics trafficking.

51. Seattle Police Department 1991.

52. *Seattle Times,* November 25, 1987 ("Crime Fight—City Council Wants Details from Chief," by Joni Balter).

53. Interview, 28:4. "I think eventually you might have a flatter organization, that's happened a lot in the private sector, where you give people at lower lev-

els of the organization more responsibility and authority to deal with customers, solve problems, and develop the product. That's a possibility in law enforcement agencies; I'm not sure it's ever going to happen just because the law is so complex. . . . I'm not sure the structure is ever going to change that much. I don't think that matters, as long as the philosophy is imbued. . . ."

54. Interview, 28:4. The decentralization that has occurred was "because we were limited by the size of the facilities."

55. *Seattle Times,* October 28, 1990 ("Buried in 911 Calls, City Tries 'Community Policing,'" by Andrew Malcolm).

56. SSCPC meeting minutes, May 2, 1990 and February 3, 1988.

57. Fleissner, Fedan, and Stotland 1991: 101.

58. Joiner to Veldwyk, April 7, 1988. The South Precinct commander had passed Veldwyk's letter on to Captain Joiner in the downtown headquarters.

59. Fleissner, Fedan, and Stotland 1991: 66.

60. *Pacific Magazine,* May 7, 1989.

61. *South District Journal,* November 18, 1987 ("Captain's Transfer Sparks Call for Chief to Resign").

62. *South District Journal,* March 4, 1987, ("Sgt. Pillon Has Been Removed from Street Duty," by Denis Law).

63. Exhibit B of Seattle Police Department 1988c shows that ACT II's primary tool was arrest. Also, the CPT annual reports for this period show that ACT II's participation on task forces in the area primarily involved serving arrest warrants. There is nothing inherently wrong with this, but, as chapters 5 and 6 make clear, this is not the way ACT I had policed crack houses.

64. There was also pressure to remake CPT to look even more like professional patrol. Conn explained that while "CPT can go to the root of the problem and rebuild citizen confidence in government and the police department . . . [t]here has been a tendency of some of the command staff to try to turn CPT into an operational crime-fighting unit. It's their natural instinct . . . [and open resistance] would be political suicide right now. This is 'in'" (Interview, 22).

65. Interview, 23:4–7.

66. Interview, 22:5.

67. A Veldwyk letter, October 25, 1988, to city council president Sam Smith calls for additional police funding and funding for other city agencies, like DCLU, that are responding to community concerns. In 1990, the South Precinct CPT prepared a long report on coordination with DCLU. The CPT developed an "advisement of violation" form to inform residents that their property was in violation of land use regulations. Voluntary compliance was encouraged. The form was created in response to DCLU's insistence that it could not handle any additional complaints and expected that South CPT's efforts would generate an extra 500 complaints. The CPT report indicated that 472 new complaints were generated, but by using the advisement of violation form 86 percent of these were cleared up voluntarily, leaving only 63 for DCLU. The effort cost 425 police hours, at $19.00 per hour ($8,075), or under $20 per residence that complied voluntarily.

68. Interview, 24:7. Referring to attempts to get information, an ACLU

spokesperson said: "You have to bird-dog the police department to an incredible level to get what you, rightfully, under state law, are entitled to get. So I guess I would say I don't think the police department has been very responsive."

69. Regarding the Drug Traffic Loitering Ordinance, I am basing my observations on the statements of City Attorney Mark Sidran in the city council hearings of July 16, 1992. The ACLU charged that, according to SPD data, more than 70 percent of those arrested under this law had been minority, many of whom were never charged, and this was harassment. In response, Sidran stated that the city would need to know the racial makeup of the population engaged in particular behaviors. This information was not available. The difference between arrests and charges was not harassment, he claimed, because the police only need probable cause to arrest but they need beyond a reasonable doubt to charge. Further, the gap was to be expected with a new enforcement tool. As the criminal justice system moves up the learning curve, a higher percentage of those arrested will be charged. While this law may miss white drug dealers, Sidran concluded, it did attack the visible dealing that threatens neighborhoods and small businesses. On the response of the mayor's office to the Weed and Seed controversy, see *Seattle Times* articles by Dick Lilly (April 6, 1992, "Seattle Wins Grant for 'Weed and Seed' Program", and May 8, 1992, "Auditors May Weed Out Seeds of Program").

70. The president of the Police Guild, Officer Ed Striedinger, was quoted in the *Seattle Times* as saying: "It's too bad [that] every time someone expresses a concern they think the department has to be retrained." Suggesting that the community may be the one that needs training in police procedures, he added: "We'll go through with it [sensitivity training], but it's a political solution to a perceived problem" (*Seattle Times,* March 8, 1991 ["Training Upsets Police Guild Chief," by Dave Birkland]). Later, commenting on the proposed police auditor, Striedinger said: "We still maintain that any problems that are being alleged are problems of perception rather than reality" (*Seattle Times,* November 12, 1991 ["Rice, Noland Propose Police Auditor," by Dick Lilly]).

71. *Seattle Times,* December 10, 1991 ("Police Auditor Gets OK," by Dick Lilly); March 17, 1992 ("Jury's Out on New Police Auditor," by Kate Shatzkin.)

72. Interview, 30:6. Even Arnette Holloway (Interview, 29:2), a strident critic of what she claims was an SPD policy to try to contain the gang and crack problem in minority neighborhoods, said that Terrence Carroll was very independent: "If the city thinks he is a team player, they may be surprised."

73. Seattle Police Department 1989a: 3–5.

74. Seattle Police Department 1989a: 7.

75. Interview, 24:6.

76. Seattle Human Rights Commission, 1990: 4.

77. Seattle Human Rights Commission, 1990: 5.

78. Seattle Human Rights Commission, 1990: 14. Rick Anderson documented one such incident of secrecy and retaliation in the *Seattle Times* (April 18, 1991 ["His Story Bears Witness to Some Police Complaints"]).

79. Walker's 1991 study of civilian review boards concluded that there is "a new national consensus on civilian review as an appropriate method for handling citizen complaints about police misconduct" (2). It is possible that both MM Bell and the SHRC felt it imprudent to recommend an external review given the resistance from the chief and the need to renegotiate the guild contract that such a change would create. I base this judgment on the fact that each study found citizens interested in a civilian review board but chose not to recommend one. It is likely that similar pragmatic concerns convinced the ACLU to recommend incremental changes in the existing system and yet conclude its report with an endorsement of an independent civilian review board, with subpoena power, that can make disciplinary recommendations.

80. Initially opposed by Noland as a police-bashing session, the intensity of distrust and community concern about the police department forced the city council to hold a public hearing. See *Seattle Times,* March 18, 1991 ("Hearing on Police Thwarted," by Dick Lilly); and March 28, 1991 ("Hearing Looks into Police Relations with Minorities," by Dick Lilly).

81. Similar recommendations appeared again in the Mayor's Task Force Report 1993.

82. *ACLU Accountability Report,* 1992: 6.

83. SSCPC meeting minutes, December 7, 1988. The reporting was discontinued, no doubt, because the first-year reporting was funded by a National Institute of Justice grant.

84. The NCJC was initially created by emergency funding from the city council in October 1988 to contract with the Neighborhood Business Group. Godefroy was hired for 10 hours per week for the NCJC in addition to her 20 hours for the SSCPC and 10 hours for the Southeast Chamber of Commerce. Beginning in January 1989, Godefroy went to 20 hours per week for the NCJC and 20 for the SSCPC under a block grant from the city to the Neighborhood Business Group (NBG) (matching grant, city and NBG each contributed $30,000) to provide the SSCPC with staffing that could also assist other precincts in establishing similar councils (SSCPC meeting minutes, October 5, 1988). By the end of 1989, when the NCJC and South Precinct commander Marquart suggested the formation of a precinctwide council, Godefroy had moved to NCJC full time.

85. The council donated $1,000 to Rainier Beach High School to support the Conflict Manager Program (SSCPC meeting minutes, May 6, 1992) and $1,341 to four area high schools for the purchase of metal detectors (SSCPC meeting minutes, November 14, 1992).

86. The Education Committee made a formal request to the council for support of a grant proposal the committee was submitting (SSCPC meeting minutes, January 6, 1993). This type of request became increasingly common in this period, when meetings included requests from visiting community groups for the council's endorsement or financial support. These were most often approved with little discussion, and the NCJC representative was assigned the task of writing a letter for the council president to sign (observations and minutes from various meetings).

87. SSCPC meeting minutes, March 30, 1993. To add insult to injury, Veldwyk's name was misspelled VelDyck.

88. SSCPC meeting minutes, September 29, 1992.

89. SSCPC meeting minutes, October 7, 1992.

90. SSCPC meeting minutes, August 27, 1993; April 7, 1993.

Chapter 8

1. *Seattle Times,* January 24, 1990 ("Redmond Plans Old Fashioned Police Beats," by Margarit Overton). Redmond is a small town just outside of Seattle.

2. Walzer 1990: 16.

3. See Foucault 1977 on the spectacle (177) and filling in the microphysics of power (213–15).

4. For a superior discussion of this phenomenon with regard to individualism, law use, and community, see Greenhouse, Yngvesson, and Engel 1994.

5. Greenhouse, Yngvesson, and Engel 1994: 119.

6. Scheingold 1991: 181–87.

7. Merry 1990: 1.

8. *Seattle Times,* December 28, 1987 ("Bad Guys Are Sometimes Outnumbered—Prostitutes, Drugs Often Go Away When Police, Citizens Get Together," by Sally MacDonald).

9. *Seattle Times,* March 14, 1988 ("Houston Experiment—The 'Community' Police Approach," by Neal Peirce).

10. *South District Journal,* June 15, 1988; July 1, 1988; April 7, 1989; October 1, 1989.

11. Tocqueville 1956: 317. "[I]t depends upon [the people] themselves whether the principle of equality is to lead them to servitude or freedom, to knowledge or barbarism, to prosperity or wretchedness."

12. Garland 1996.

13. Booth 1997.

14. Booth 1997. Kraska (1993), argues that federal funding for the war on drugs has been a major catalyst in the military for overcoming the initial resistance to change. Federal funding is also an important leveraging tool for overcoming resistance to change among patrol officers.

15. Booth 1997. Initially the military was resistant (like officers in departments moving to community policing), but political pressure to send a message triumphed, as Congress sought to combine (1) efforts to assist cities struggling to manage the consequences of their inability to solve urban problems and (2) a response to the post–cold war military's need to find a new justification for its budgets. See also Kraska 1993: 175.

16. Booth 1997. The use of SWAT teams by local law enforcement, mostly trained by active or retired U.S. military personnel, has risen more than 500 percent since 1980. Some are deployed on permanent patrol, wearing camouflage and body armor and carrying the automatic submachine guns used by Navy Seals.

17. Booth 1997.

18. According to Fresno police chief Winchester, SWAT teams "overwhelm suspects. They don't need to shoot" (Booth 1997). They depend on the (increased and increasingly militarized) visibility of their power as coercive agents of the state and the invisibility of their discretion to act as members of particular communities.

19. *Seattle Times,* March 29, 1991.

20. Fleissner, Fedan, and Stotland 1991: 67; emphasis added. Stuart Hall (1978) observed that police departments operate as primary definers in framing crime control debates. Here that function is extended to defining the community itself.

21. Tomlins 1993: 7.

22. Skogan (1988) contrasts preservationist crime prevention (in defense of the status quo) with insurgent crime prevention (challenging existing power relations).

23. Radin 1989.

24. Greenstone and Peterson 1973.

25. Foucault 1988: 162.

26. Scheingold 1984.

27. Bennett 1988: 51. "The potential for confusion and disorientation inherent in personalized, dramatic, fragmented news leaves people vulnerable to old, familiar, reassuring images of how the world works—images that drive bothersome details out of mind."

28. Machiavelli, 1988.

29. Hall 1978; Taylor 1982.

30. Sennett 1970; Altshuler 1970: 44.

31. Foucault 1988: 153–62.

32. Wilson 1968, 1983; Tonry 1995.

33. Attorney General Edwin Meese, quoted in Kraska 1993: 168. As Kraska, (174) argues, drug czar William Bennett recognized that successfully exporting the military model would require the United States to prove its willingness to use its military domestically. One such attempt led to a massive multiagency task force deployed in the northern California King Range Conservation Area (Operation Green Harvest) in search of marijuana growing. Regarding this effort, a researcher at the University of California reported that residents complained of "persistent trespassing and harassment by federal forces, citizens ambushed and held at gunpoint without explanation, the seizure and destruction of private property, and surveillance of local residents."

34. *Seattle Times,* June 13, 1988 ("Residents March to Protest Rainier Beach Crack House," by Dick Lilly). The speaker was a member of Neighbors Against Drugs, which also applied pressure on corporate leadership in the entertainment industry. The group, along with the local chapter of the Guardian Angels, spoke out strongly against the 1988 movie *Colors* for glorifying gang life. See *Seattle Times,* April 14, 1988 ("Movie Glorifies and Promotes Gangs, Opponents Complain," by Kit Boss).

35. Katznelson 1976; Kraska 1993.

Bibliography

Abel, Richard. 1982. "The Contradictions of Informal Justice." In Richard Abel, ed., *The Politics of Informal Justice*, 267–321. New York: Academic.

Ackelsberg, Martha. 1992. "Feminist Analysis of Public Policy." *Comparative Politics* 24, no. 4: 477–93.

ACLU Accountability Report. 1992. "Recommendations for Changes in Seattle Police Operations to Improve Accountability and the Complaint Review Process, July 10, 1992." Report prepared by the American Civil Liberties Union of Washington.

Alinsky, Saul. 1971. *Rules for Radicals: A Practical Primer for Realistic Radicals.* New York: Random House.

Altshuler, Alan. 1970. *Community Control: The Black Demand for Participation in Large American Cities.* New York: Pegasus.

Angell, John E. 1971. "Toward an Alternative to the Classic Police Organizational Arrangements: A Democratic Model." *Criminology* 9:185–207.

Appleby, Joyce. 1993. "Historians, Community, and the Pursuit of Jefferson: Comment on Professor Tomlins." In *Studies in American Political Development: An Annual* 4:35–44. New Haven: Yale University Press.

Bayley, David. 1988. "Community Policing: A Report from the Devil's Advocate." In Jack Greene and Stephen Mastrofski, eds., *Community Policing: Rhetoric or Reality*, 225–39. New York: Praeger.

Bayley, David, and James Garofalo. 1989. "The Management of Violence by Police Patrol Officers." *Criminology* 27:1–25.

Bayley, David, and Clifford Shearing. 1996. "The Future of Policing." *Law and Society Review* 30, no. 3: 585–606.

Bennett, W. Lance. 1988. *News: The Politics of Illusion.* New York: Longmans.

Berkley, George. 1969. *The Democratic Policeman.* Boston: Beacon.

Bernstein, Jerome. 1971. "Manpower—TWO and the Blackstone Rangers." In Edgar Cahn and Barry Passett, eds., *Citizen Participation: Effecting Community Change*, 250–72. New York: Praeger.

Bittner, Egon. 1970. *The Functions of Police in Modern Society.* Washington, DC: Government Printing Office.

Black, Donald. 1978. "Mobilizing the Law." In Peter Manning and John Van Maanen, eds., *Policing: A View from the Street*, 167–86. Santa Monica: Goodyear.

Black, Donald. 1991. "The Social Organization of Arrest: Citizen Discretion." In

Carl Klockars and Stephen Mastrofski, eds., *Thinking About Police*, 334–52. New York: McGraw-Hill.

Block, Richard. 1971. "Fear of Crime and Fear of the Police." *Social Problems* 19:91–101.

Booth, William. 1997. "Exploding Number of SWAT Teams Sets Off Alarms." *Washington Post* home page (washingtonpost.com), June 17.

Borden, David. 1971. "Participation on the Block." In Edgar Cahn and Barry Passett, eds., *Citizen Participation: Effecting Community Change*, 184–99. New York: Praeger.

Bordua, David, ed. 1967. *The Police: Six Sociological Essays*. New York: Wiley.

Boyte, Harry. 1992. "The Critic Critiqued." In *From the Ground Up: Essays on Grassroots and Workplace Democracy*, by George Bennello, with commentaries, Boston: Southend.

Braithwaite, John. 1989. *Crime, Shame, and Reintegration*. New York: Cambridge University Press.

Brown, Lee. 1989. "Community Policing: A Practical Guide for Police Officials." *The Police Chief* (August): 72–82.

Brown, Richard Maxwell. 1969. "Historical Patterns of Violence in America." In *The History of Violence in America*, 154–226. New York: Bantam.

Browning, Rufus, Dale Marshall, and David Tabb, eds. 1990. *Racial Politics in American Cities*. New York: Longmans.

"Census 90: Population Changes in Seattle, 1980–1990." 1991. *Current Planning Research Bulletin* 51 (April).

Chambliss, William. 1978. *On the Take: From Petty Crooks to Presidents*. Bloomington: Indiana University Press.

Clark, Kenneth, and Jeanette Hopkins, eds. *A Relevant War against Poverty: A Study of Community Action Programs and Observable Social Change*. New York: Harper and Row.

Cohen, Joshua, and Joel Rogers. 1986. *On Democracy*. New York: Penguin.

Cohen, Stanley. 1979. "The Punitive City: Notes on the Dispersal of Social Control." *Contemporary Crises* 3:339–63.

Cohen, Stanley. 1985. *Visions of Social Control*. Cambridge: Polity.

Coleman, James. 1988. "Social Capital in the Creation of Human Capital." *American Journal of Sociology* 94:S95–120.

Cordner, Gary. 1988. "A Problem-Oriented Approach to Community-Oriented Policing." In Jack Greene and Stephen Mastrofski, eds., *Community Policing: Rhetoric or Reality*, 135–53. New York: Praeger.

Crank, John. 1994. "Watchman and Community: Myth and Institutionalization in Policing." *Law and Society Review* 28 (May): 325–51.

Crawford, Adam. 1996. "The Spirit of Community: Rights, Responsibilities, and the Communitarian Agenda." *Journal of Law and Society* 23, no. 2 (June): 247–63.

Dahrendorf, Ralf. 1985. *Law and Order*. Boulder: Westview.

Davis, Robert, Barbara Smith, Arthur Lurigio, and Wesley Skogan. 1991. *Community Response to Crack: Grassroots Anti-drug Program*. New York: Victim Services Agency.

Donovan, John. 1980. *The Politics of Poverty*. Washington, DC: University Press of America.

Eck, John, and Dennis Rosenbaum. 1994. "The New Police Order: Effectiveness, Equity, and Efficiency in Community Policing." In Dennis Rosenbaum, ed., *The Challenge of Community Policing: Testing the Promises*, 3–27. Beverly Hills: Sage.

Elkin, Stephen. 1987. *City and Regime in the American Republic*. Chicago: University of Chicago Press.

Ericson, Richard, Kevin Haggerty, and Kevin Carriere. 1993. "Community Policing as Communications Policing." In Dieter Dolling and Thomas Feltes, eds., *Community Policing: Comparative Aspects of Community Oriented Police Work*, 37–70. Holzkirchen: Felix-Verlag.

Esman, Milton, and Norman Uphoff. 1984. *Local Organizations: Intermediaries in Rural Development*. Ithaca: Cornell University Press.

Etzioni, Amitai. 1993. *The Spirit of Community: Rights, Responsibilities, and the Communitarian Agenda*. New York: Crown.

Evans, Sara, and Harry Boyte. 1982. "Schools for Action: Radical Uses of Social Space." *Democracy* (fall): 55–65.

Ewick, Patricia, and Susan Silbey. 1995. "Subversive Stories and Hegemonic Tales: Toward a Sociology of Narrative." *Law and Society Review* 29, no. 2: 197–227.

Farrell, Michael. 1988. "The Development of the Community Patrol Officer Program: Community-Oriented Policing in the New York City Police Department." In Jack Greene and Stephen Mastrofski, eds., *Community Policing: Rhetoric or Reality*, 73–89. New York: Praeger.

Fleissner, Dan, Nicholas Fedan, and Ezra Stotland. 1991. *South Seattle Crime Reduction Project: A Descriptive Study of Community/Police Cooperation in the City of Seattle*. Washington, DC: National Institute of Justice.

Fogelson, Robert. 1977. *Big City Police*. Cambridge: Harvard University Press.

Foucault, Michel. 1977. *Discipline and Punish: The Birth of the Prison*. New York: Vintage.

Foucault, Michel. 1980. *Power/Knowledge: Selected Interviews and Other Writings*. New York: Pantheon.

Foucault, Michel. 1988. "The Political Technology of Individuals." In Luther Martin, Huck Gutman, and Patrick Hutton, eds., *Technologies of the Self: A Seminar with Michel Foucault*, 145–62. Amherst: University of Massachusetts Press.

Fraser, Nancy. 1992. "Rethinking the Public Sphere: A Contribution to the Critique of Actually Existing Democracy." In Francis Barker, Peter Hulme, and Margaret Iversen, eds., *Post-Modernism and the Re-Reading of Modernity*, 197–232. New York: St. Martin's.

Garland, David. 1996. "The Limits of the Sovereign State: Strategies of Crime Control in Contemporary Society." *British Journal of Criminology* 36 (autumn): 445–71.

Geller, William, ed. 1985. *Police Leadership In America: Crisis and Opportunity*. New York: Praeger.

Germann, A. C., 1973. "Community Policing: An Assessment." In Paul Cromwell and George Keefer, eds., *Police-Community Relations*, 9–12. St. Paul: West.

Giddens, A. 1976. *Central Problems in Social Theory: Action, Structure, and Contradiction in Social Analysis.* Berkeley: University of California Press.

Goldstein, Herman. 1990. *Problem Oriented Policing.* New York: McGraw-Hill.

Goodwyn, Lawrence. 1978. *The Populist Moment: A Short History of the Agrarian Revolt in America.* New York: Oxford University Press.

Greene, Jack, and Stephen Mastrofski, eds. 1988. *Community Policing: Rhetoric or Reality?* New York: Praeger.

Greene, Jack, and Carl Klockars. 1991. "What Police Do." In Carl Klockars and Stephen Mastrofski, eds., *Thinking about Police: Contemporary Readings*, 273–85. New York: McGraw-Hill.

Greene, Jack, and Ralph Taylor. 1988. "Community Based Policing and Foot Patrol: Issues of Theory and Evaluation." In Jack Greene and Stephen Mastrofski. eds., *Community Policing: Rhetoric or Reality?* 195–225. New York: Praeger.

Greenstone, J. David, and Paul Peterson. 1973. *Race and Authority in Urban Politics: Community Participation and the War on Poverty.* New York: Russell Sage.

Habermas, Jurgen. 1989. *The Structural Transformation of the Public Sphere: An Inquiry into a Category of Bourgeois Society.* Cambridge: MIT Press.

Hall, Stuart, et al. 1978. *Policing the Crisis: Mugging, the State, and Law and Order.* New York: Holmes and Meier.

Handler, Joel. 1990. *Law and the Search for Community.* Philadelphia: University of Pennsylvania Press.

Hanson, Russell. 1985. *The Democratic Imagination in America.* Princeton: Princeton University Press.

Harrington, Christine. 1985. *Shadow Justice: The Ideology and Institutionalization of Alternatives to Court.* Westport: Greenwood.

Harrington, Christine. 1993. "Community Organizing through Conflict Resolution." In Sally Eagle Merry and Neal Milner, eds., *The Possibility of Popular Justice: A Case Study of Community Mediation in the United States*, 401–35. Ann Arbor: University of Michigan Press.

Harrington, Michael. "The Politics of Poverty." In Jerome Larner and Irving Howe, eds., *Poverty: Views from the Left*, 13–39. New York: Morrow.

Hofrichter, Richard. 1982. "Neighborhood Justice and the Social Control Problems of American Capitalism: A Perspective." In Richard Abel, ed., *The Politics of Informal Justice*, 207–48. New York: Academic.

Hofstadter, Richard. 1955. *The Age of Reform.* New York: Random House.

Holmes, Stephen. 1993. *The Anatomy of Anti-liberalism.* Cambridge: Harvard University Press.

Kappler, Victor, Mark Blumberg, and Gary Potter. 1993. *The Mythology of Crime and Criminal Justice.* Prospect Heights, IL: Waveland.

Katznelson, Ira. 1976. "The Crisis of the Capitalist City: Urban Politics and

Social Control." In Willis Hawley and Michael Lipsky, eds., *Theoretical Perspectives on Urban Politics* 214–29. Brunswick, NJ: Prentice-Hall.

Katznelson, Ira. 1981. *City Trenches.* Chicago: University of Chicago Press.

Kelling, George. 1985. "Order Maintenance, the Quality of Life, and Police: A Line of Argument." In William Geller, ed., *Police Leadership in America: Crisis and Opportunity,* 296–309. New York: Praeger.

Kelling, George. 1988. "Police and Communities: The Quiet Revolution." *Perspective on Policing,* Washington, DC: National Institute of Justice.

Kelling, George. 1992. "Measuring What Matters: A New Way of Thinking about Crime and Public Order." *The City Journal*: 21–32.

Kelling, George, and William Bratton. 1993. "Implementing Community Policing: The Administrative Problem." *Perspectives on Policing.* Washington, DC: National Institute of Justice.

Kelling, George, and Katherine Coles. 1996. *Fixing Broken Windows: Restoring Order and Reducing Crime in Our Communities.* New York: Free Press.

Kelling, George, and Mark Moore. 1988. "From Policing to Reform to Community: The Evolving Strategy of the Police." In Jack Greene and Stephen Mastrofski, eds., *Community Policing: Rhetoric or Reality?* 3–27. New York: Praeger.

Kelling, George, Robert Wasserman, and Hubert Williams. 1988. "Police Accountability and Community Policing." *Perspectives on Policing.* Washington, DC: National Institute of Justice.

Kelman, Mark. 1987. *A Guide to Critical Legal Studies.* Cambridge: Harvard University Press.

Key, V. O. 1935. "Police Graft." *American Journal of Sociology* 60 (March): 624–36.

King, Michael. 1991. "The Political Construction of Crime Prevention: A Contrast between the French and British Experience." In Steven Stenson, ed., *The Politics of Crime Control,* 87–108. London, Sage.

Klockars, Carl. 1985. "Order Maintenance, the Quality of Urban Life, and Police: A Different Line of Argument." In William Geller, ed., *Police Leadership In America: Crisis and Opportunity,* 309–22. New York: Praeger.

Klockars, Carl. 1988. "The Rhetoric of Community Policing." In Jack Greene and Stephen Mastrofski, eds., *Community Policing: Rhetoric or Reality?* 239–59. New York: Praeger.

Klockars, Carl, and Stephen Mastrofski, eds. 1991. *Thinking about the Police.* New York: McGraw-Hill.

Kraska, Peter, ed. 1993. *Altered States of Mind: Critical Observations of the Drug War.* New York: Garland.

Krieger, James. 1994. *Too Many, Too Young. A Report by the Seattle-King County Department of Public Health.* Seattle: King County Department of Public Health.

Kymlicka, Will. 1989. *Liberalism, Community, and Culture.* Oxford: Clarendon.

Lacey, Nicola, and Lucia Zedner. 1995. "Discourses of Community in Criminal Justice." *Journal of Law and Society* 22, no. 3 (1995): 301–26.

Logan, John, and Harvey Molotch. 1987. *Urban Fortunes: The Political-Economy of Place.* Berkeley: University of California Press.

Lustig, Jeffrey, R. 1982. *Corporate Liberalism: The Origins of Modern American Political Theory, 1890–1920.* Berkeley: University of California Press.

Lyons, William, and Nancy McPherson. 1998. *When the Heat is On: Seattle Leadership Sessions,* Seattle: Seattle Police Department.

Machiavelli, Niccolo. 1988. *The Prince.* New York: Cambridge University Press.

Manning, Peter. 1977. *Police Work: The Social Organization of Policing.* Cambridge: MIT Press.

Manning, Peter. 1988. "Community Policing as a Drama of Control." In Jack Greene and Stephen Mastrofski, eds., *Community Policing: Rhetoric or Reality?* 27–47. New York: Praeger.

Marx, Karl. [1852] 1987. *The 18th Brumaire of Louis Bonaparte,* New York: International Publishers.

Mastrofski, Stephen. 1988. "Community Policing as Reform: A Cautionary Tale." In Jack Greene and Stephen Mastrofski, eds., *Community Policing: Rhetoric or Reality?* 47–69. New York: Praeger.

Mayor's Task Force Report. 1993. "Police-Community Relations Task Force: Recommendations and Report Identifying Means to Improve Police-Community Relations." Seattle: Mayor's Office.

McCann, Michael. 1986. *Taking Reform Seriously: Perspectives on Public Interest Liberalism.* New York: Cornell University Press.

McEwen, Craig, and Richard Maiman. 1984. "Mediation in Small Claims Courts: Achieving Compliance through Consent." *Law and Society Review* 18:11–49.

McGahey, Richard. 1986. "Economic Conditions, Neighborhood Organization, and Urban Crime." In Albert Reiss and Michael Tonry, eds., *Communities and Crime,* 232–64. Chicago: University of Chicago Press.

Mencke, Ben, Mervin White, and William Carey. 1982. "Police Professionalism: Pursuit of Excellence or Political Power?" In Jack Greene, ed. *Managing Police Work,* 75–106. Beverly Hills: Sage.

Merry, Sally Engle. 1990. *Getting Justice and Getting Even: Legal Consciousness among Working-Class Americans.* Chicago: University of Chicago Press.

Merton, Robert. 1969. "The Latent Functions of the Machine." In Edward Banfield, ed., *Urban Government,* 223–33. New York: Free Press.

Mill, John Stuart. 1975. *Three Essays.* Oxford: Oxford University Press.

Miller, Lisa. 1994. "Competing Visions of Drug Policy and Crime Control: An Exploration of the Seattle Drug Traffic Loitering Ordinance." University of Washington, manuscript.

Moore, Mark, and Mark Kleiman. 1989. "The Police and Drugs." *Perspectives on Policing.* Washington, DC: National Institute of Justice.

Morgan, Murray. 1960. *Skid Road.* New York: Ballantine.

Muir, William. 1977. *Police: Street Corner Politicians.* Chicago: University of Chicago Press.

National Institute of Justice. 1992. *Research in Brief,* "Community Policing in Seattle: A Model Partnership between Citizens and Police." August.

Oettmeier, Timothy, and Lee Brown. 1988. "Developing a Neighborhood Oriented Policing Style." In Jack Greene and Stephen Mastrofski, eds., *Community Policing: Rhetoric or Reality?* 121–35. New York: Praeger.

Okin, Susan Moller. 1989. *Justice, Gender, and the Family.* New York: Basic Books.

Okin, Susan Moller. 1991. "Gender, the Public and the Private." In David Held, ed., *Political Theory Today,* 67–90. Stanford: Stanford University Press.

Olson, Mancur. 1965. *The Logic of Collective Action.* Cambridge: Harvard University Press.

Peterson, Paul. 1981. *City Limits.* Chicago: University of Chicago Press.

Polsky, Andrew. 1991. *The Rise of the Therapeutic State.* Princeton: Princeton University Press.

Putnam, Robert. 1993. "The Prosperous Community: Social Capital and Public Life." *American Prospect* (spring): 35–42.

Quinney, Richard. 1980. *Class, State, and Crime.* New York: Longmans.

Radin, Margaret Jane. 1989. "The Constitution and the Liberal Conception of Property." In Michael McCann and Gerald Houseman, eds., *Judging the Constitution,* 205–24. Glenview, IL: Scott Foresman.

Reiders, Lisa, and Roy Roberg. 1990. "Community Policing: A Critical Review of Underlying Assumptions." *Journal of Police Science and Administration* 17:105–11.

Reiss, A. 1971. *The Police and the Public.* New Haven: Yale University Press.

Reiss, A. 1986. "Why Are Communities Important in Understanding Crime?" In Albert Reiss and Michael Tonry, eds., *Communities and Crime,* 1–28. Chicago: University of Chicago Press.

Reiss, Albert, and Michael Tonry, eds. 1986. *Communities and Crime.* Chicago: University of Chicago Press.

Reuss-Ianni, Elizabeth. 1983. *Two Cultures of Policing: Street Cops and Management Cops.* New Brunswick, NJ: Transaction Books.

Rosenbaum, Dennis. 1986. "The Problem of Crime Control." In Dennis Rosenbaum, ed., *Community Crime Prevention: Does It Work?* 11–14. Beverly Hills: Sage.

Rosenbaum, Dennis, ed. 1994. *The Challenge of Community Policing: Testing the Promises,* Beverly Hills: Sage.

Rosenburg, Ginger. 1971. "Model Cities—Dayton Plays the Game." In Edgar Cahn and Barry Passett, eds., *Citizen Participation: Effecting Community Change,* 271–86. New York: Praeger.

Sadd, Susan, and Randolph Grinc. 1994. "Innovative Neighborhood Oriented Policing: An Evaluation of Community Policing Programs in Eight Cities." In Dennis Rosenbaum, ed., *The Challenge of Community Policing: Testing the Promises,* 27–53. Beverly Hills: Sage.

Sale, Roger. 1976. *Seattle: Past to Present.* Seattle: University of Washington Press.

Santos, Boaventura de Sousa. 1982. "Law and Community: The Changing Nature of State Power in Late Capitalism." In Richard Abel, ed., *The Politics of Informal Justice,* 249–66. New York: Academic.

Scheingold, Stuart. 1974. *The Politics of Rights: Lawyers, Public Policy, and Political Change.* New Haven: Yale University Press.

Scheingold, Stuart. 1984. *The Politics of Law and Order: Street Crime and Public Policy*. New York: Longmans.

Scheingold, Stuart. 1991. *The Politics of Street Crime: Criminal Process and Cultural Obsession*. Philadelphia: Temple University Press.

Schuerman, Leo, and Solomon Kobrin. 1986. "Community Careers in Crime." In Albert Reiss and Michael Tonry, eds., *Communities and Crime*, 68–99. Chicago: University of Chicago Press.

Scott, James C. 1990. *Domination and the Arts of Resistance: Hidden Transcripts*. New Haven: Yale University Press.

Seattle Human Rights Commission. 1990. "Report Regarding the Monitoring and Investigation of Citizen Complaints of Police Harassment." November.

Seattle Police Department. 1923. *History of the Seattle Police Department, 1923*. Seattle: Press of Grettner-Diers.

Seattle Police Department. 1978. *Department Organizational Study: A Staff Report, 1977–1978*.

Seattle Police Department. 1980. "Reorganization Project, 1970–1980." Report to the mayor, September 15.

Seattle Police Department. 1982. *From Then until Today: History of the Seattle Police Department, 1859–1982*. Seattle: Seattle Police Department.

Seattle Police Department. 1988a. "Civil Abatement Law." Report, April.

Seattle Police Department. 1988b "South Seattle Crime Reduction Project." Quarterly report.

Seattle Police Department. 1988c. "South Seattle Crime Reduction Project, Year-End Report."

Seattle Police Department. 1989a. "Internal Complaint Handling: A Review and Evaluation." Report submitted to the City of Seattle Office of Management and Budget by MM Bell, Urban Policy Research, Peter Moy and Associates, Lukin and Associates, November 15.

Seattle Police Department. 1989b. "Seattle Police Department Management Study." Report submitted to the city of Seattle by Carroll Buracker & Associates.

Seattle Police Department. 1990. "South Precinct DCLU Project Closure Report." January.

Seattle Police Department. 1991. *Community-Police Team South Precinct*.

Seattle Police Department 1994 Annual Report. 1994. Seattle: Seattle Police Department.

Seattle Police Relief Association. 1900. *History of the Seattle Police Department*.

Sennett, Richard. 1970. *The Uses of Disorder: Personal Identity and City Life*. New York: Knopf.

Sharp, Elaine. 1990. *Urban Politics and Administration: From Service Delivery to Economic Development*. New York: Longmans.

Sherman, Lawrence. 1986. "Policing Communities: What Works?" In Albert Reiss and Michael Tonry, eds., *Communities and Crime*, 344–78. Chicago: University of Chicago Press.

Sherman, Lawrence. 1997. "Communities and Crime Prevention." In *Preventing*

Crime: What Works, What Doesn't, What's Promising? A Report to the United States Congress, prepared for the National Institute of Justice by Lawrence Sherman, Denise Gottfredson, Doris MacKenzie, John Eck, Peter Rueter, and Shawn Bushway, 1–36. (Published on the internet at <http://www.ncjrs.org/works>.)

Sherman, Lawrence, P. Gartin, and M. Buergen. 1989. "Hot Spots of Predatory Crime: Routine Activities and the Criminology of Place." *Criminology* 27 (February): 27–55.

Silberman, Charles. 1978. *Criminal Violence, Criminal Justice.* New York: Random House.

Skogan, Wesley. 1988. "Community Organizations and Crime." In Michael Tonry and Norval Morris, eds., *Crime and Justice*, 39–67. v10. Chicago: University of Chicago Press 39–67.

Skogan, Wesley. 1990. *Disorder and Decline: Crime and the Spiral of Decay in American Neighborhoods.* New York: Free Press.

Skogan, Wesley, and Michael Maxfield. 1981. *Coping with Crime: Individual and Neighborhood Responses.* Beverley Hills: Sage.

Skolnick, Jerome, and David Bayley. 1986. *The New Blue Line: Police Innovation in Six American Cities.* New York: Free Press.

Skolnick, Jerome, and David Bayley. 1988. *Community Policing: Issues and Practices around the World.* Washington, DC: National Institute of Justice.

Skolnick, Jerome, and James Fyfe. 1993. *Above the Law: Police and the Excessive Use of Force.* New York: Free Press.

"Southeast Seattle Action Plan." 1991. Report prepared by Southeast Effective Development.

"Southeast Seattle Background Report." 1989. Report prepared by Southeast Effective Development.

"Southeast Seattle Revitalization Plan." 1991. Report prepared by the Rainier Chamber of Commerce, Southeast Effective Development, and the College of Architecture and Urban Design of the University of Washington.

Sparrow, Malcolm. 1988. "Implementing Community Policing." *Perspective on Policing*. Washington, DC: National Institute of Justice.

Spitzer, Steven. 1982. "The Dialectics of Formal and Informal Control." In Richard Abel, ed., *The Politics of Informal Justice*, 167–207. New York: Academic.

Spitzer, Steven. 1991. "Policing the Past." Paper presented at the Law and Society annual meetings. Amsterdam, June.

SSCPC Flyer, "Expedited Evictions for Drug-Related Activities."

Stern, Gerald. 1976. *The Buffalo Creek Disaster: The Story of the Survivors' Unprecedented Lawsuit.* New York: Random House.

Stone, Clarence, and Heywood Sanders 1987. *The Politics of Urban Development.* Lawrence: University Press of Kansas.

Stone, Debra. 1988. *Policy Paradox and Political Reason.* Glenview, IL: Scott, Foresman.

Taylor, Michael. 1982. *Community, Anarchy, and Liberty.* New York: Cambridge University Press.

Tinder, Glen. 1991. *Political Thinking: The Perennial Questions.* New York: Harper Collins.

Tocqueville, Alexis de. 1956. *Democracy in America.* Edited and abridged by Richard Heffner. New York: Mentor Books.

Tomlins, Christopher. 1993. "Law, Police, and the Pursuit of Happiness in the New American Republic." In *Studies in American Political Development: An Annual,* 4:3–33. New Haven: Yale University Press.

Tonry, Michael. 1995. *Malign Neglect: Race, Crime, and Punishment in America.* New York: Oxford University Press.

Trojanowicz, Robert, and Bonnie Bucqueroux. *1990. Community Policing: A Contemporary Perspective.* Cincinnati: Anderson.

Walker, Samuel. 1977. *A Critical History of Police Reform.* Lexington: Lexington Books.

Walker, Samuel. 1980. *Popular Justice: A History of American Criminal Justice.* New York: Oxford University Press.

Walker, Samuel. 1984. "'Broken Windows' and Fractured History: The Use and Misuse of History in Recent Police Patrol Analysis." *Justice Quarterly* 1: 75–90.

Walker, Samuel. 1991. "Civilian Review of the Police: A National Survey of the 50 Largest Cities." Research funded by the University of Nebraska-Omaha.

Walzer, Michael. 1990. "The Communitarian Critique of Liberalism." *Political Theory* 18, no. 1 (February): 1990.

Weatheritt, Mollie. 1988. "Community Policing: Rhetoric of Reality?" In Jack Greene and Stephen Mastrofski, eds., *Community Policing: Rhetoric or Reality?* 153–77. New York: Praeger.

Weisburd, David, and Jerome McElroy. 1988. "Enacting the CPO Role: Findings from the New York City Pilot Program in Community Policing." In Jack Greene and Stephen Mastrofski, eds., *Community Policing: Rhetoric or Reality?* 89–103. New York: Praeger.

Williams, G. O. 1950–51. "History of the Seattle Police Department." *Sheriff and Police Reporter* 12, nos. 8–12; 13, nos. 1–6, 8. Article in 12 installments.

Wilson, James Q. 1968. *Varieties of Police Behavior: The Management of Law and Order.* Cambridge: Harvard University Press.

Wilson, James Q. 1983. *Thinking about Crime.* New York: Basic Books.

Wilson, James Q., and George Kelling. 1982. "Broken Windows." *Atlantic Monthly,* March, 29–38.

Winthrop, John. [1630] 1988. "A Modell of Christian Charity." In Michael Levy, ed., *American Political Thought: An Anthology,* 26. Chicago: Dorsey Press.

Wilson, James Q., and George Kelling. 1989. "Making Neighborhoods Safe." *Atlantic Monthly,* February, 46–52.

Wittgenstein, Ludwig. 1937. *Culture and Values,* 27. Chicago: University of Chicago Press.

Wolfe, Tom. 1969. *The Electric Kool-aid Acid Test.* New York: Bantam.

Wycoff, Mary Ann. 1988. "The Benefits of Community Policing: Evidence and Conjecture." In Jack Greene and Stephen Mastrofski, eds., *Community Policing: Rhetoric or Reality*, 103–21. New York: Praeger.

Yates, Douglas. 1973. *Neighborhood Democracy: The Politics and Impacts of Decentralization.* Lexington: Lexington Books.

Yngvesson, Barbara. 1988. "Making Law at the Doorway: The Clerk, the Court, and the Construction of Community in a New England Town." *Law and Society Review* 22:409–49.

Zinn, Howard. 1968. *Disobedience and Democracy: Nine Fallacies of Law and Order.* New York: Random House.

Index

accountability, 1–2, 5, 9–12, 23–25, 35, 45–47, 58, 78–81, 83–92, 106, 112–13, 116, 121–23, 137, 144, 155–60, 174, 177, 180, 182, 184
aggressive order maintenance, 10–11, 40, 129–31, 143–46, 149, 156, 165
American Civil Liberties Union (ACLU), 1, 158–60, 197n. 2
anti-crime teams, 88–92, 125–33, 146, 149, 153–55

Bayley, David, 35
Boeing, 59–67, 74
Braithewaite, John, 202n. 61

capitalism, 32–33, 45–47, 58–59, 107–8, 110, 114, 176, 185
citizen patrols, 80–85, 107–8, 133, 165, 167, 177, 179, 183
city council, 2, 46, 57–59, 67, 74–75, 78, 83, 85, 89, 108, 111–12, 117–19, 121, 144–45, 150, 156–59, 169, 197n. 3, 222n. 69
Cohen, Stanley, 8–10, 18
community, 2, 58, 77
  ambiguity of, 18, 22–23, 25, 167
  communitarian account of, 16, 19–25
  co-production of social order, 15–16, 39, 77–79, 92, 105–8, 116, 122, 130
  definition of, 25–27, 139, 151, 153, 164, 172–74, 181
  and informal social controls, 8, 13, 15–33, 36, 39, 43–44, 55, 57, 110
  liberal account of, 19–20
  revitalization of, 6–8, 15–16, 23, 33, 36, 57, 72, 74, 79, 85, 91, 93–94, 98, 100, 136, 164, 167, 169–70, 175, 177, 182
community police teams, 83, 127–33, 144, 146, 148–49, 153–55, 169
courts, 1, 69, 92, 94, 100–101, 109, 129, 143–44, 178
Crawford, Adam, 15, 199nn. 11, 12, 200n. 32
crime, 2–3, 36, 50, 57–58, 66–69, 72, 80, 85, 94–95, 98, 114, 166
  crime-fighting strategy, 40, 44, 84, 109–10, 128, 151, 153, 166, 172, 177
  prevention of, 35, 53, 77–78, 82, 84, 91, 93–98, 101, 117, 121, 136–50, 164–66
  root causes of, 17–18, 83, 126, 137, 176
critical public scrutiny, 4, 7–12, 19–25, 28, 30–33, 37, 39, 78–81, 84, 90, 93, 101, 139, 163, 165, 168, 172, 174, 180–83

democracy, 3–4, 8–12, 19, 21, 37, 51, 54, 169, 172
  democratic forms of social control, 16–17, 24, 31, 52, 149, 163–64, 174–76, 183–84
  democratic moderation, 4, 7–12, 29, 79, 84, 90, 93, 102–4, 163–65, 168, 171, 179–80

disciplinary forms of social control, 3–4, 8–12, 18–19, 24, 52, 79, 163, 166, 168, 174–76, 183–84
discretion. *See* policing, discretion in
discursive struggle, 4, 17–18, 21–23, 25, 37–39, 44, 52, 58, 77, 89, 104, 135–36, 167, 169–70, 179, 183–84
disorder, 10–11, 19, 23–24, 29, 36, 42–44, 47, 48, 50, 79, 87, 129–31, 140–46, 148–50, 156, 164–66, 172, 183–85

Eck, John, 40–42, 51–55
enforcement. *See* law enforcement
equity, 41–42, 53–54

fear, 2, 9, 11–13, 15, 23, 36, 39–44, 45, 50, 53, 59, 63, 82, 87, 89, 107, 109–10, 117, 118, 150, 159, 164, 166, 170–72, 178–79, 182, 184–85
force. *See* violence
Foucault, Michel, 10–12, 197n. 8

Garland, David, 171
Goldstein, Herman, 40, 47
Greene, Jack, 51

hot lines, 81, 87, 95, 125, 138, 140, 180, 183

informal social controls. *See* community
insulation, 21, 23, 30, 37, 39, 48–49, 84, 104, 109, 113–15, 127, 133, 135, 159, 169, 172, 175, 177–79, 180–84

Kelling, George, 3, 10–11, 43–44, 50–51, 198n. 24
Klockars, Carl, 48

Lacey, Nicola, 15, 199n. 12
law enforcement, 1, 10, 37, 40, 42, 89, 106–9, 128–31, 143–50, 165–67, 173, 177, 180
  mobilizing the law, 23, 57–59, 69, 74, 78, 82, 87–88, 102, 111, 122–23, 136, 140–46, 220n. 40
legitimacy, 4, 11–12, 21, 37, 39, 50, 140, 170–73, 178, 184–85

Manning, Peter, 51
Mastrofski, Stephen, 50
Moore, Mark, 42–43
Mothers Against Police Harassment (MAPH), 139–40, 156, 174, 219n. 18

Neighbors Against Drugs (NAD), 79–80, 85–92, 99–104, 139, 156, 174
normalization, 7–9, 79, 163–64, 168, 171, 173–74, 178–80, 182

Operation Results, 79–85, 90–91, 99–104, 139, 156, 174, 179

police-community partnerships, 5, 8–13, 15–17, 23, 36, 39–45, 54, 57–60, 69, 74–75, 92–104, 118, 128, 136–62, 164–66, 168, 170, 172, 177–78, 182
police-community relations, 16, 199n. 4
policing
  communitarian account of, 36–38
  discretion in, 48–49, 111–13
  misconduct of, 12, 43, 46, 110–13, 121–23, 136, 146, 155–59, 165, 173, 177, 220n. 42
  patrol strategies of, 37, 42–43, 52, 79–81, 88–92, 117, 129–32, 146–50, 165, 171
  pro-active, 15, 43, 78, 80, 90, 92, 111, 117, 119–20, 126, 141, 152–55, 176, 180
  professional, 35–55, 87, 108–10, 113–17, 120, 126–27, 135, 151, 153–55, 165–68, 171–72, 174, 179, 180–81

and property, 1–2, 69, 74, 81, 95, 102, 104, 107, 110, 132, 136–37, 141–44, 147, 165, 173, 176–78
problem solving, 15, 36, 40–44, 53–54, 93, 132, 153, 164, 168, 170–71, 178, 185

reciprocity, 7–8, 20–21, 26–33, 55, 77–78, 84–85, 91, 101–5, 136, 163, 166, 168–69, 173–75, 181, 184. *See also* social capital
redlining, 66, 69, 70, 74, 147, 220n. 47
Reiss, A., 57–58
responsiveness, 1–2, 47, 51, 85–87, 95, 102, 112, 121, 129–31, 139, 142, 145, 148–49, 151–53, 156–58, 161, 173, 181
rights, 1, 19–20, 141, 165, 179–80
due process, 84
of officers, 122–23
privacy, 20–23
Rosenbaum, Dennis, 40–42, 51–55

Scheingold, Stuart, 79, 102, 167, 178, 199n. 11
Sherman, Lawrence, 46, 210n. 2
Skogan, Wesley, 198nn. 23, 25, 18, 200n. 42, 202n. 1, 77, 214n. 11
Skolnick, Jerome, 35
social capital, 7–9, 27–29, 31–32, 37, 93–98, 101, 136, 164, 166, 170, 173, 175, 184–85. *See also* reciprocity
Southeast Effective Development (SEED), 60, 62, 66, 68–75, 78, 100
Southeast Seattle Community Organization (SESCO), 60, 66, 69–75, 78, 100, 138
South Seattle Crime Prevention Council (SSCPC), 5–6, 8, 12–13, 62, 79–80, 83, 85, 91–104, 118–20, 136–56, 160–62, 174
surveillance, 7–12, 78, 81, 90, 101–2, 163, 168, 176, 180–83

targeting, 98, 136, 146–50, 164, 169, 173, 181, 183
Tomlins, Christopher, 35–38, 47, 176
Tonry, Michael, 197n. 9, 202n. 61

unemployment, 65

vigilantism, 107–8, 165, 177, 179–80, 211n. 13
violence, 19, 49, 80, 84, 89, 176, 179

Walker, Samuel, 223n. 79
Weed and Seed, 1–2, 12, 156, 177, 184, 197n. 1
Wilson, James Q., 43–44, 50–51

Zedner, Lucia, 15, 17, 199n. 12